MARK WAID · PETER KRAUSE

IRREDEEMABLE

VOLUME 2

IRREDEEM

Ross Richie - Chief Executive Officer

Matt Gagnon - Editor-in-Chief

Adam Fortier - VP-New Business

Wes Harris - VP-Publishing

Lance Kreiter - VP-Licensing & Merchandising

Chip Mosher - Marketing Director

Bryce Carlson - Managing Editor

Ian Brill - Editor

Dafna Pleban - Editor

Christopher Burns - Editor

Shannon Watters - Assistant Editor

Eric Harburn - Assistant Editor

Adam Staffaroni - Assistant Editor

Brian Latimer - Lead Graphic Designer

Stephanie Gonzaga - Graphic Designer

Phil Barbaro - Operations

Ivan Salazar - Marketing Manager

Devin Funches - Marketing Assistant

IRREDEEMABLE Volume Two — June 2011. Published by BOOM! Studios, a division of Boom Entertainment, Inc. Irredeemable is Copyright © 2011 Boom Entertainment, Inc. and Mark Waid. Originally published in single magazine form as IRREDEEMABLE 5-8. Copyright © 2009 Boom Entertainment, Inc. and Mark Waid. All rights reserved. BOOM! Studios™ and the BOOM! Studios logo are trademarks of Boom Entertainment, Inc., registered in various countries and categories. All characters, events, and institutions depicted herein are fictional. Any similarity between any of the names, characters, persons, events, and/or institutions in this publication to actual names, characters, and persons, whether living or dead, events, and/or institutions is unintended and purely coincidental. BOOM! Studios does not read or accept unsolicited submissions of ideas, stories, or artwork.

A catalog record of this book is available from OCLC and from the BOOM! Studios website, www.boom-studios.com, on the Librarians Page.

BOOM! Studios, 6310 San Vicente Boulevard, Suite 107, Los Angeles, CA 90048-5457. Printed in China. Second Printing. ISBN: 978-1-60886-000-5

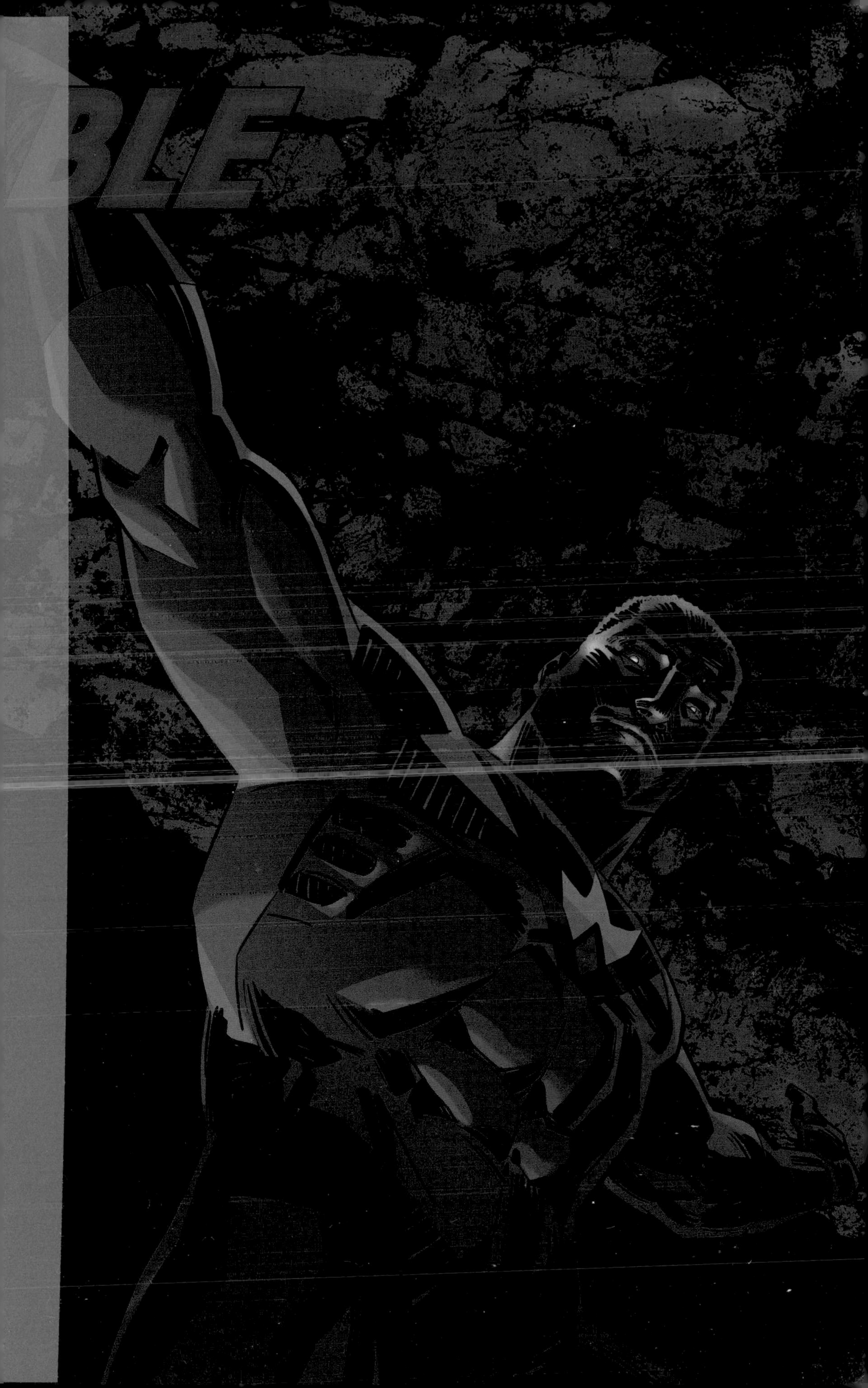
BLE

CREATED & WRITTEN BY: **MARK WAID**

ARTIST: **PETER KRAUSE**

COLORIST: **ANDREW DALHOUSE**
LETTERER: **ED DUKESHIRE**
EDITOR: **MATT GAGNON**

COVER: **GENE HA**
COLORS/ **MATTHEW WILSON**

PELTONIAN CHARACTER DESIGN: **PAUL AZACETA**

TRADE DESIGN: **ERIKA TERRIQUEZ**

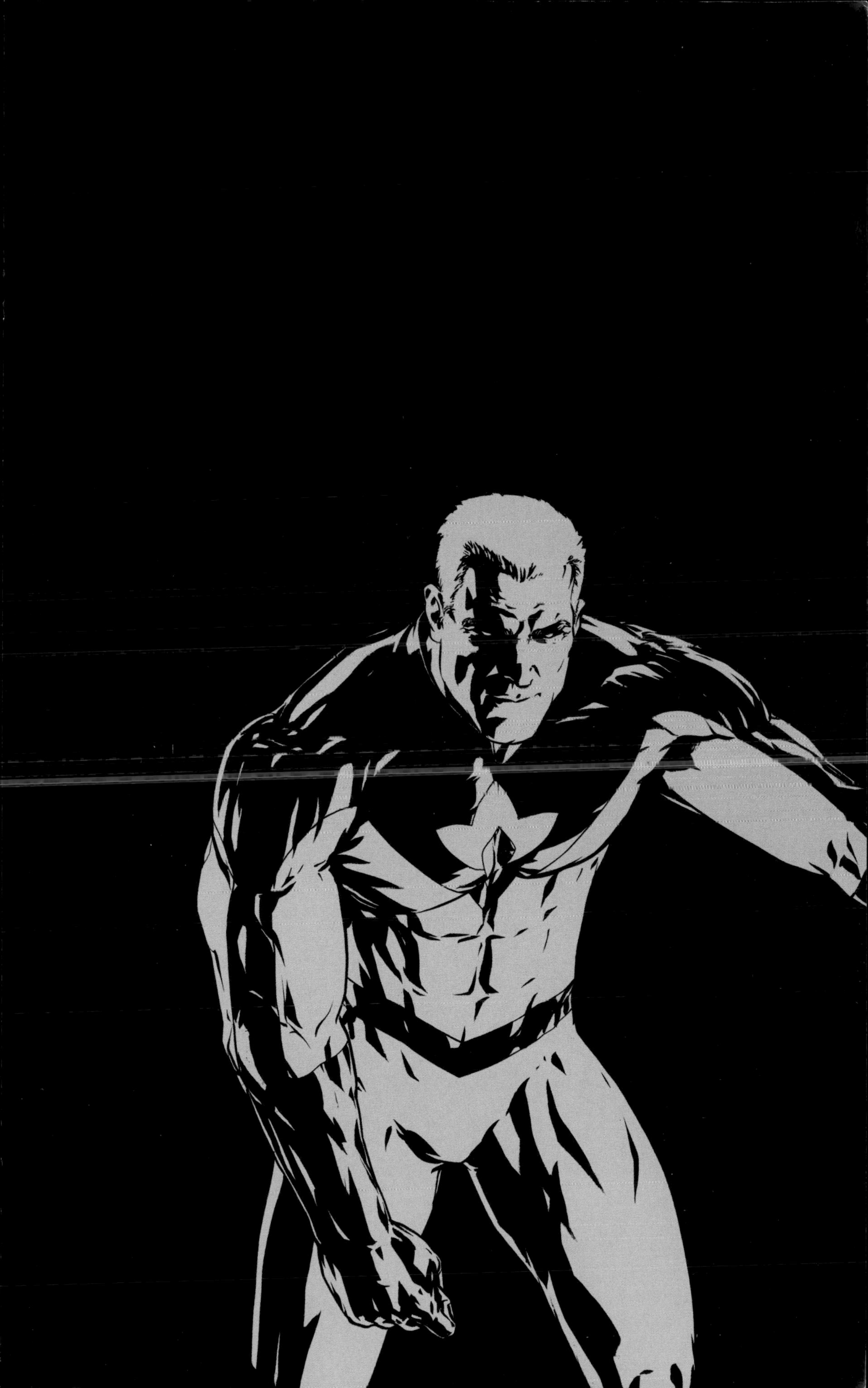

CHAPTER 5

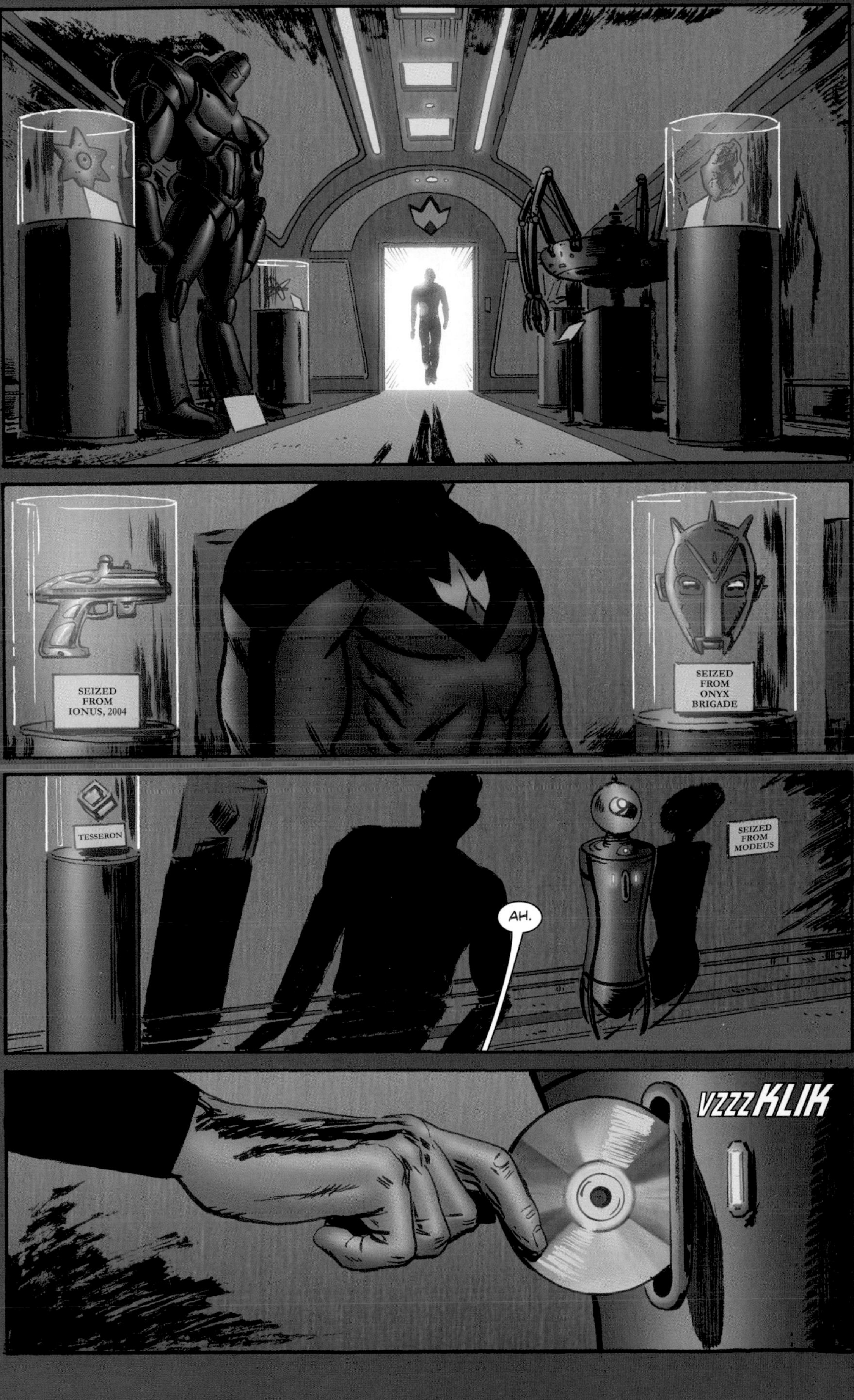
SEIZED FROM IONUS, 2004
SEIZED FROM ONYX BRIGADE
TESSERON
SEIZED FROM MODEUS
AH.
VZZZKLIK

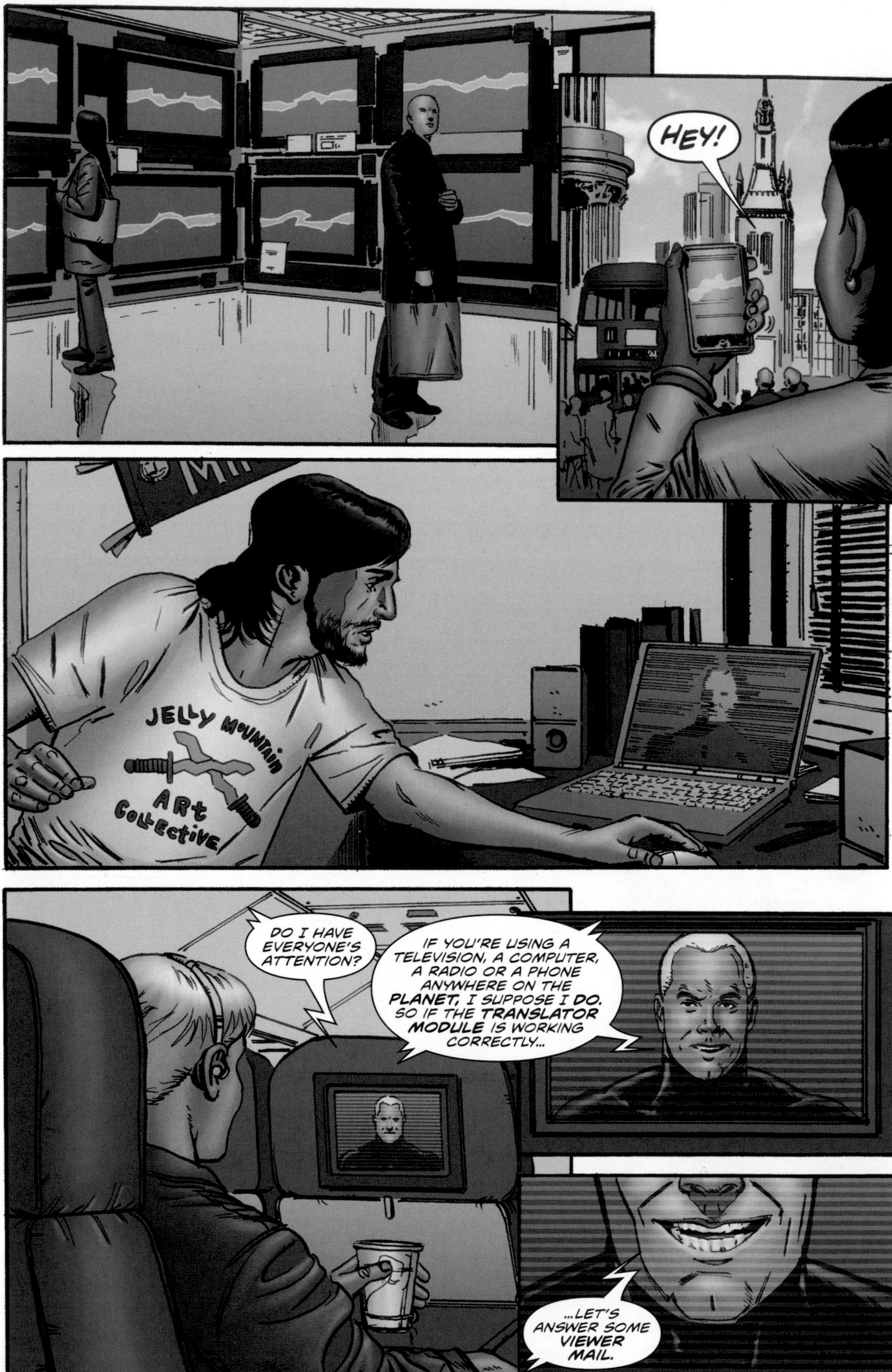
HEY!
JELLY MOUNTAIN ART COLLECTIVE
DO I HAVE EVERYONE'S ATTENTION?
IF YOU'RE USING A TELEVISION, A COMPUTER, A RADIO OR A PHONE ANYWHERE ON THE PLANET, I SUPPOSE I DO. SO IF THE TRANSLATOR MODULE IS WORKING CORRECTLY...
...LET'S ANSWER SOME VIEWER MAIL.

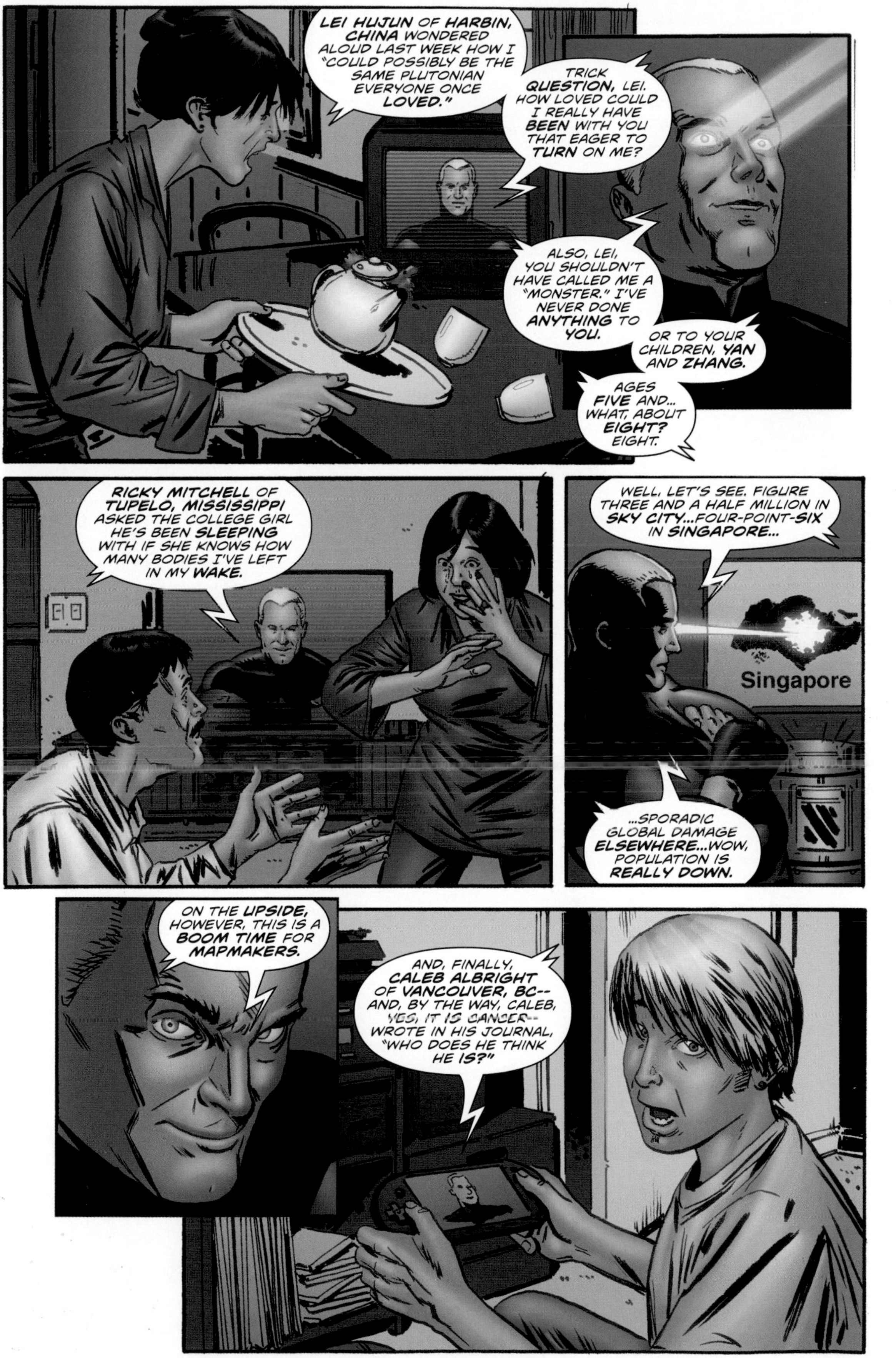
LEI HUJUN OF HARBIN, CHINA WONDERED ALOUD LAST WEEK HOW I "COULD POSSIBLY BE THE SAME PLUTONIAN EVERYONE ONCE LOVED."
TRICK QUESTION, LEI. HOW LOVED COULD I REALLY HAVE BEEN WITH YOU THAT EAGER TO TURN ON ME?
ALSO, LEI, YOU SHOULDN'T HAVE CALLED ME A "MONSTER." I'VE NEVER DONE ANYTHING TO YOU.
OR TO YOUR CHILDREN, YAN AND ZHANG.
AGES FIVE AND... WHAT, ABOUT EIGHT? EIGHT.
RICKY MITCHELL OF TUPELO, MISSISSIPPI ASKED THE COLLEGE GIRL HE'S BEEN SLEEPING WITH IF SHE KNOWS HOW MANY BODIES I'VE LEFT IN MY WAKE.
WELL, LET'S SEE. FIGURE THREE AND A HALF MILLION IN SKY CITY...FOUR-POINT-SIX IN SINGAPORE...
Singapore
...SPORADIC GLOBAL DAMAGE ELSEWHERE...WOW, POPULATION IS REALLY DOWN.
ON THE UPSIDE, HOWEVER, THIS IS A BOOM TIME FOR MAPMAKERS.
AND, FINALLY, CALEB ALBRIGHT OF VANCOUVER, BC-- AND, BY THE WAY, CALEB, YES, IT IS CANCER-- WROTE IN HIS JOURNAL, "WHO DOES HE THINK HE IS?"

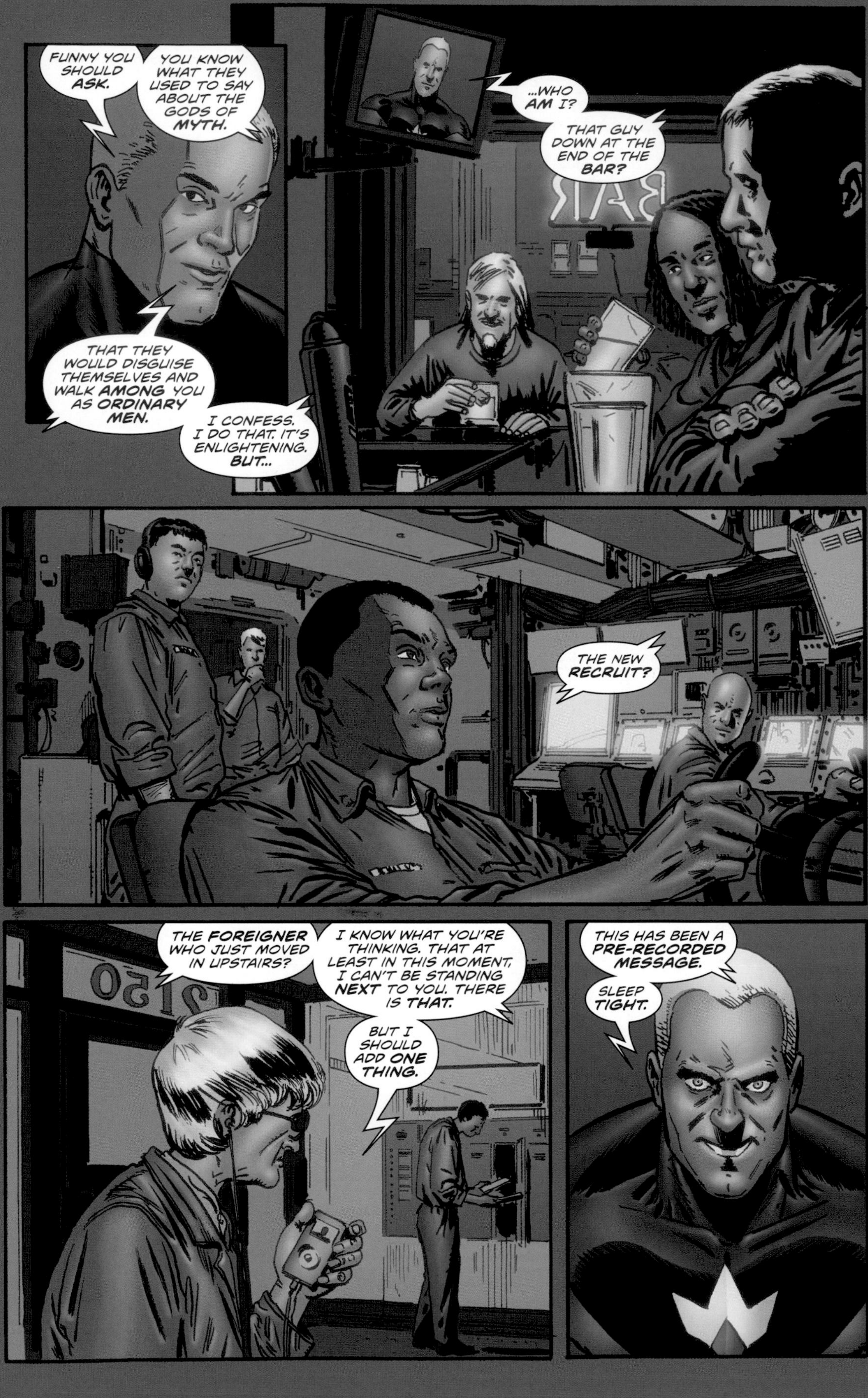
FUNNY YOU SHOULD ASK.
YOU KNOW WHAT THEY USED TO SAY ABOUT THE GODS OF MYTH.
THAT THEY WOULD DISGUISE THEMSELVES AND WALK AMONG YOU AS ORDINARY MEN.
I CONFESS. I DO THAT. IT'S ENLIGHTENING. BUT...
...WHO AM I?
THAT GUY DOWN AT THE END OF THE BAR?
BAR
THE NEW RECRUIT?
2150
THE FOREIGNER WHO JUST MOVED IN UPSTAIRS?
I KNOW WHAT YOU'RE THINKING. THAT AT LEAST IN THIS MOMENT, I CAN'T BE STANDING NEXT TO YOU. THERE IS THAT.
BUT I SHOULD ADD ONE THING.
THIS HAS BEEN A PRE-RECORDED MESSAGE.
SLEEP TIGHT.

HOME | WORLD | U.S. | REGION | BUSINESS | TECHNOLOGY | HEALTH | SPORTS | OPINION | ARTS

NATION TODAY

WORLD ON FIRE

Plutonian creates global panic; Casualties in the thousands.

>> MORE

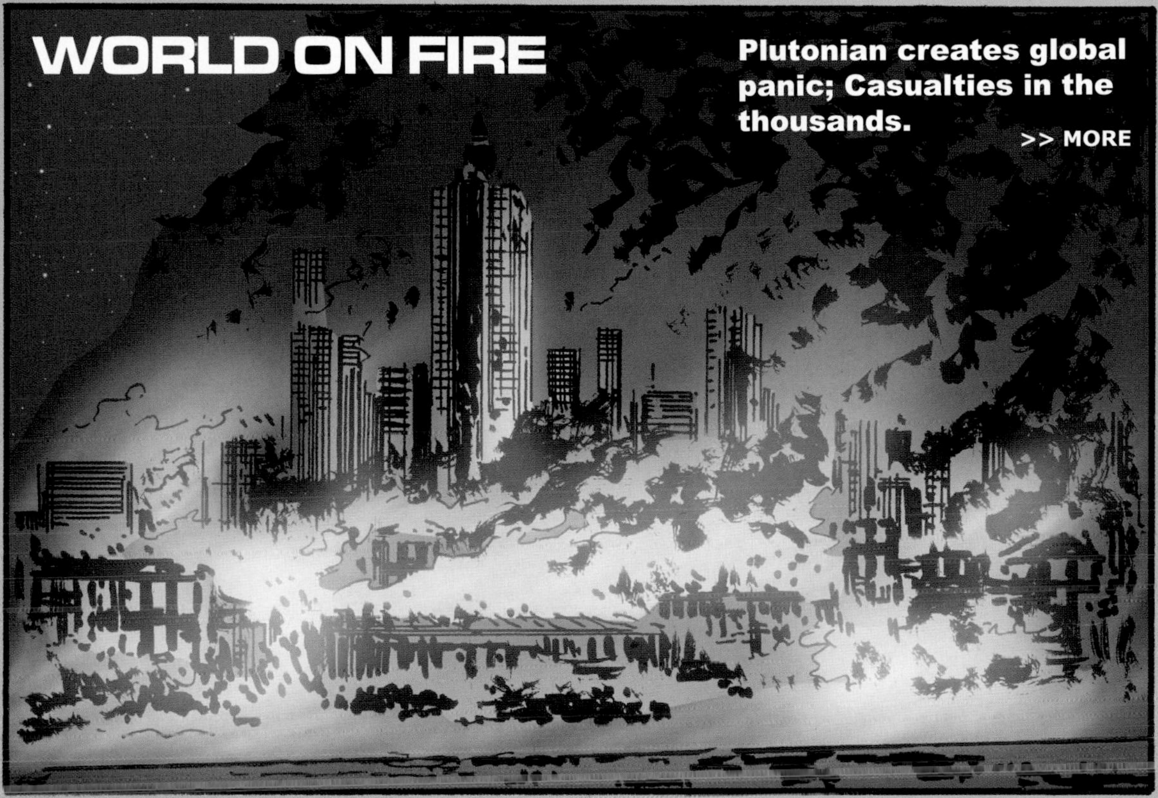

PLUTONIAN: WHAT HAPPENED?

Champion turned psychopath; Now history's greatest mass-murderer.

>> MORE

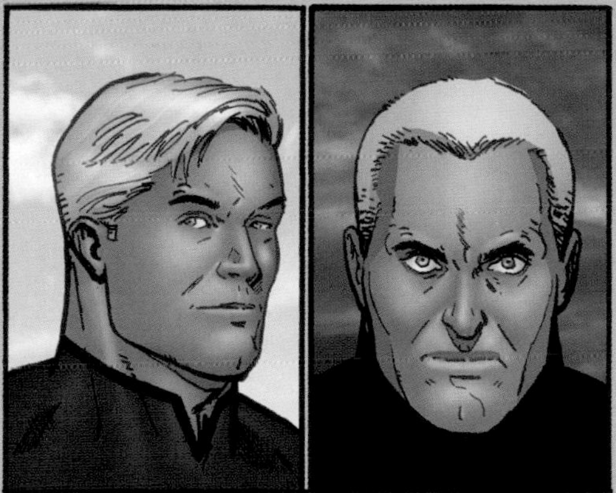

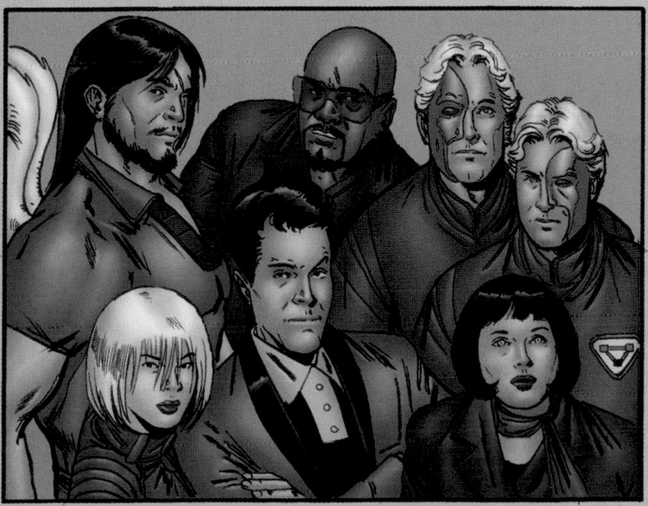

WHERE ARE THE HEROES?

Plutonian's former allies, The Paradigm, MIA; Are they even still alive?

>> MORE

HISTORY: Paradigm Origins
DOSSIER: Paradigm Members

HOME | WORLD | U.S. | REGION | BUSINESS | TECHNOLOGY | HEALTH | SPORTS | OPINION | ARTS

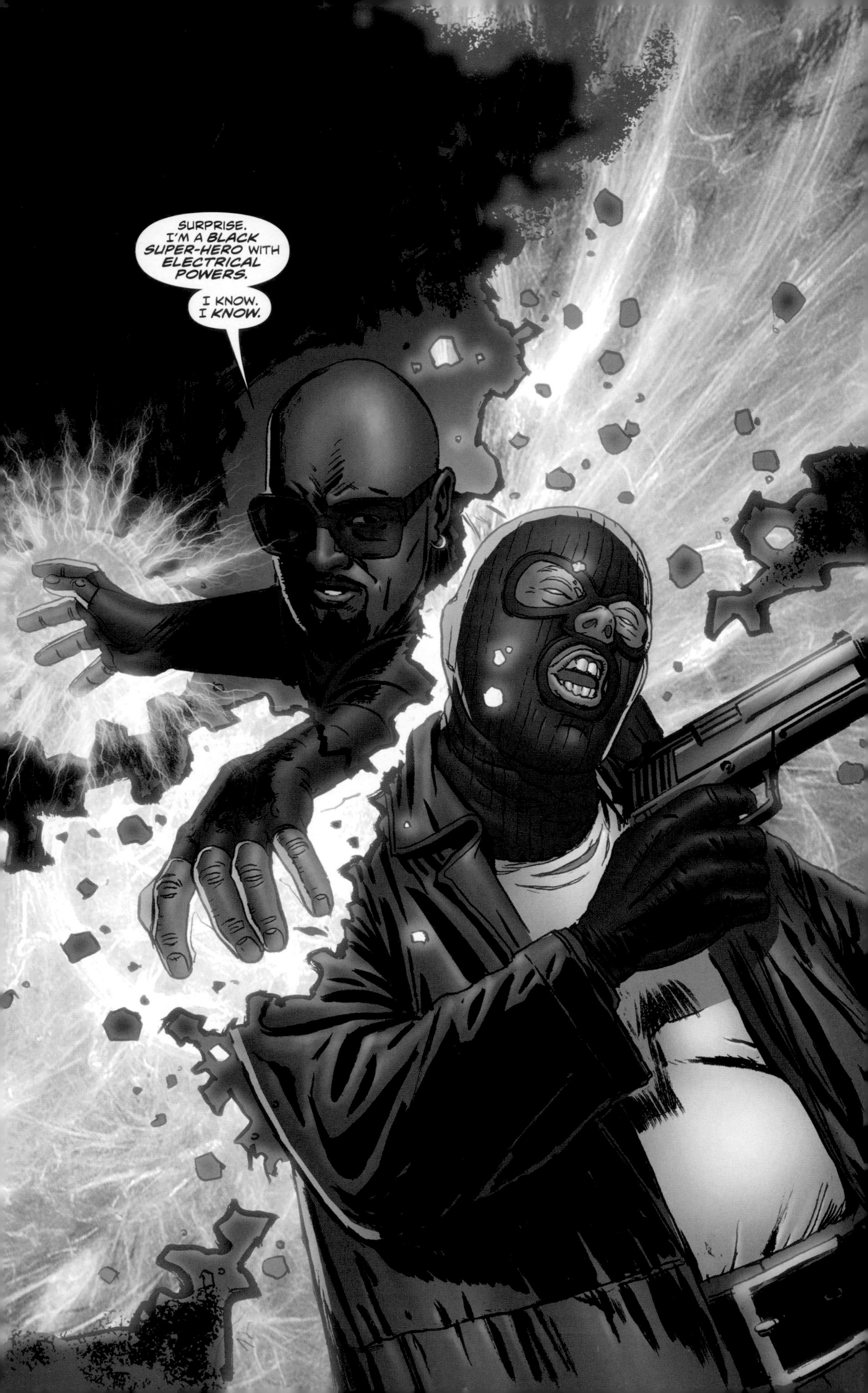
SURPRISE. I'M A BLACK SUPER-HERO WITH ELECTRICAL POWERS.
I KNOW. I KNOW.

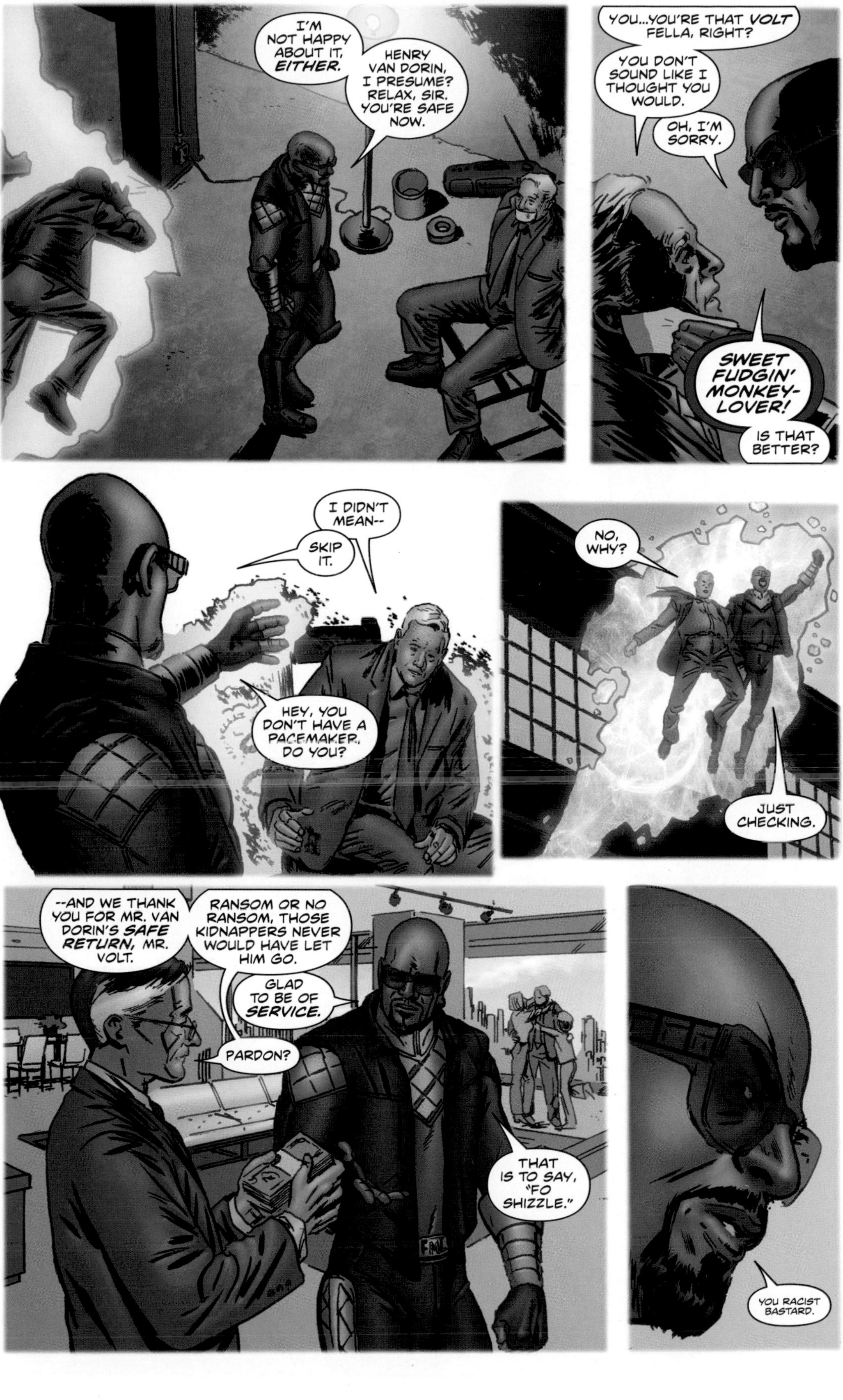
I'M NOT HAPPY ABOUT IT, EITHER.
HENRY VAN DORIN, I PRESUME? RELAX, SIR. YOU'RE SAFE NOW.
YOU...YOU'RE THAT VOLT FELLA, RIGHT?
YOU DON'T SOUND LIKE I THOUGHT YOU WOULD.
OH, I'M SORRY.
SWEET FUDGIN' MONKEY-LOVER!
IS THAT BETTER?
I DIDN'T MEAN--
SKIP IT.
HEY, YOU DON'T HAVE A PACEMAKER, DO YOU?
NO, WHY?
JUST CHECKING.
--AND WE THANK YOU FOR MR. VAN DORIN'S SAFE RETURN, MR. VOLT.
RANSOM OR NO RANSOM, THOSE KIDNAPPERS NEVER WOULD HAVE LET HIM GO.
GLAD TO BE OF SERVICE.
PARDON?
THAT IS TO SAY, "FO SHIZZLE."
YOU RACIST BASTARD.

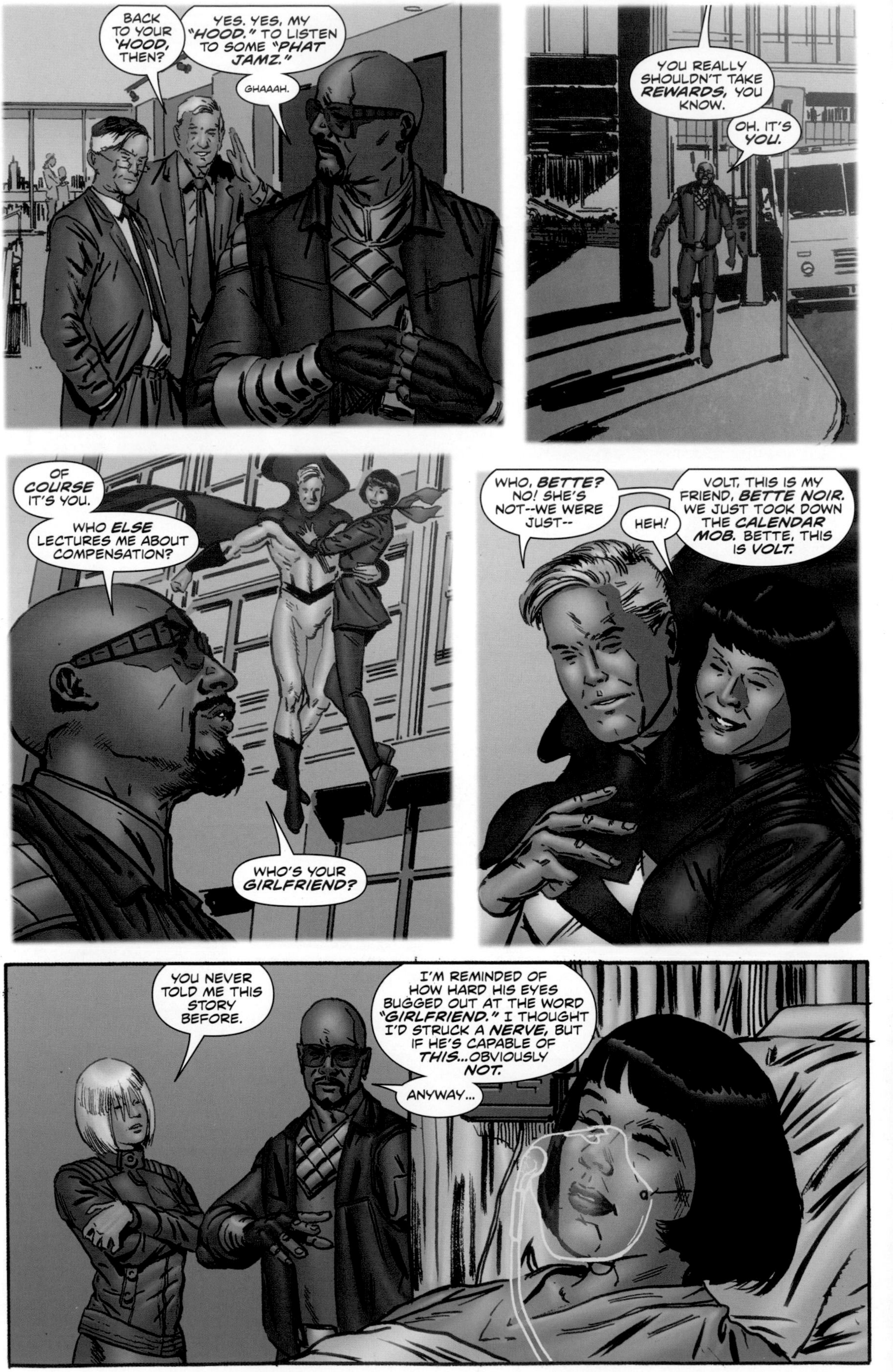
BACK TO YOUR 'HOOD, THEN?
YES. YES, MY "HOOD." TO LISTEN TO SOME "PHAT JAMZ."
GHAAAH.
YOU REALLY SHOULDN'T TAKE REWARDS, YOU KNOW.
OH. IT'S YOU.
OF COURSE IT'S YOU.
WHO ELSE LECTURES ME ABOUT COMPENSATION?
WHO'S YOUR GIRLFRIEND?
WHO, BETTE? NO! SHE'S NOT--WE WERE JUST--
VOLT, THIS IS MY FRIEND, BETTE NOIR. WE JUST TOOK DOWN THE CALENDAR MOB. BETTE, THIS IS VOLT.
HEH!
YOU NEVER TOLD ME THIS STORY BEFORE.
I'M REMINDED OF HOW HARD HIS EYES BUGGED OUT AT THE WORD "GIRLFRIEND." I THOUGHT I'D STRUCK A NERVE, BUT IF HE'S CAPABLE OF THIS...OBVIOUSLY NOT.
ANYWAY...

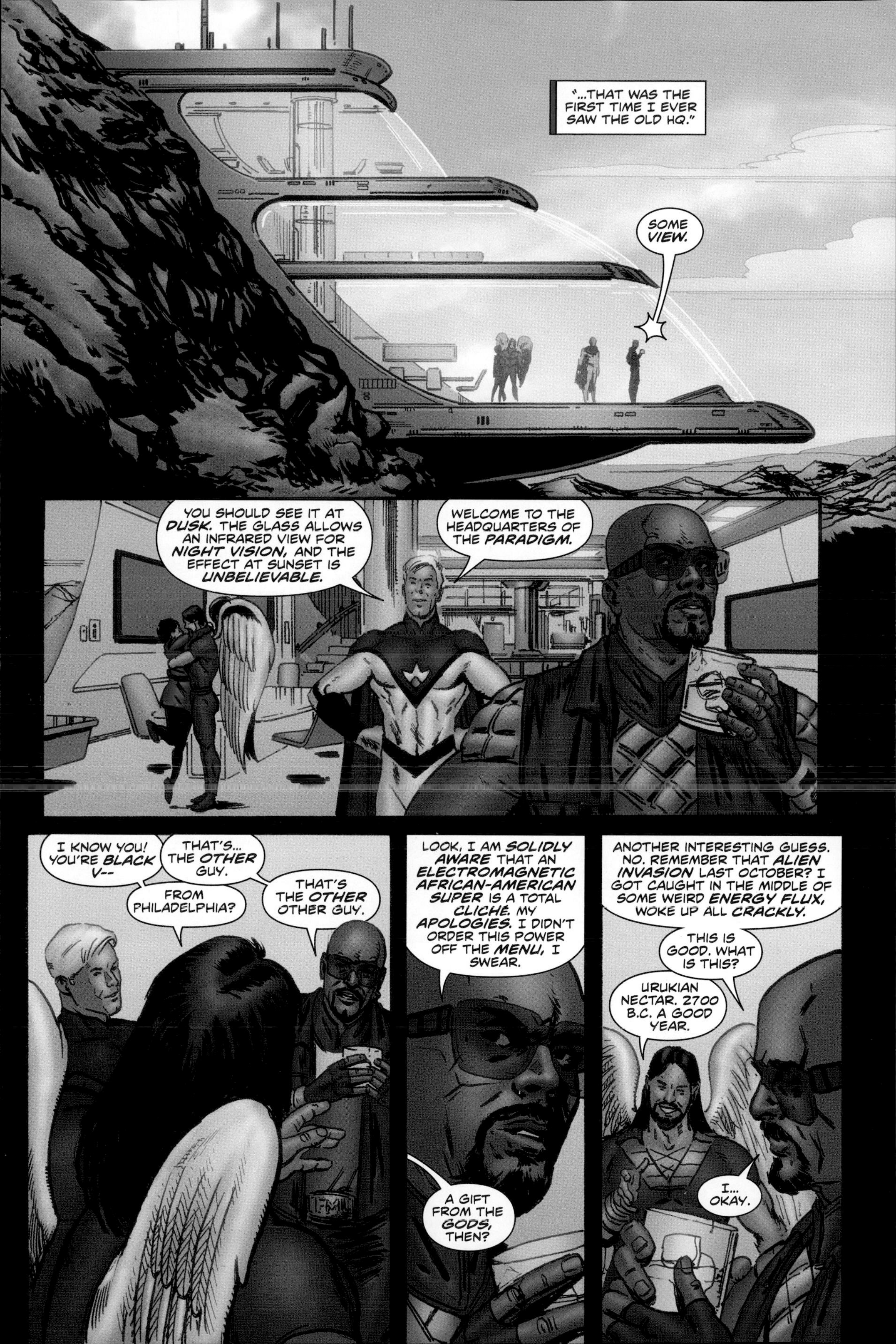
"...THAT WAS THE FIRST TIME I EVER SAW THE OLD HQ."
SOME VIEW.
YOU SHOULD SEE IT AT DUSK. THE GLASS ALLOWS AN INFRARED VIEW FOR NIGHT VISION, AND THE EFFECT AT SUNSET IS UNBELIEVABLE.
WELCOME TO THE HEADQUARTERS OF THE PARADIGM.
I KNOW YOU! YOU'RE BLACK V--
THAT'S... THE OTHER GUY.
FROM PHILADELPHIA?
THAT'S THE OTHER OTHER GUY.
LOOK, I AM SOLIDLY AWARE THAT AN ELECTROMAGNETIC AFRICAN-AMERICAN SUPER IS A TOTAL CLICHÉ. MY APOLOGIES. I DIDN'T ORDER THIS POWER OFF THE MENU, I SWEAR.
A GIFT FROM THE GODS, THEN?
ANOTHER INTERESTING GUESS. NO. REMEMBER THAT ALIEN INVASION LAST OCTOBER? I GOT CAUGHT IN THE MIDDLE OF SOME WEIRD ENERGY FLUX, WOKE UP ALL CRACKLY.
THIS IS GOOD. WHAT IS THIS?
URUKIAN NECTAR. 2700 B.C. A GOOD YEAR.
I... OKAY.

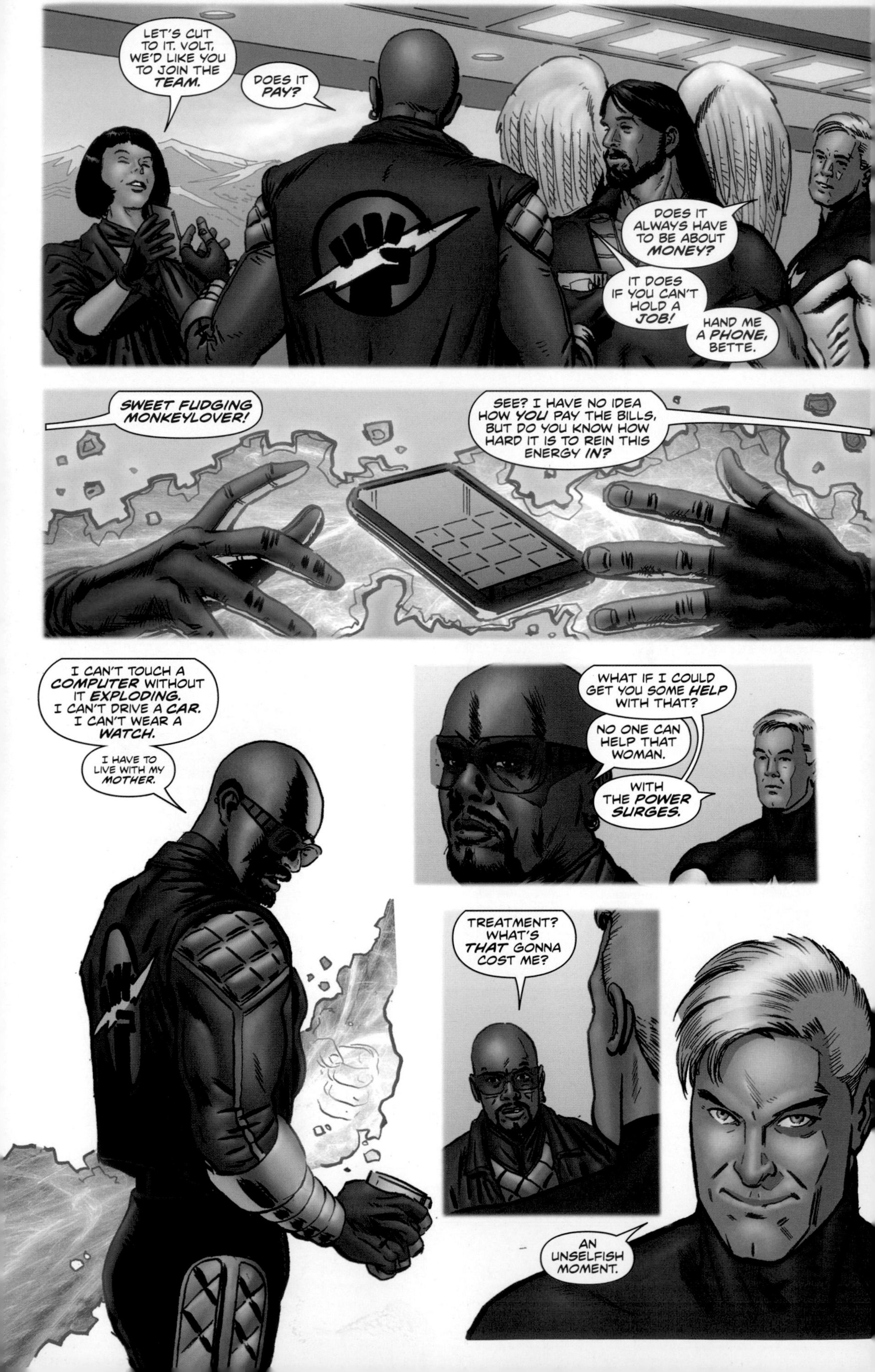
LET'S CUT TO IT. VOLT, WE'D LIKE YOU TO JOIN THE TEAM.
DOES IT PAY?
DOES IT ALWAYS HAVE TO BE ABOUT MONEY?
IT DOES IF YOU CAN'T HOLD A JOB!
HAND ME A PHONE, BETTE.
SWEET FUDGING MONKEYLOVER!
SEE? I HAVE NO IDEA HOW YOU PAY THE BILLS, BUT DO YOU KNOW HOW HARD IT IS TO REIN THIS ENERGY IN?
I CAN'T TOUCH A COMPUTER WITHOUT IT EXPLODING. I CAN'T DRIVE A CAR. I CAN'T WEAR A WATCH.
I HAVE TO LIVE WITH MY MOTHER.
WHAT IF I COULD GET YOU SOME HELP WITH THAT?
NO ONE CAN HELP THAT WOMAN.
WITH THE POWER SURGES.
TREATMENT? WHAT'S THAT GONNA COST ME?
AN UNSELFISH MOMENT.

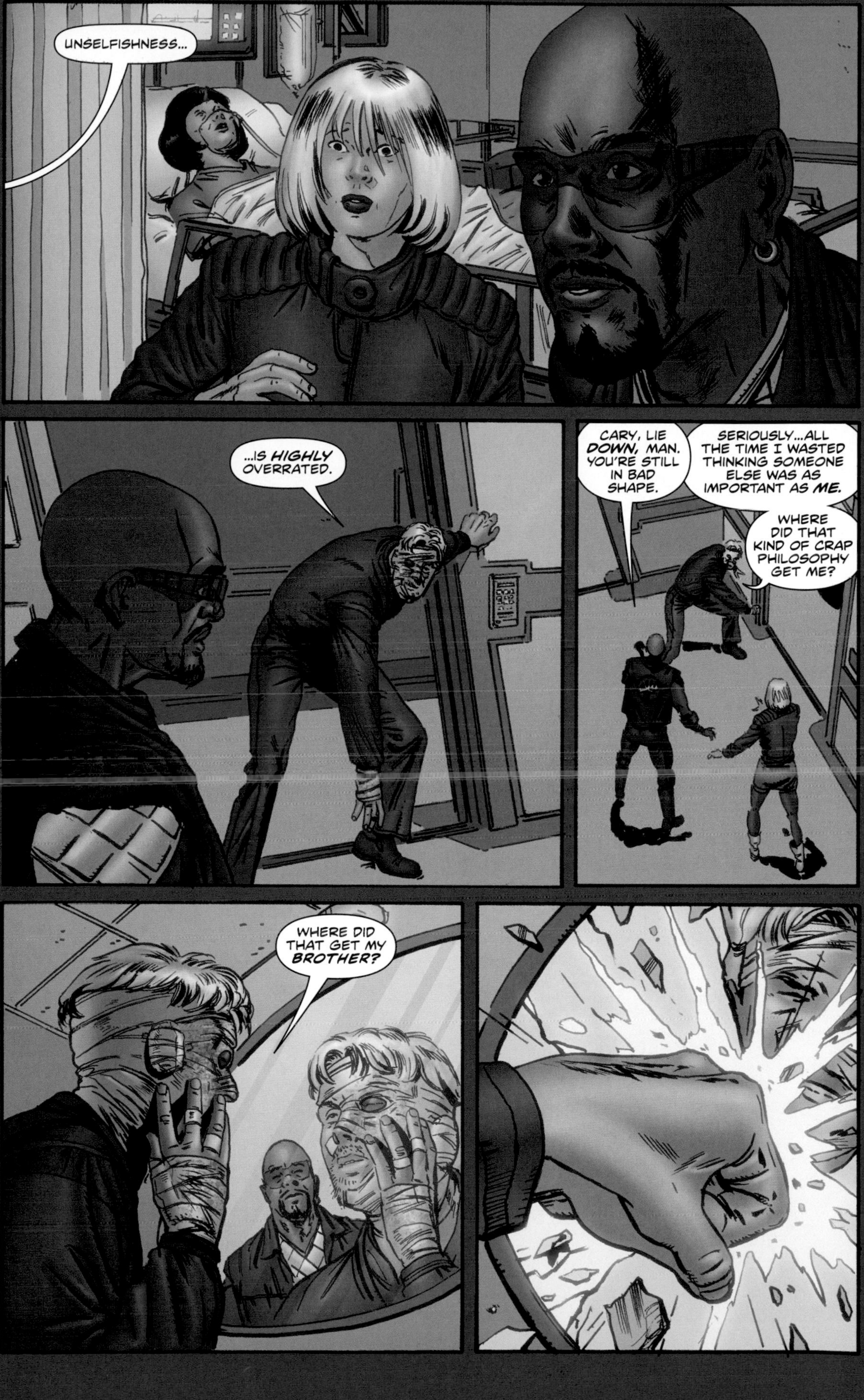
UNSELFISHNESS...
...IS HIGHLY OVERRATED.
CARY, LIE DOWN, MAN. YOU'RE STILL IN BAD SHAPE.
SERIOUSLY...ALL THE TIME I WASTED THINKING SOMEONE ELSE WAS AS IMPORTANT AS ME.
WHERE DID THAT KIND OF CRAP PHILOSOPHY GET ME?
WHERE DID THAT GET MY BROTHER?

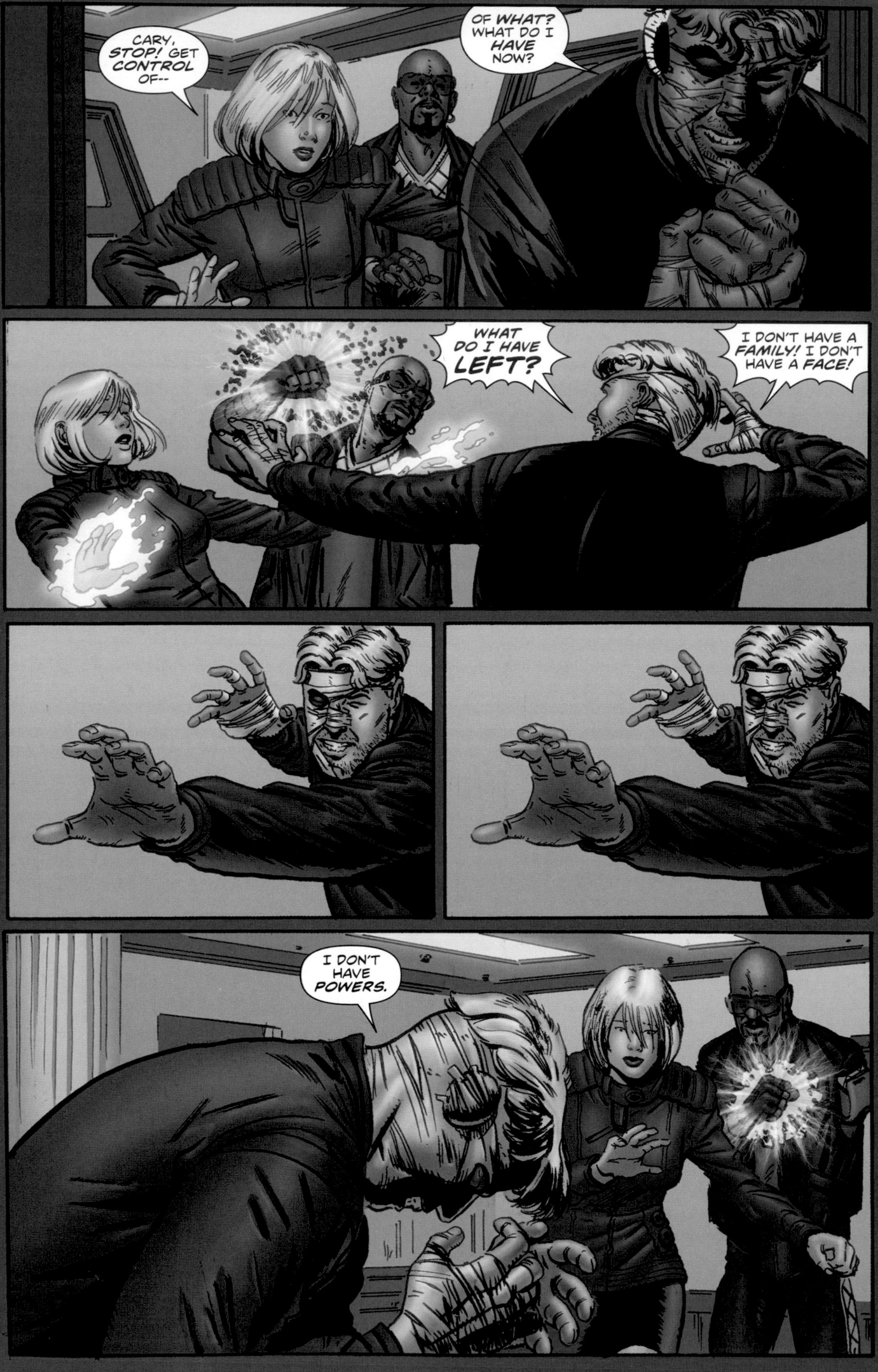

CARY, STOP! GET CONTROL OF--
OF WHAT? WHAT DO I HAVE NOW?
WHAT DO I HAVE LEFT?
I DON'T HAVE A FAMILY! I DON'T HAVE A FACE!
I DON'T HAVE POWERS.

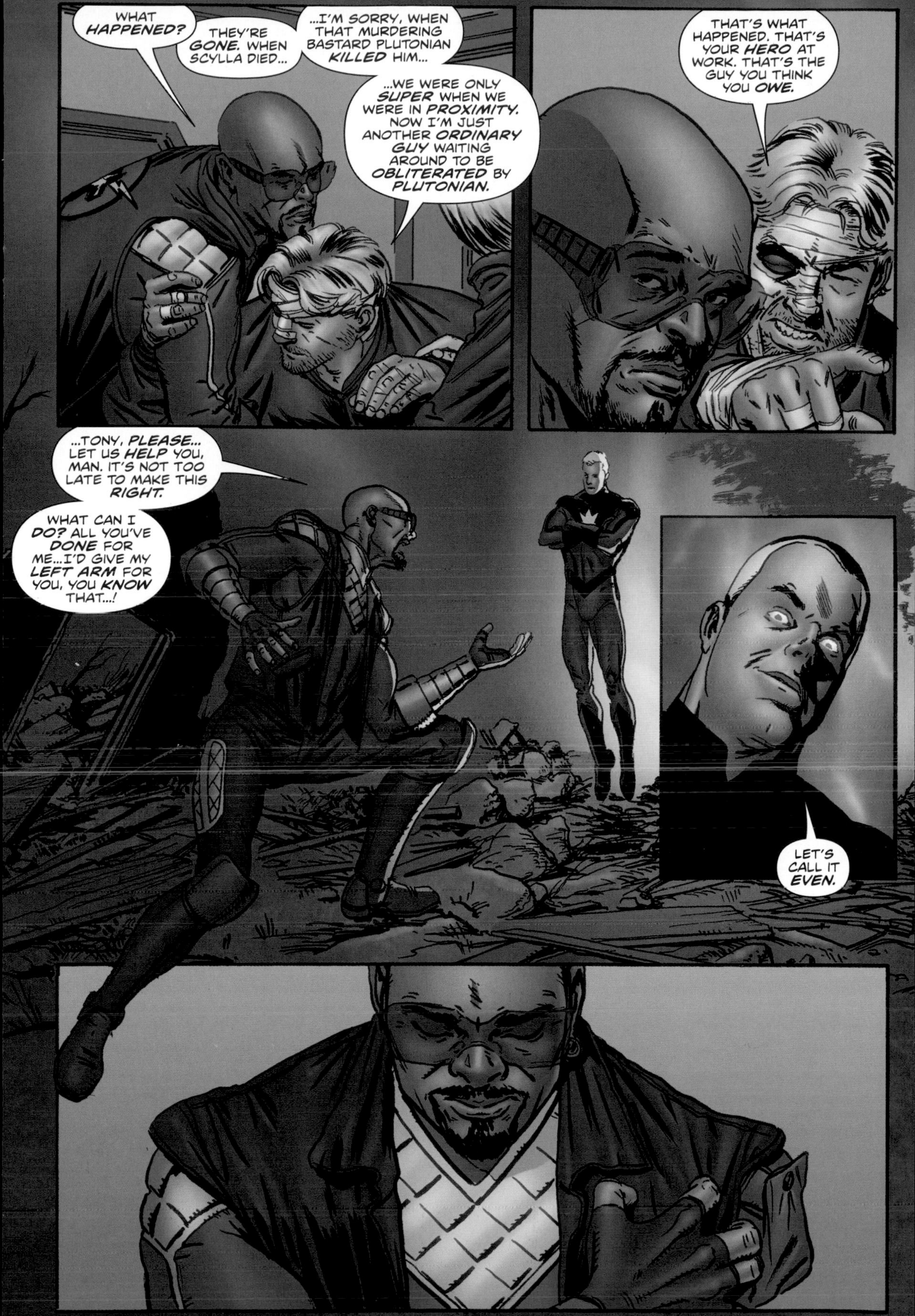
WHAT HAPPENED?
THEY'RE GONE. WHEN SCYLLA DIED...
...I'M SORRY, WHEN THAT MURDERING BASTARD PLUTONIAN KILLED HIM...
...WE WERE ONLY SUPER WHEN WE WERE IN PROXIMITY. NOW I'M JUST ANOTHER ORDINARY GUY WAITING AROUND TO BE OBLITERATED BY PLUTONIAN.
THAT'S WHAT HAPPENED. THAT'S YOUR HERO AT WORK. THAT'S THE GUY YOU THINK YOU OWE.
...TONY, PLEASE... LET US HELP YOU, MAN. IT'S NOT TOO LATE TO MAKE THIS RIGHT.
WHAT CAN I DO? ALL YOU'VE DONE FOR ME...I'D GIVE MY LEFT ARM FOR YOU, YOU KNOW THAT...!
LET'S CALL IT EVEN.

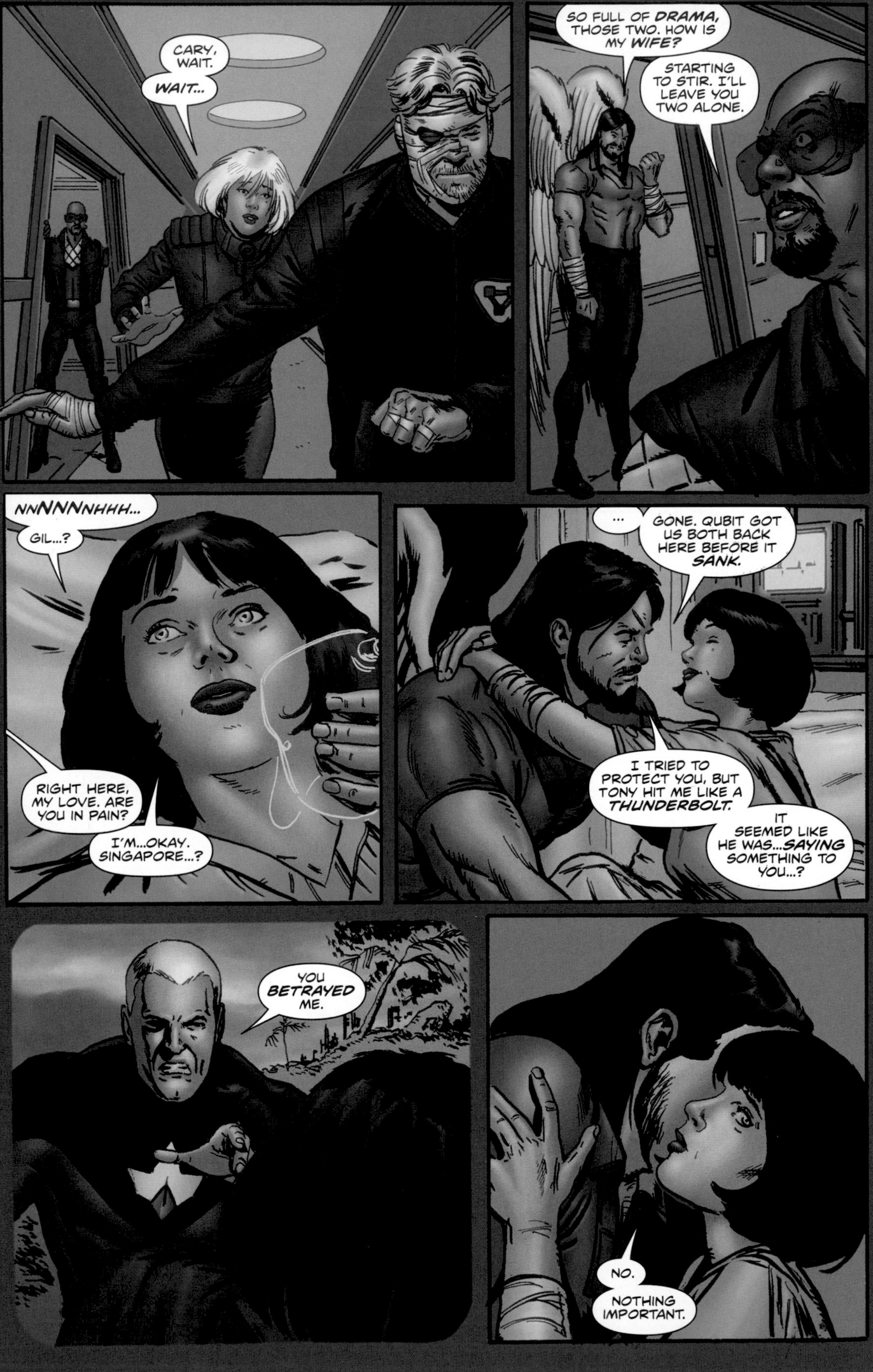

CARY, WAIT.
WAIT...
SO FULL OF DRAMA, THOSE TWO. HOW IS MY WIFE?
STARTING TO STIR. I'LL LEAVE YOU TWO ALONE.
NNNNNHHH...
GIL...?
RIGHT HERE, MY LOVE. ARE YOU IN PAIN?
I'M...OKAY. SINGAPORE...?
...
GONE. QUBIT GOT US BOTH BACK HERE BEFORE IT SANK.
I TRIED TO PROTECT YOU, BUT TONY HIT ME LIKE A THUNDERBOLT.
IT SEEMED LIKE HE WAS...SAYING SOMETHING TO YOU...?
YOU BETRAYED ME.
NO.
NOTHING IMPORTANT.

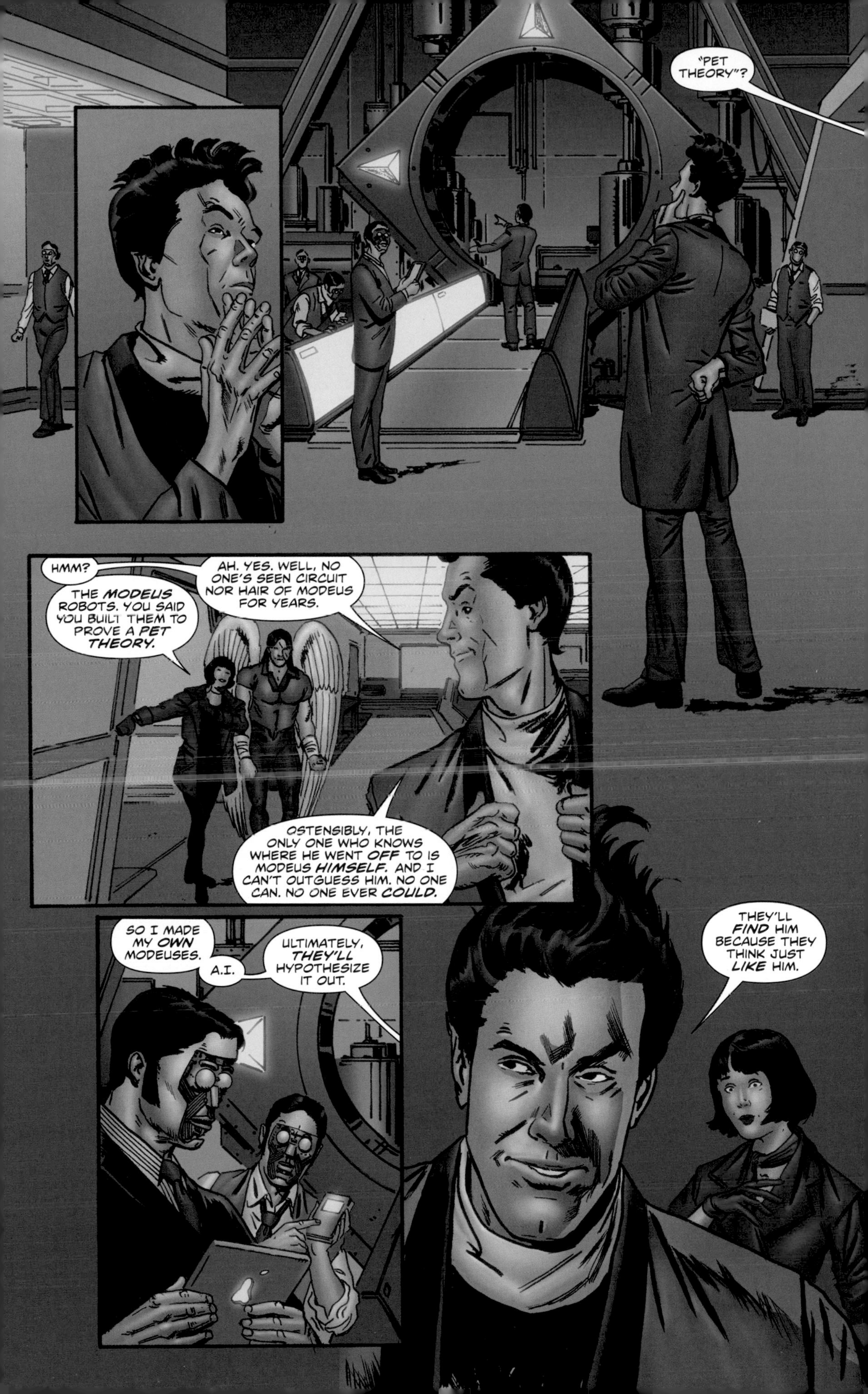
"PET THEORY"?
HMM?
THE MODEUS ROBOTS. YOU SAID YOU BUILT THEM TO PROVE A PET THEORY.
AH. YES. WELL, NO ONE'S SEEN CIRCUIT NOR HAIR OF MODEUS FOR YEARS.
OSTENSIBLY, THE ONLY ONE WHO KNOWS WHERE HE WENT OFF TO IS MODEUS HIMSELF. AND I CAN'T OUTGUESS HIM. NO ONE CAN. NO ONE EVER COULD.
SO I MADE MY OWN MODEUSES.
A.I.
ULTIMATELY, THEY'LL HYPOTHESIZE IT OUT.
THEY'LL FIND HIM BECAUSE THEY THINK JUST LIKE HIM.

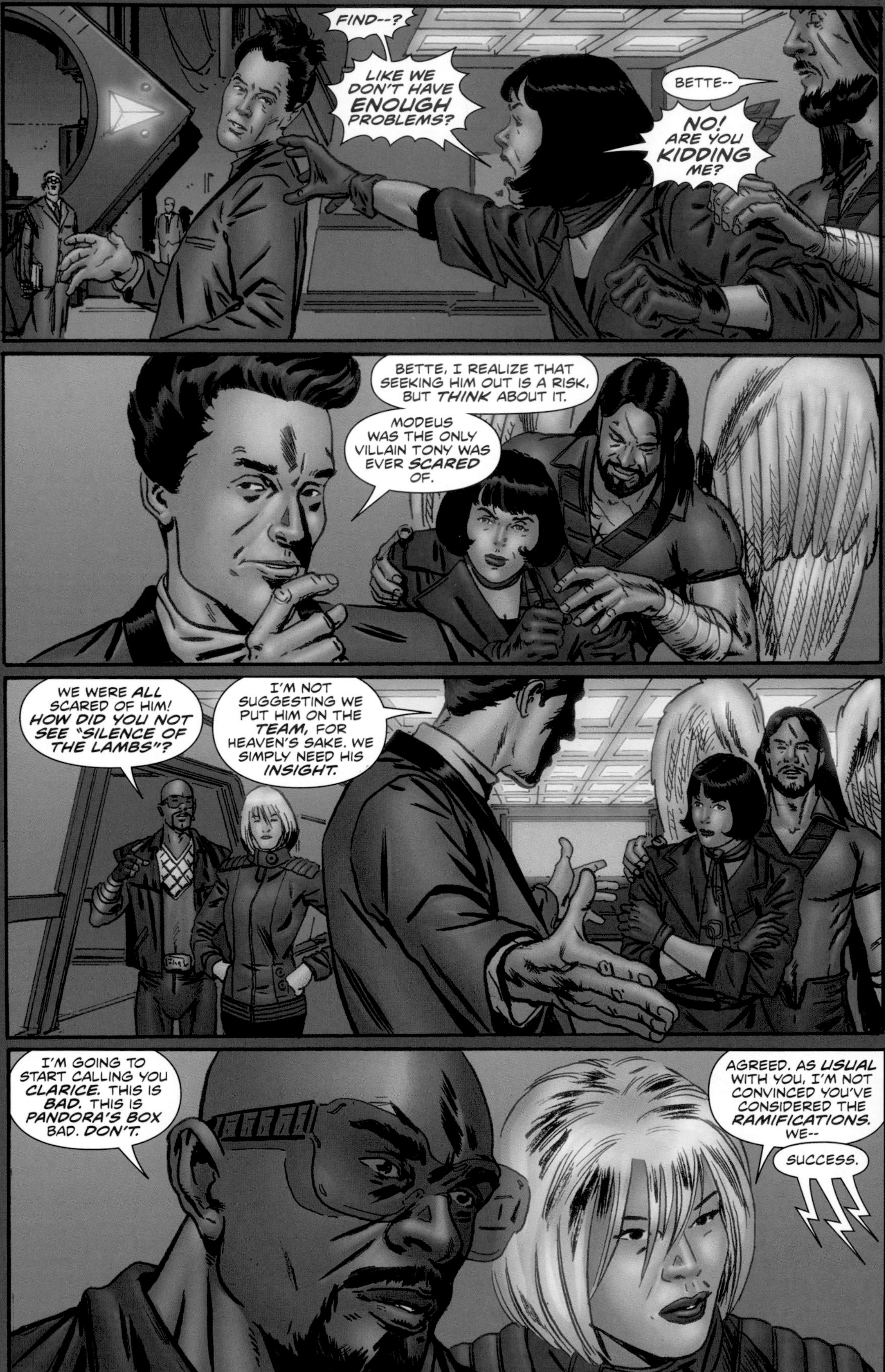
FIND--?
LIKE WE DON'T HAVE ENOUGH PROBLEMS?
BETTE--
NO! ARE YOU KIDDING ME?
BETTE, I REALIZE THAT SEEKING HIM OUT IS A RISK, BUT THINK ABOUT IT.
MODEUS WAS THE ONLY VILLAIN TONY WAS EVER SCARED OF.
WE WERE ALL SCARED OF HIM! HOW DID YOU NOT SEE "SILENCE OF THE LAMBS"?
I'M NOT SUGGESTING WE PUT HIM ON THE TEAM, FOR HEAVEN'S SAKE. WE SIMPLY NEED HIS INSIGHT.
I'M GOING TO START CALLING YOU CLARICE. THIS IS BAD. THIS IS PANDORA'S BOX BAD. DON'T.
AGREED. AS USUAL WITH YOU, I'M NOT CONVINCED YOU'VE CONSIDERED THE RAMIFICATIONS. WE--
SUCCESS.

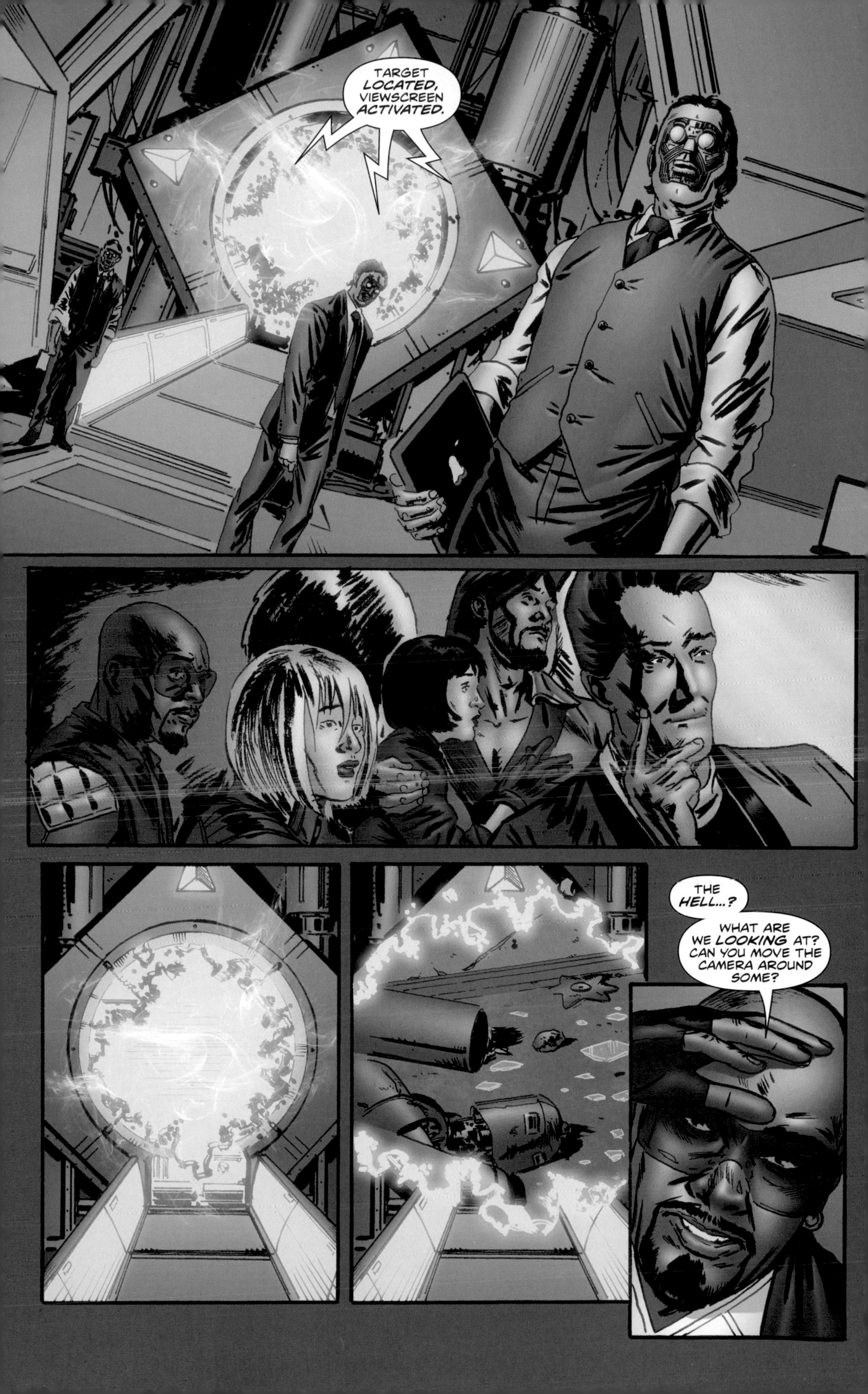
TARGET LOCATED, VIEWSCREEN ACTIVATED.
THE HELL...?
WHAT ARE WE LOOKING AT? CAN YOU MOVE THE CAMERA AROUND SOME?

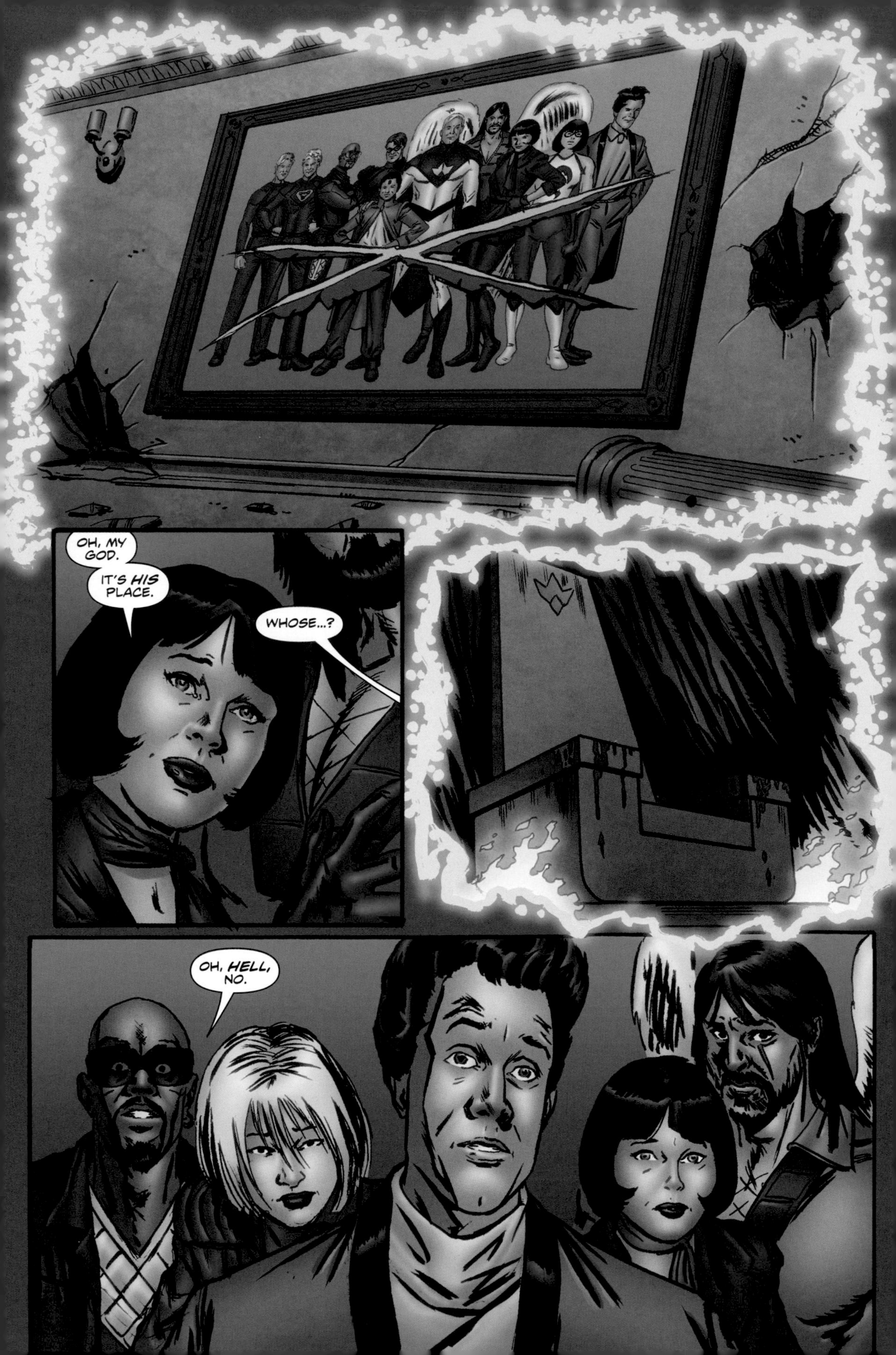
OH, MY GOD.
IT'S *HIS* PLACE.
WHOSE...?
OH, *HELL,* NO.

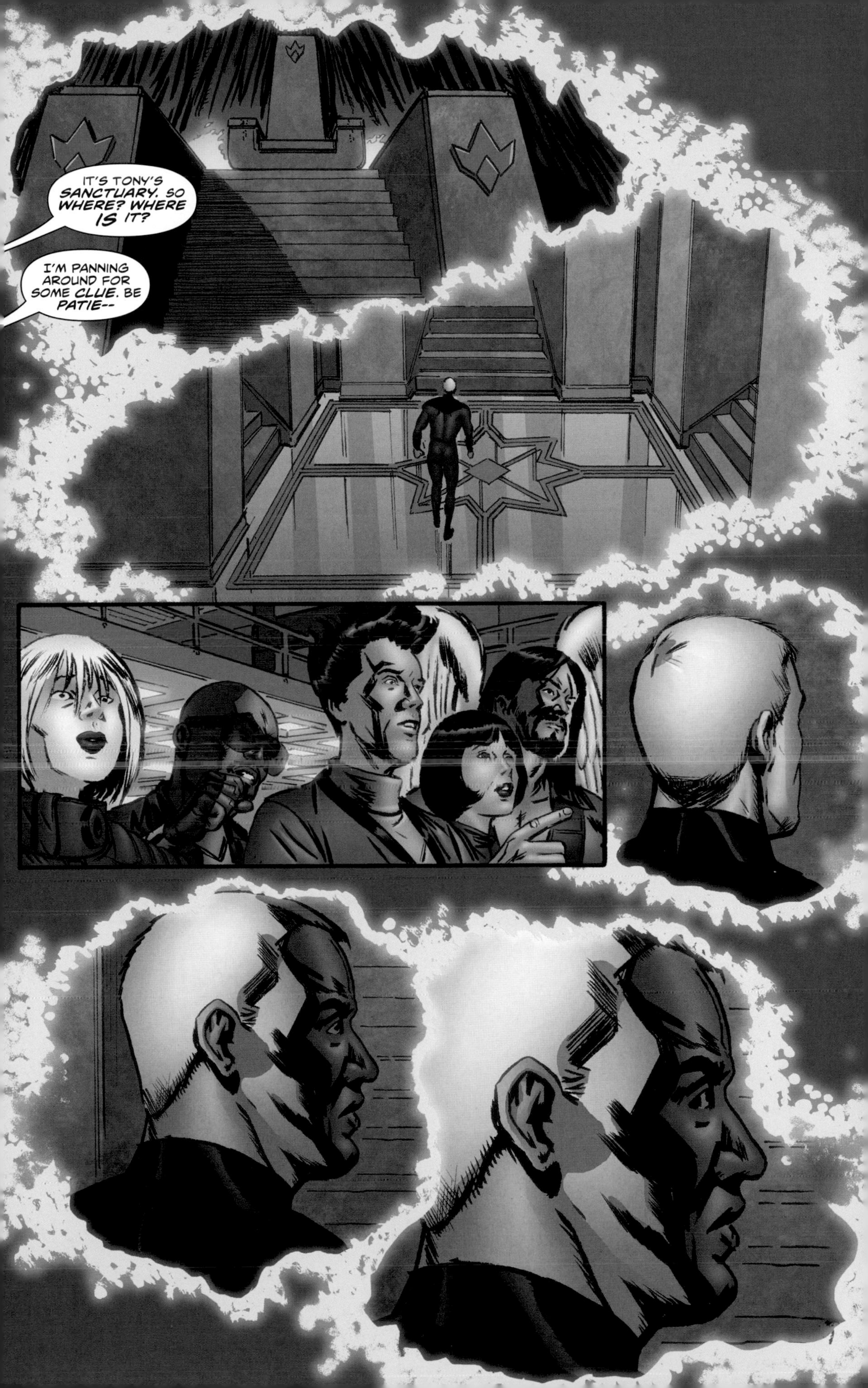
IT'S TONY'S SANCTUARY. SO WHERE? WHERE IS IT?
I'M PANNING AROUND FOR SOME CLUE. BE PATIE--

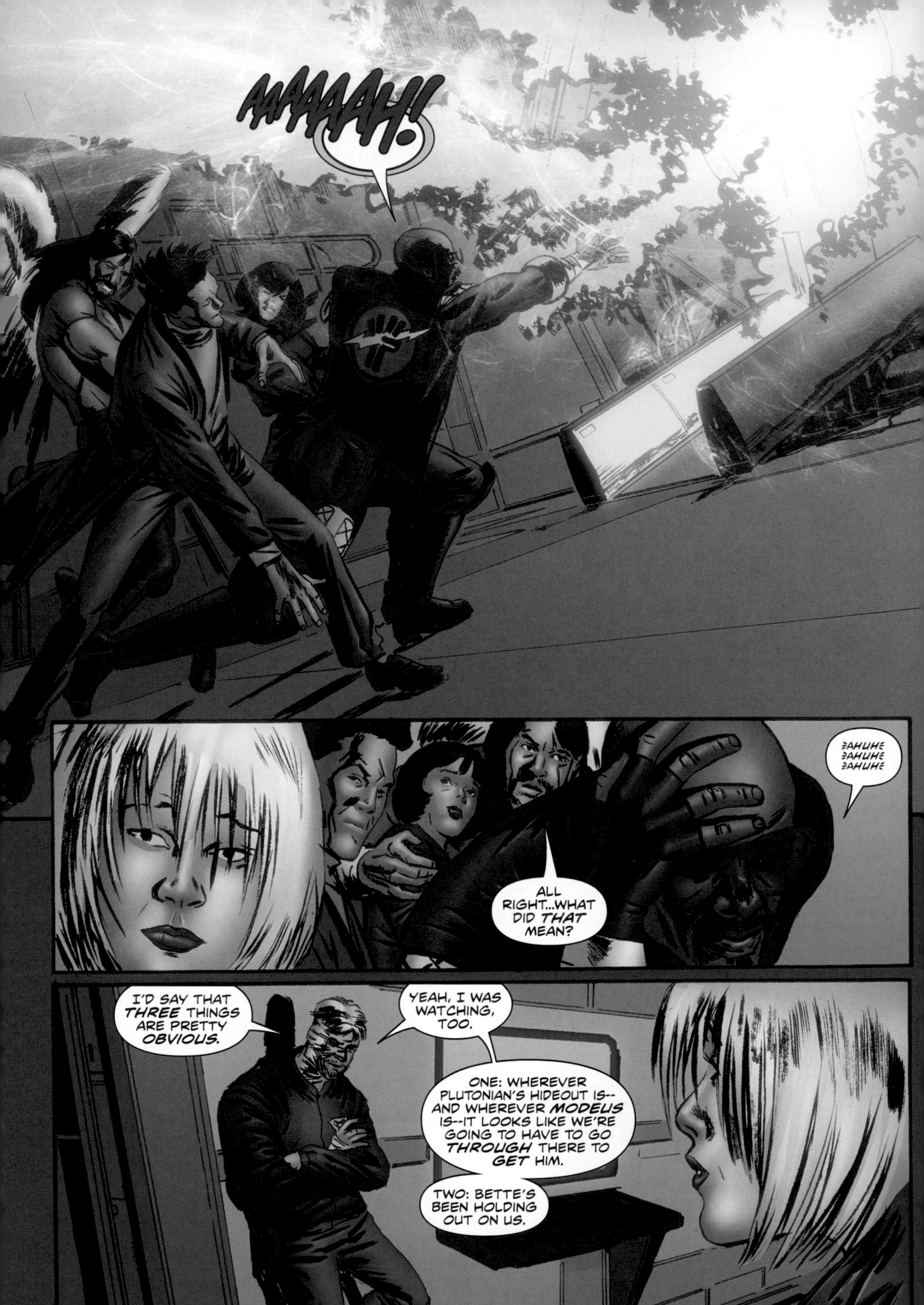
AAAAAAH!
AHUH AHUH AHUH
ALL RIGHT...WHAT DID *THAT* MEAN?
I'D SAY THAT *THREE* THINGS ARE PRETTY *OBVIOUS.*
YEAH, I WAS WATCHING, TOO.
ONE: WHEREVER PLUTONIAN'S HIDEOUT IS--AND WHEREVER *MODEUS* IS--IT LOOKS LIKE WE'RE GOING TO HAVE TO GO *THROUGH* THERE TO *GET* HIM.
TWO: BETTE'S BEEN HOLDING OUT ON US.

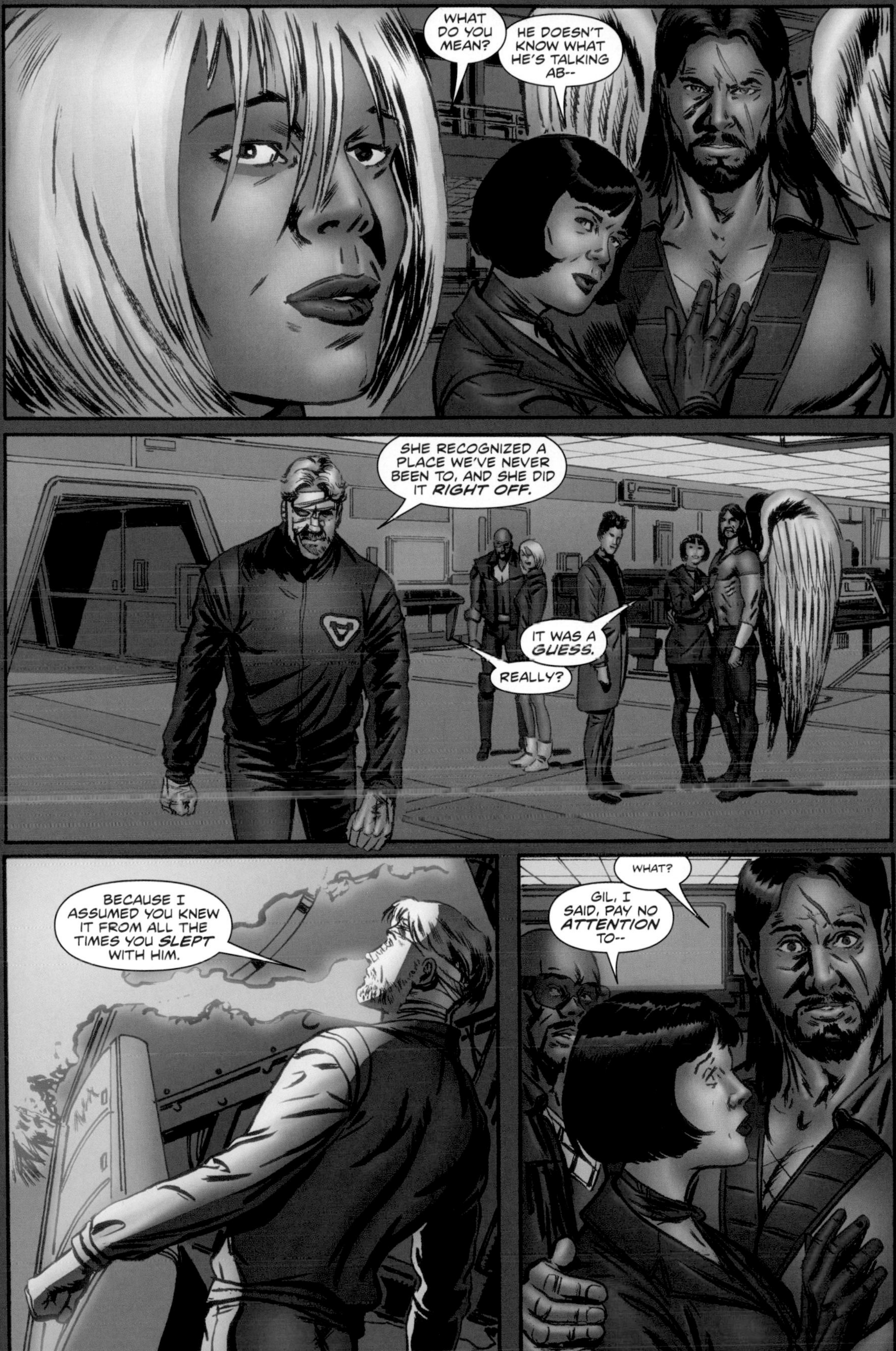
WHAT DO YOU MEAN?
HE DOESN'T KNOW WHAT HE'S TALKING AB--
SHE RECOGNIZED A PLACE WE'VE NEVER BEEN TO, AND SHE DID IT *RIGHT OFF.*
IT WAS A *GUESS.*
REALLY?
BECAUSE I ASSUMED YOU KNEW IT FROM ALL THE TIMES YOU *SLEPT* WITH HIM.
WHAT?
GIL, I SAID, PAY NO *ATTENTION* TO--

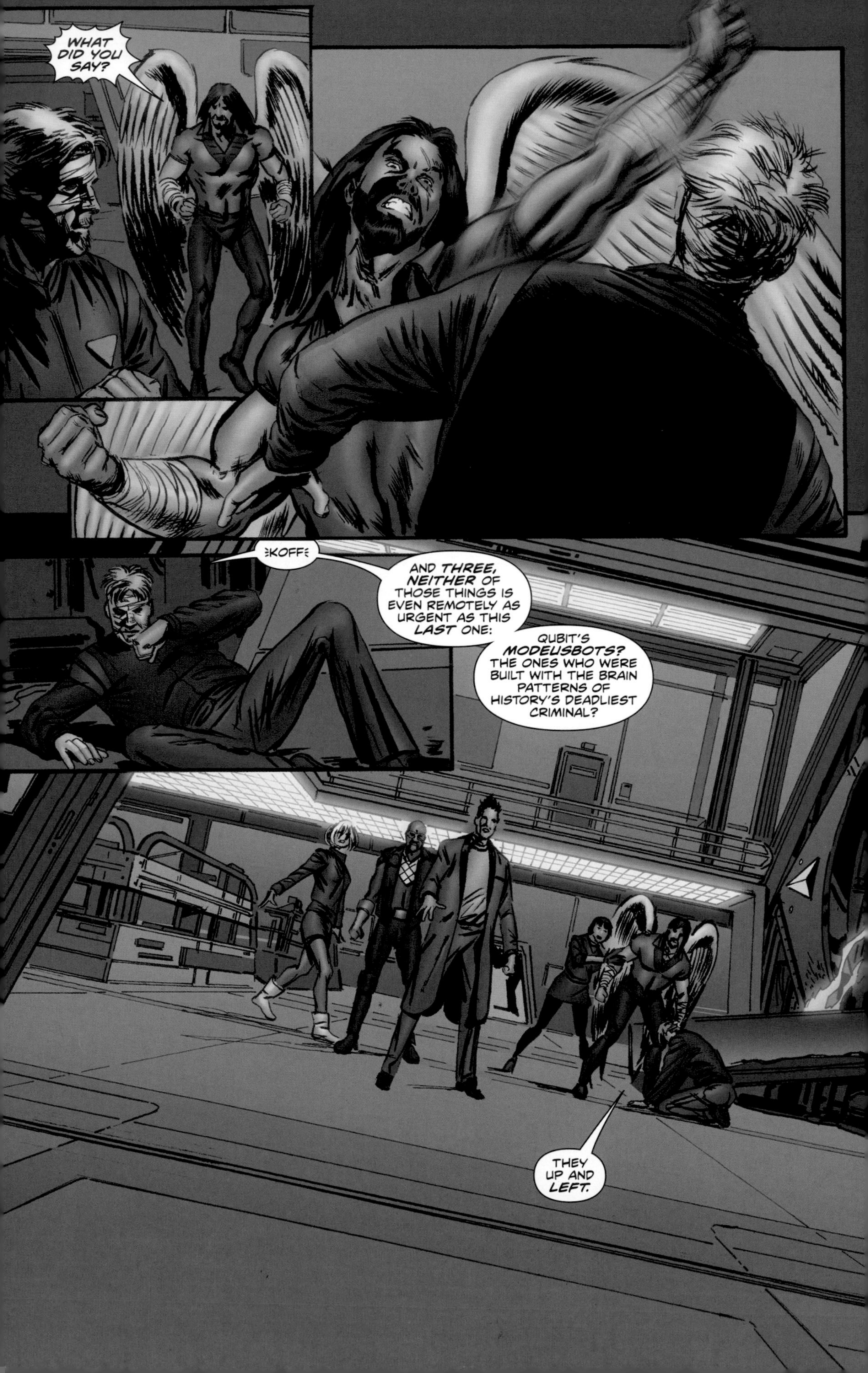
WHAT DID YOU SAY?
KOFF
AND THREE, NEITHER OF THOSE THINGS IS EVEN REMOTELY AS URGENT AS THIS LAST ONE:
QUBIT'S MODEUSBOTS? THE ONES WHO WERE BUILT WITH THE BRAIN PATTERNS OF HISTORY'S DEADLIEST CRIMINAL?
THEY UP AND LEFT.

CHAPTER 6

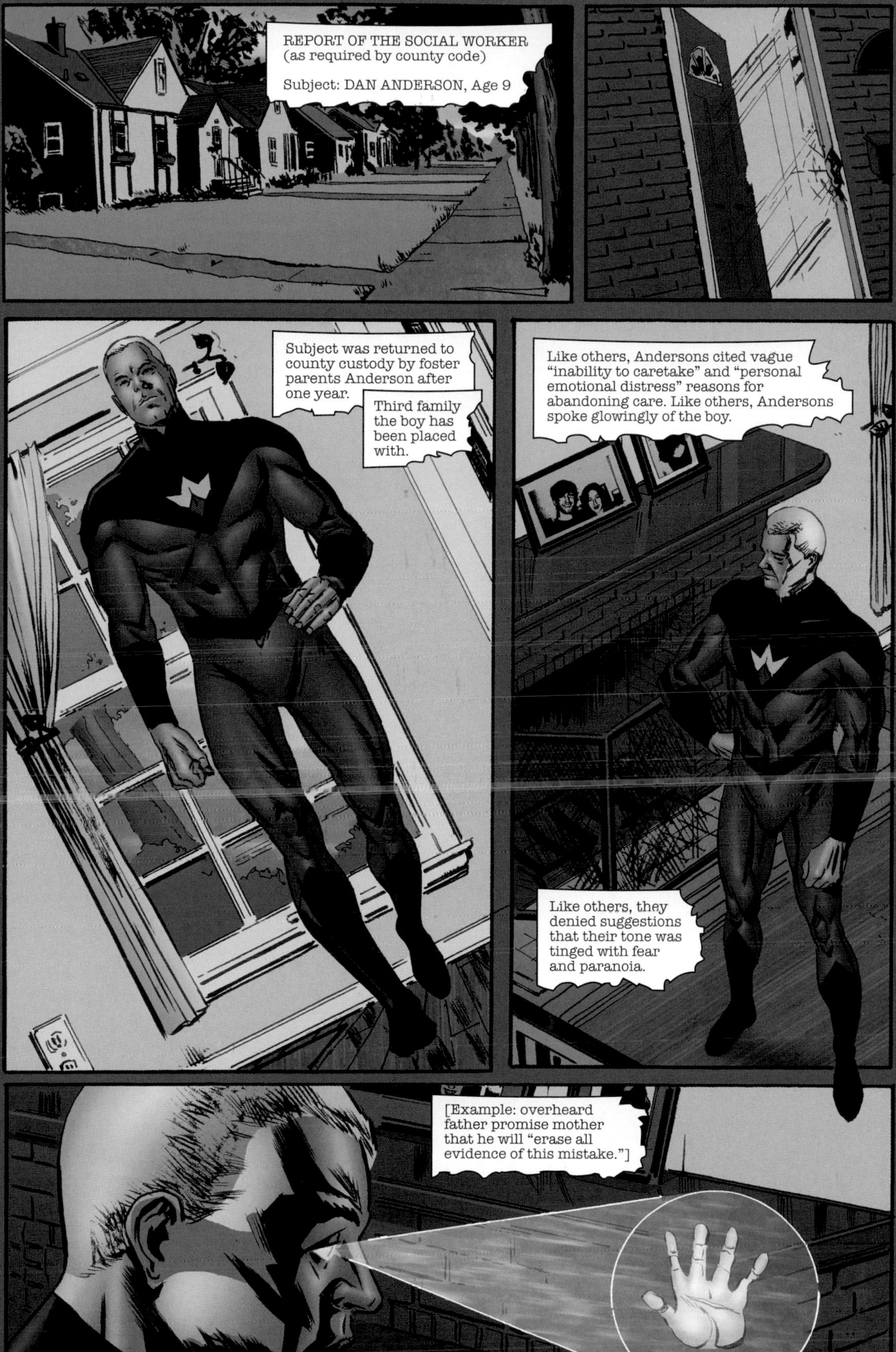
REPORT OF THE SOCIAL WORKER
(as required by county code)
Subject: DAN ANDERSON, Age 9
Subject was returned to county custody by foster parents Anderson after one year.
Third family the boy has been placed with.
Like others, Andersons cited vague "inability to caretake" and "personal emotional distress" reasons for abandoning care. Like others, Andersons spoke glowingly of the boy.
Like others, they denied suggestions that their tone was tinged with fear and paranoia.
[Example: overheard father promise mother that he will "erase all evidence of this mistake."]

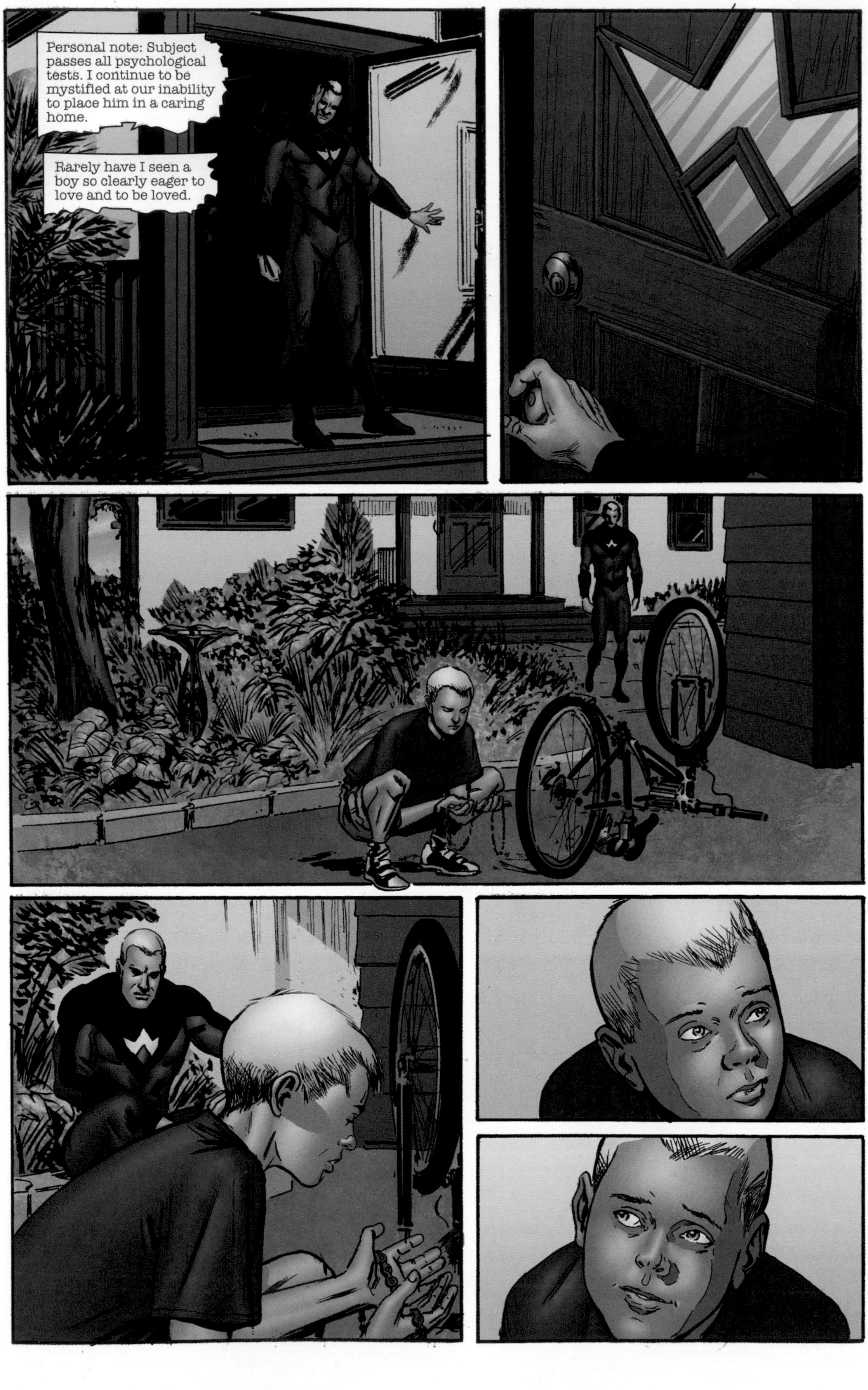
Personal note: Subject passes all psychological tests. I continue to be mystified at our inability to place him in a caring home.
Rarely have I seen a boy so clearly eager to love and to be loved.

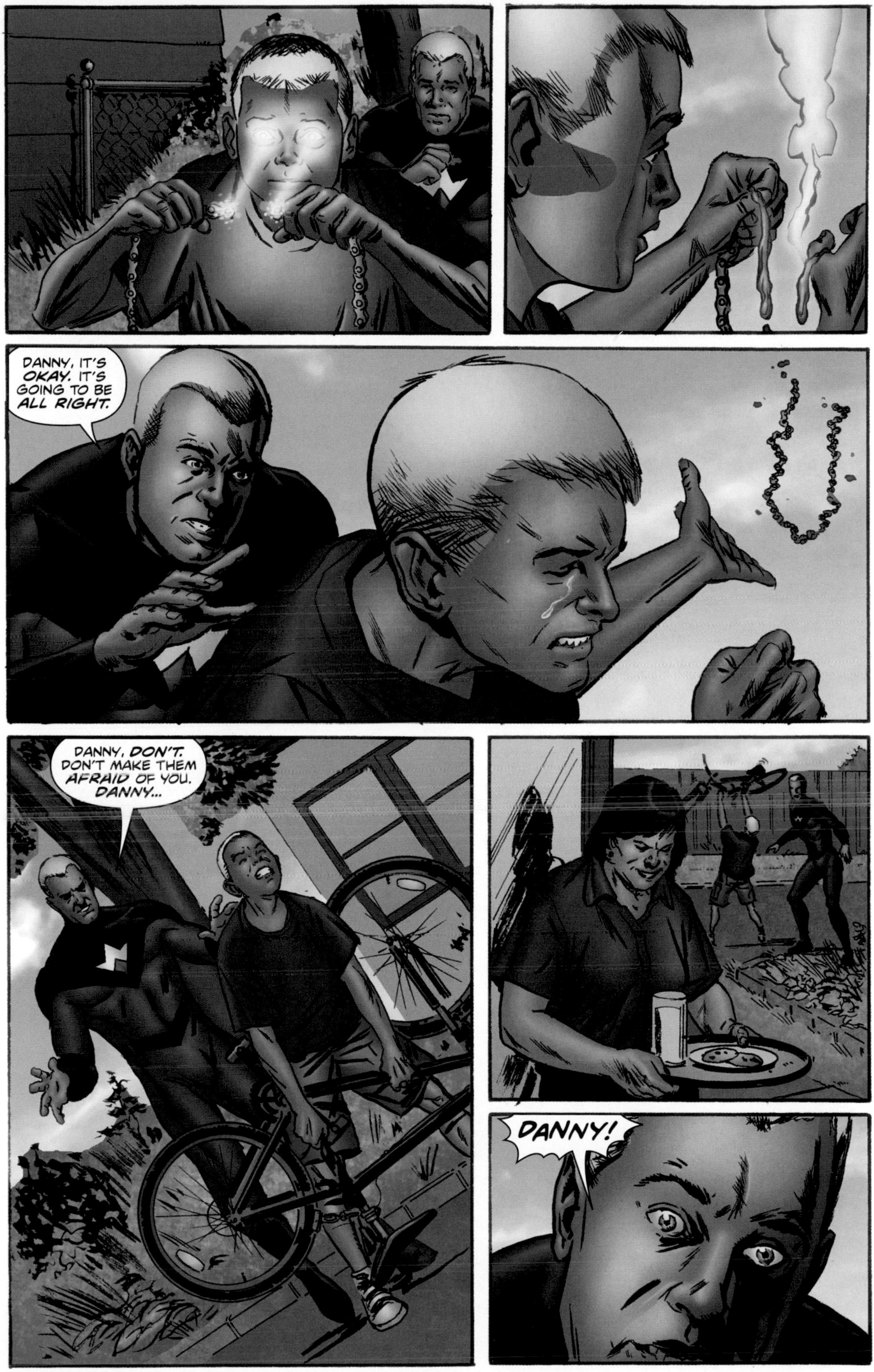
DANNY, IT'S *OKAY*. IT'S GOING TO BE *ALL RIGHT*.
DANNY, *DON'T*. DON'T MAKE THEM *AFRAID* OF YOU. *DANNY*...
DANNY!

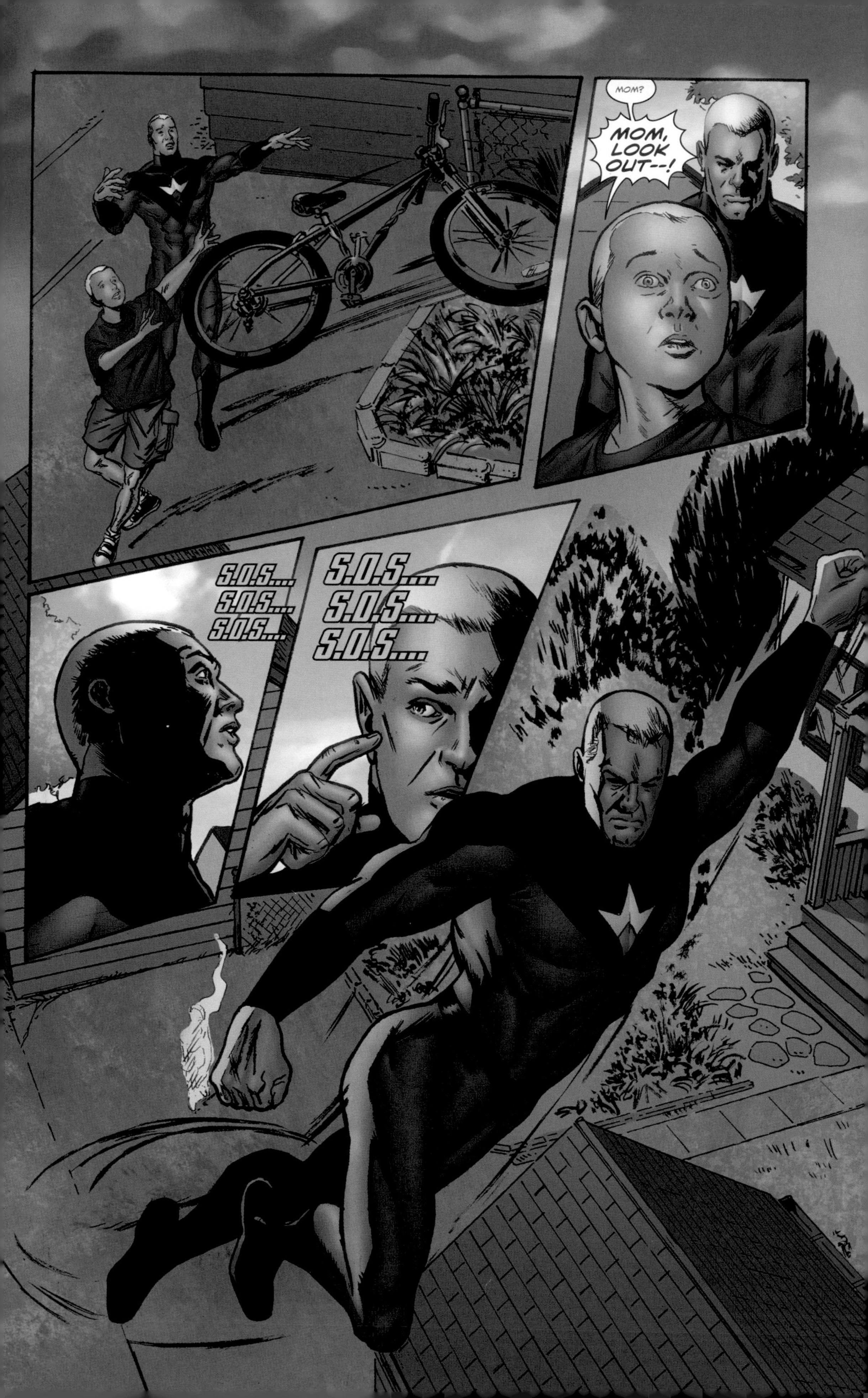
MOM?
MOM, LOOK OUT--!
S.O.S.... S.O.S.... S.O.S....
S.O.S.... S.O.S.... S.O.S....

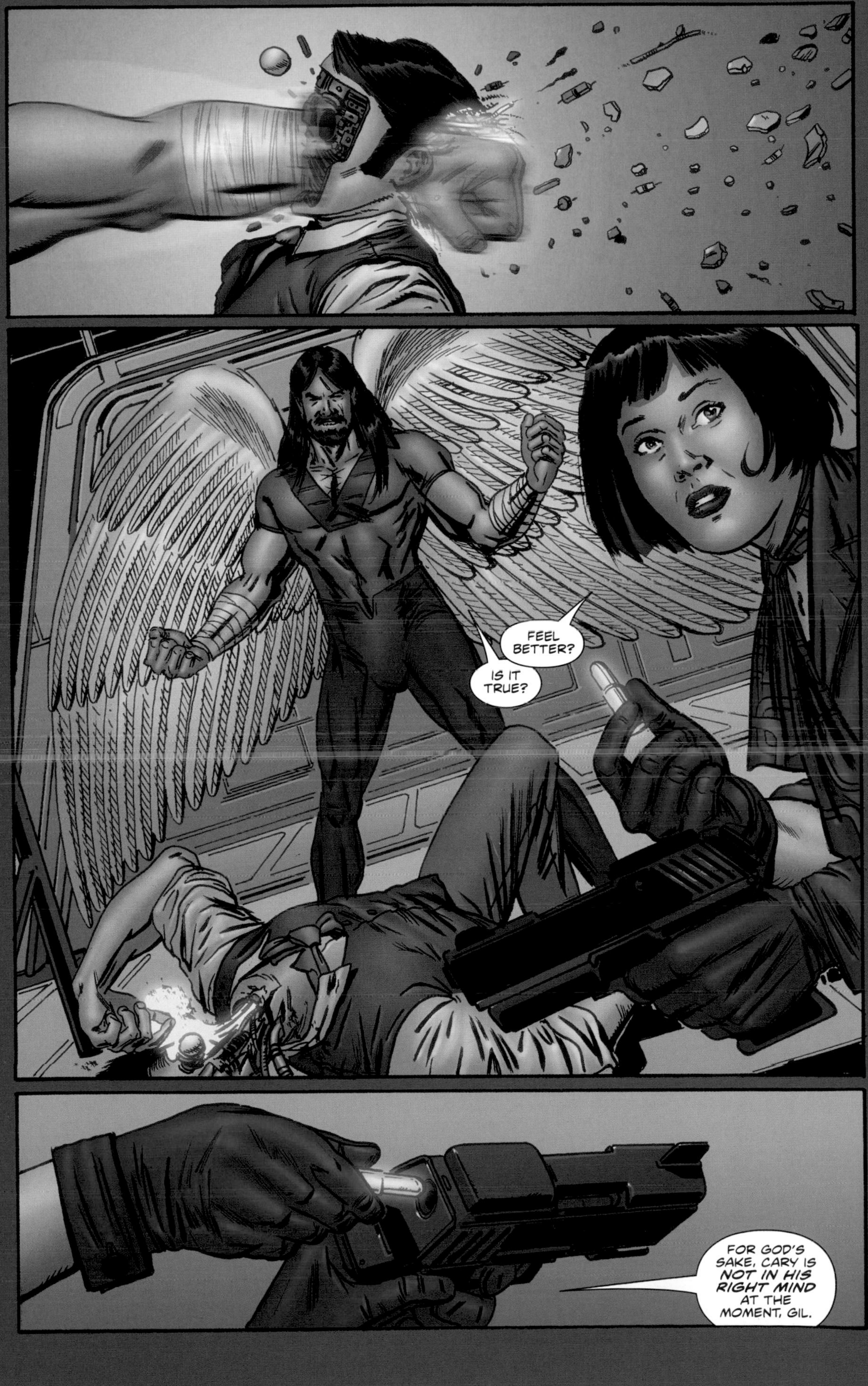
FEEL BETTER?
IS IT TRUE?
FOR GOD'S SAKE, CARY IS *NOT IN HIS RIGHT MIND* AT THE MOMENT, GIL.

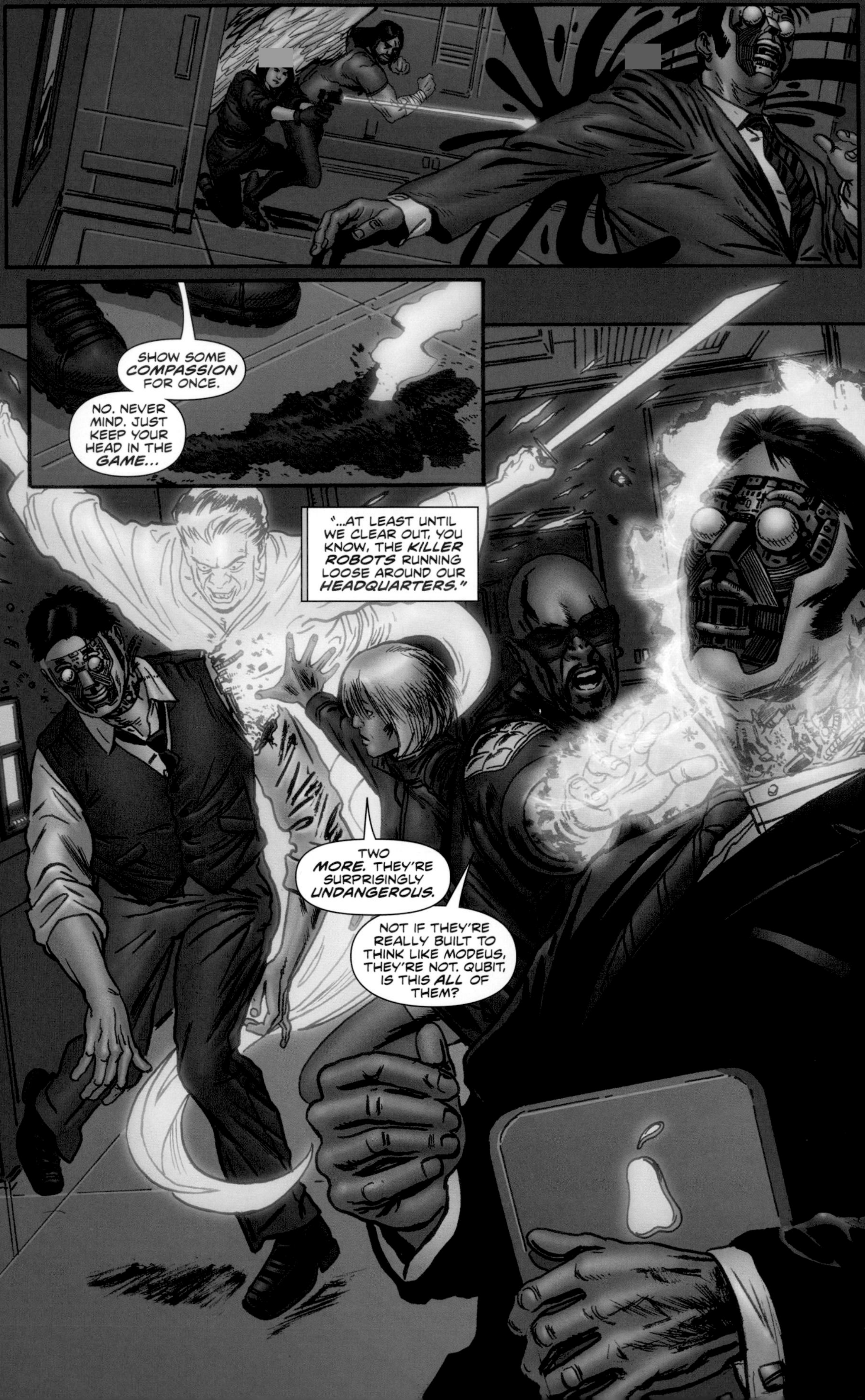
SHOW SOME COMPASSION FOR ONCE.
NO. NEVER MIND. JUST KEEP YOUR HEAD IN THE GAME...
"...AT LEAST UNTIL WE CLEAR OUT, YOU KNOW, THE KILLER ROBOTS RUNNING LOOSE AROUND OUR HEADQUARTERS."
TWO MORE. THEY'RE SURPRISINGLY UNDANGEROUS.
NOT IF THEY'RE REALLY BUILT TO THINK LIKE MODEUS, THEY'RE NOT. QUBIT, IS THIS ALL OF THEM?

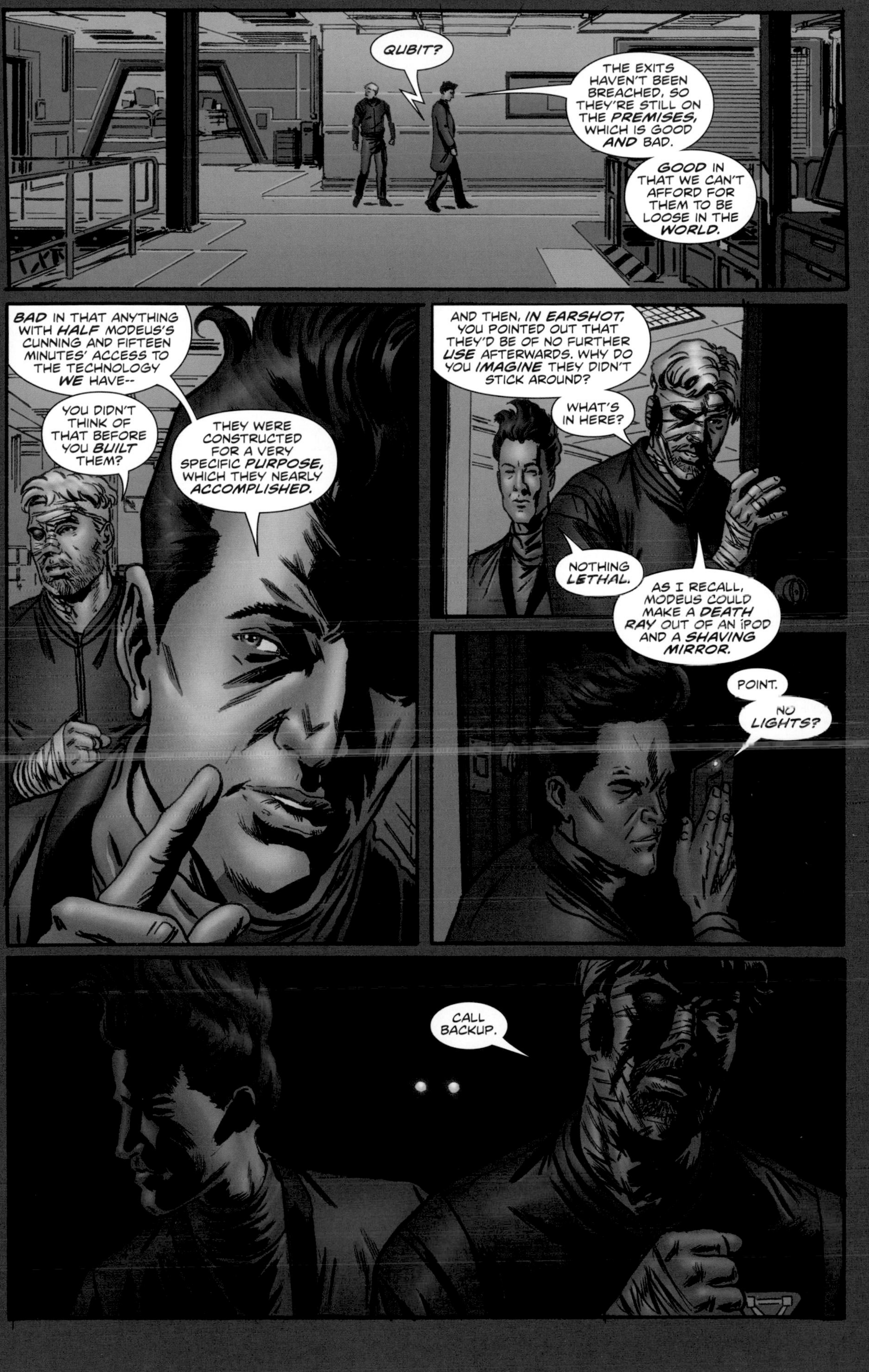
QUBIT?
THE EXITS HAVEN'T BEEN BREACHED, SO THEY'RE STILL ON THE PREMISES, WHICH IS GOOD AND BAD.
GOOD IN THAT WE CAN'T AFFORD FOR THEM TO BE LOOSE IN THE WORLD.
BAD IN THAT ANYTHING WITH HALF MODEUS'S CUNNING AND FIFTEEN MINUTES' ACCESS TO THE TECHNOLOGY WE HAVE--
YOU DIDN'T THINK OF THAT BEFORE YOU BUILT THEM?
THEY WERE CONSTRUCTED FOR A VERY SPECIFIC PURPOSE, WHICH THEY NEARLY ACCOMPLISHED.
AND THEN, IN EARSHOT, YOU POINTED OUT THAT THEY'D BE OF NO FURTHER USE AFTERWARDS. WHY DO YOU IMAGINE THEY DIDN'T STICK AROUND?
WHAT'S IN HERE?
NOTHING LETHAL.
AS I RECALL, MODEUS COULD MAKE A DEATH RAY OUT OF AN iPOD AND A SHAVING MIRROR.
POINT.
NO LIGHTS?
CALL BACKUP.

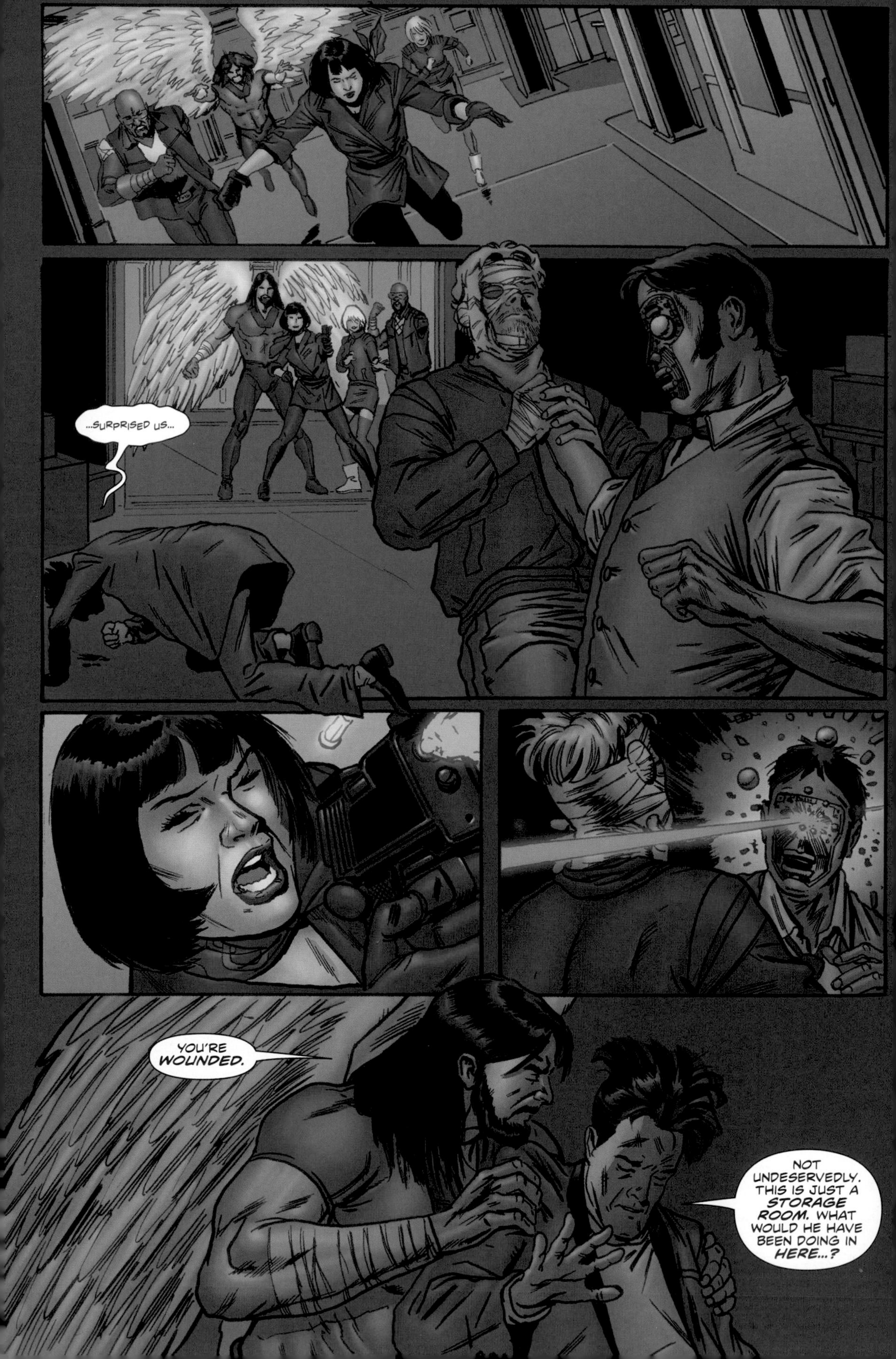
...SURPRISED US...
YOU'RE WOUNDED.
NOT UNDESERVEDLY. THIS IS JUST A STORAGE ROOM. WHAT WOULD HE HAVE BEEN DOING IN HERE...?

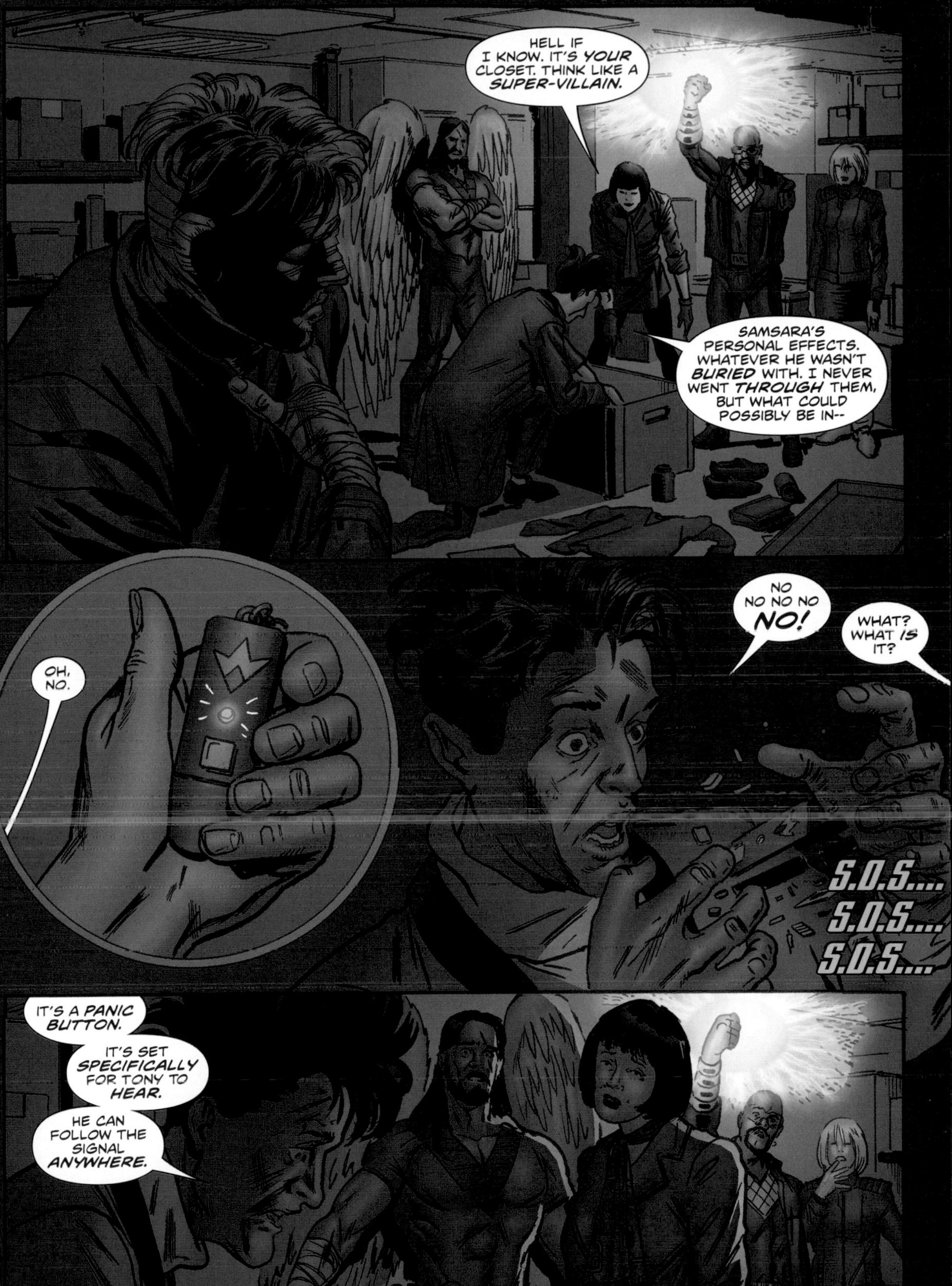
HELL IF I KNOW. IT'S *YOUR* CLOSET. THINK LIKE A *SUPER-VILLAIN.*
SAMSARA'S PERSONAL EFFECTS. WHATEVER HE WASN'T *BURIED* WITH. I NEVER WENT *THROUGH* THEM, BUT WHAT COULD POSSIBLY BE IN--
OH, NO.
NO NO NO NO *NO!*
WHAT? WHAT *IS* IT?
S.O.S.... S.O.S.... S.O.S....
IT'S A *PANIC BUTTON.*
IT'S SET *SPECIFICALLY* FOR TONY TO *HEAR.*
HE CAN FOLLOW THE SIGNAL *ANYWHERE.*

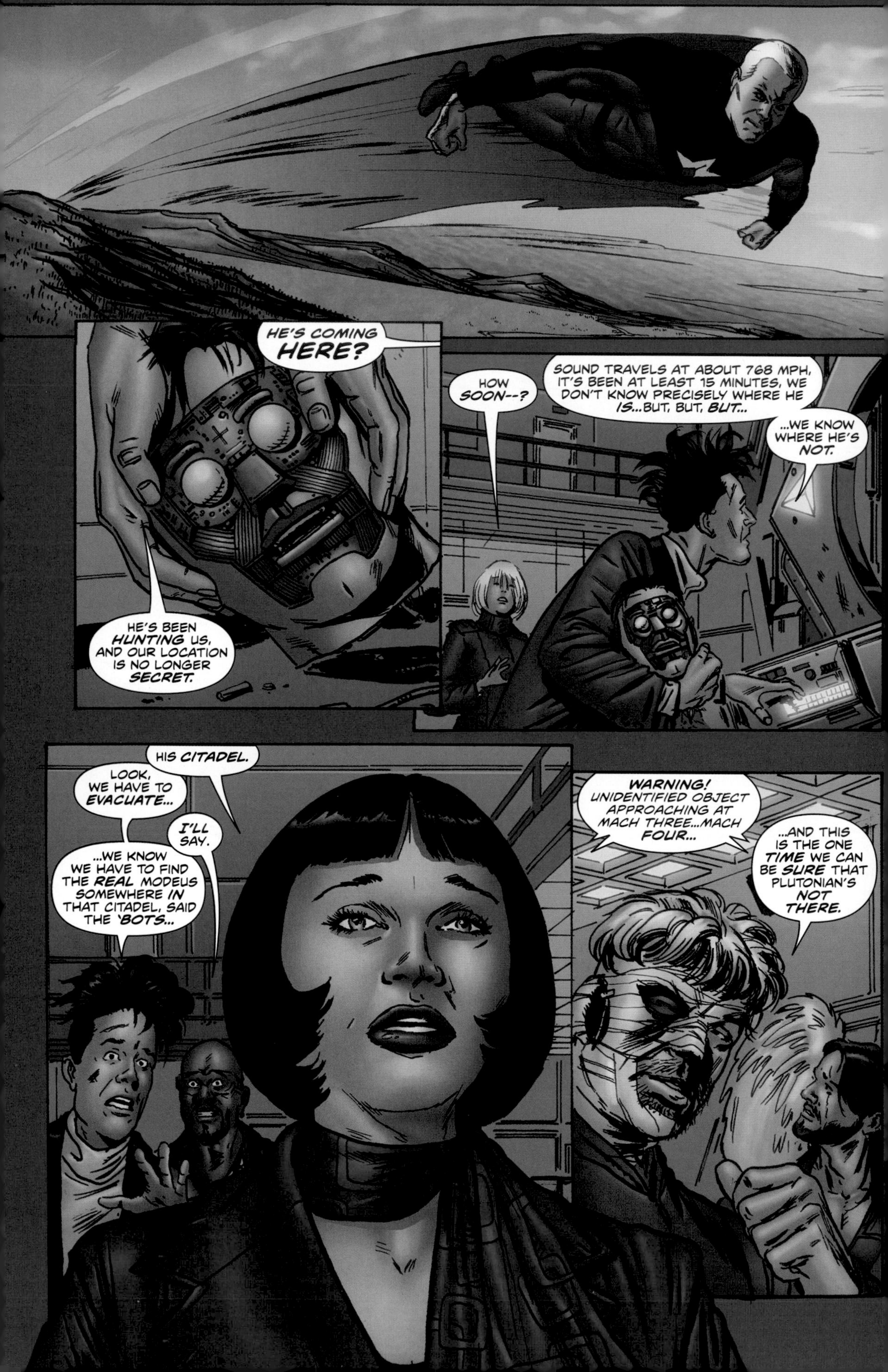

HE'S COMING HERE?
HE'S BEEN HUNTING US, AND OUR LOCATION IS NO LONGER SECRET.
HOW SOON--?
SOUND TRAVELS AT ABOUT 768 MPH, IT'S BEEN AT LEAST 15 MINUTES, WE DON'T KNOW PRECISELY WHERE HE IS...BUT, BUT, BUT...
...WE KNOW WHERE HE'S NOT.
HIS CITADEL.
LOOK, WE HAVE TO EVACUATE...
I'LL SAY.
...WE KNOW WE HAVE TO FIND THE REAL MODEUS SOMEWHERE IN THAT CITADEL, SAID THE 'BOTS...
WARNING! UNIDENTIFIED OBJECT APPROACHING AT MACH THREE...MACH FOUR...
...AND THIS IS THE ONE TIME WE CAN BE SURE THAT PLUTONIAN'S NOT THERE.

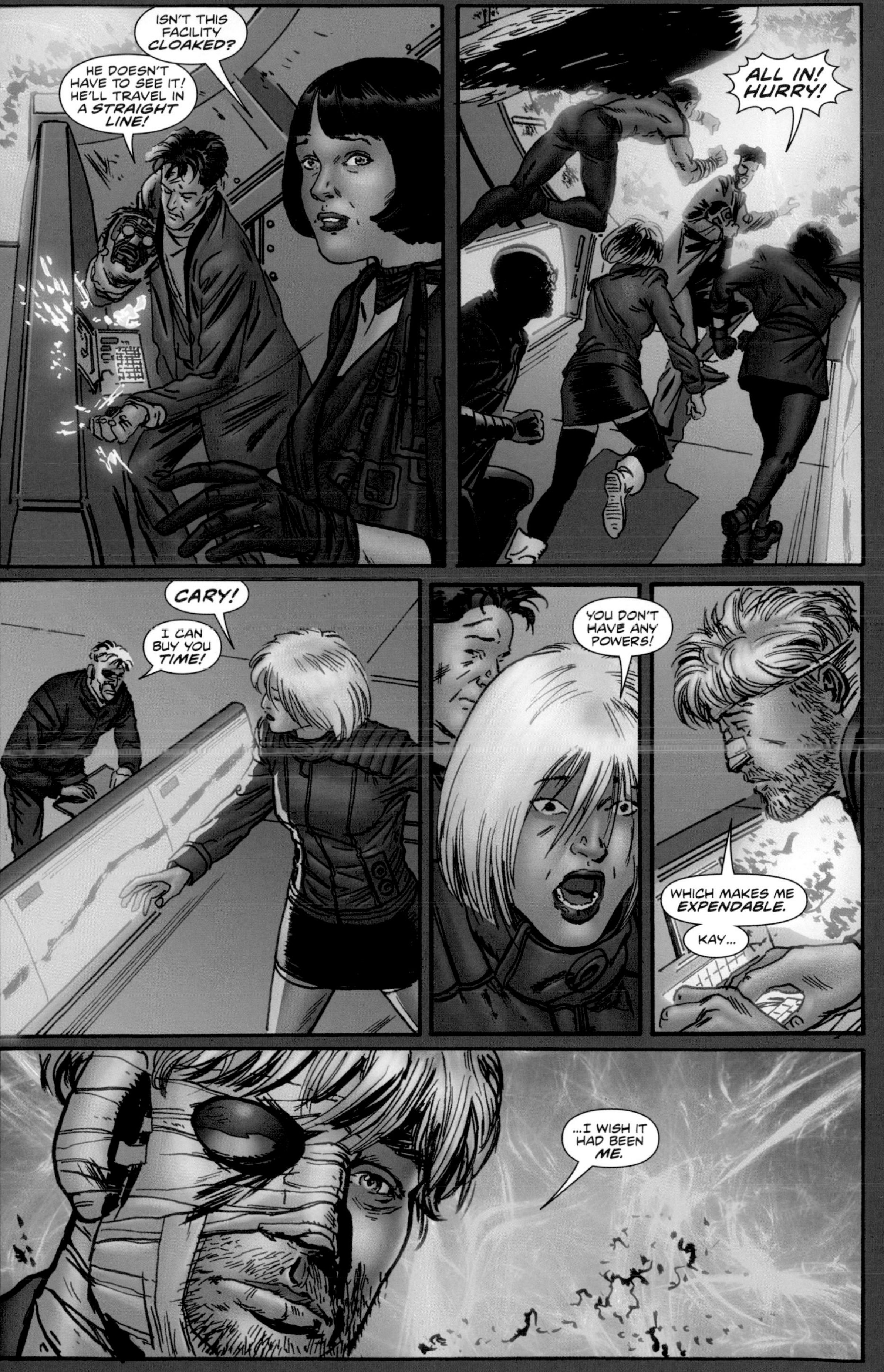
ISN'T THIS FACILITY CLOAKED?
HE DOESN'T HAVE TO SEE IT! HE'LL TRAVEL IN A STRAIGHT LINE!
ALL IN! HURRY!
CARY!
I CAN BUY YOU TIME!
YOU DON'T HAVE ANY POWERS!
WHICH MAKES ME EXPENDABLE.
KAY...
...I WISH IT HAD BEEN ME.

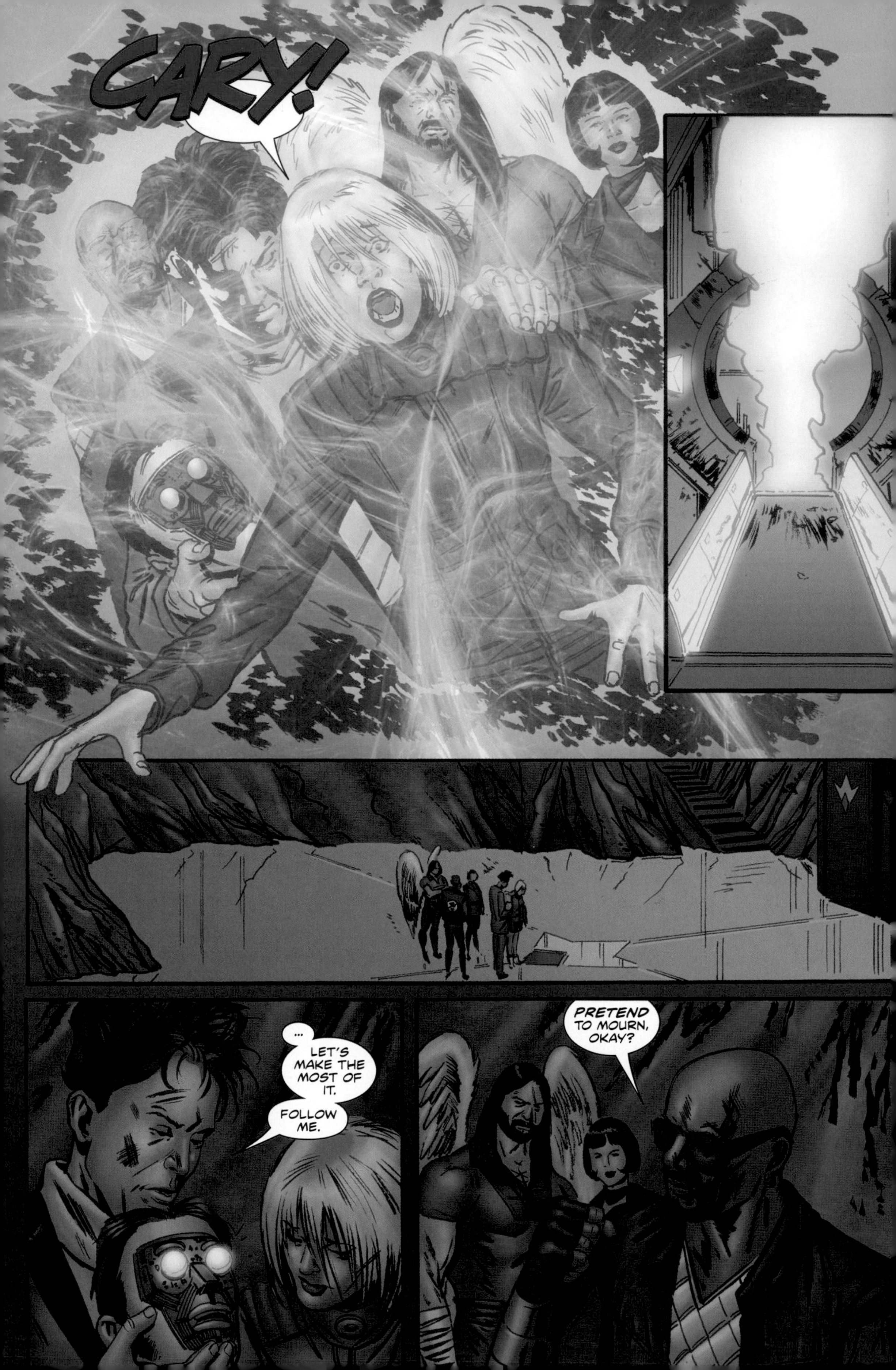
CARY!
...
LET'S MAKE THE MOST OF IT.
FOLLOW ME.
PRETEND TO MOURN, OKAY?

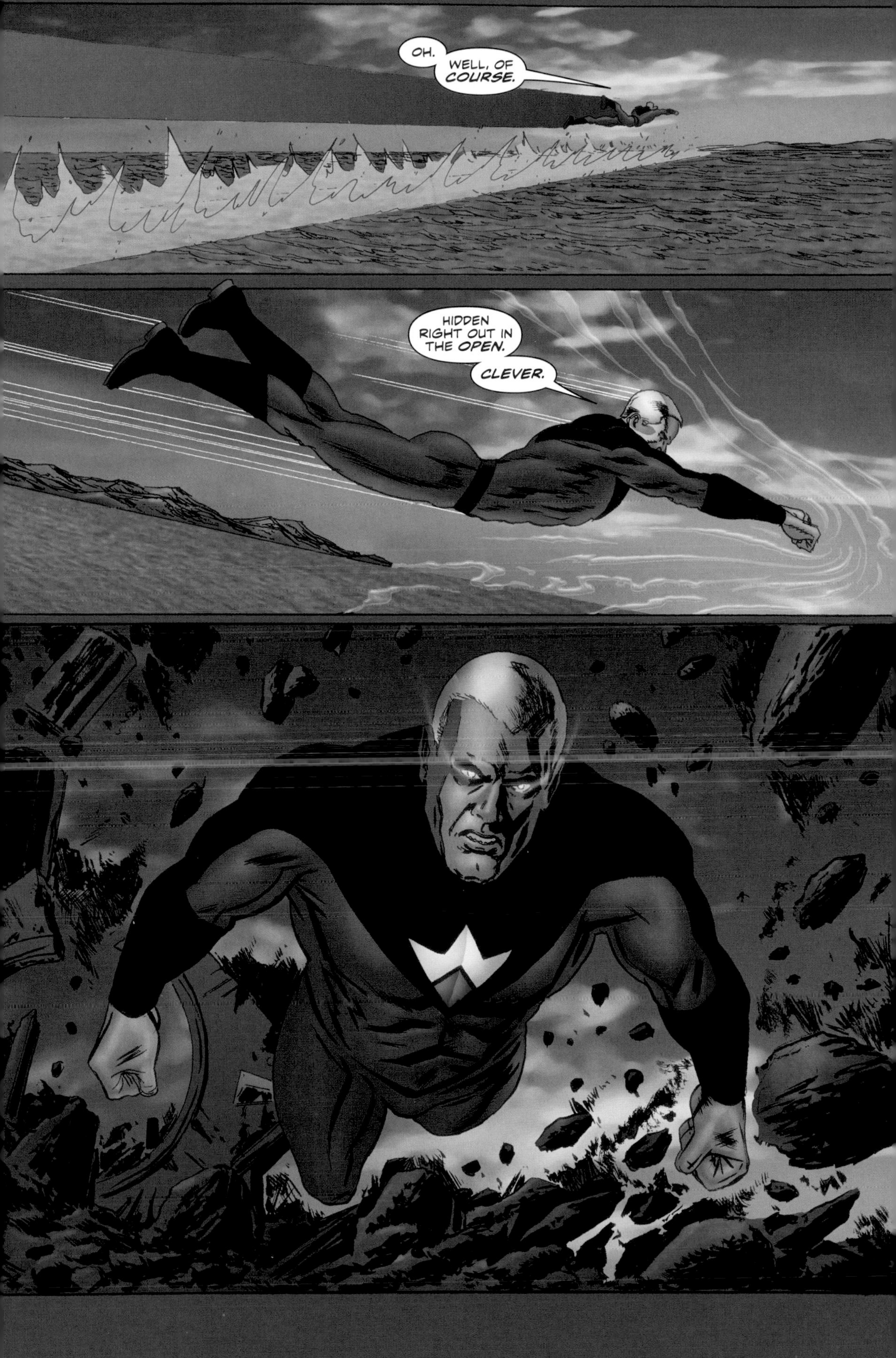
OH.
WELL, OF COURSE.
HIDDEN RIGHT OUT IN THE OPEN.
CLEVER.

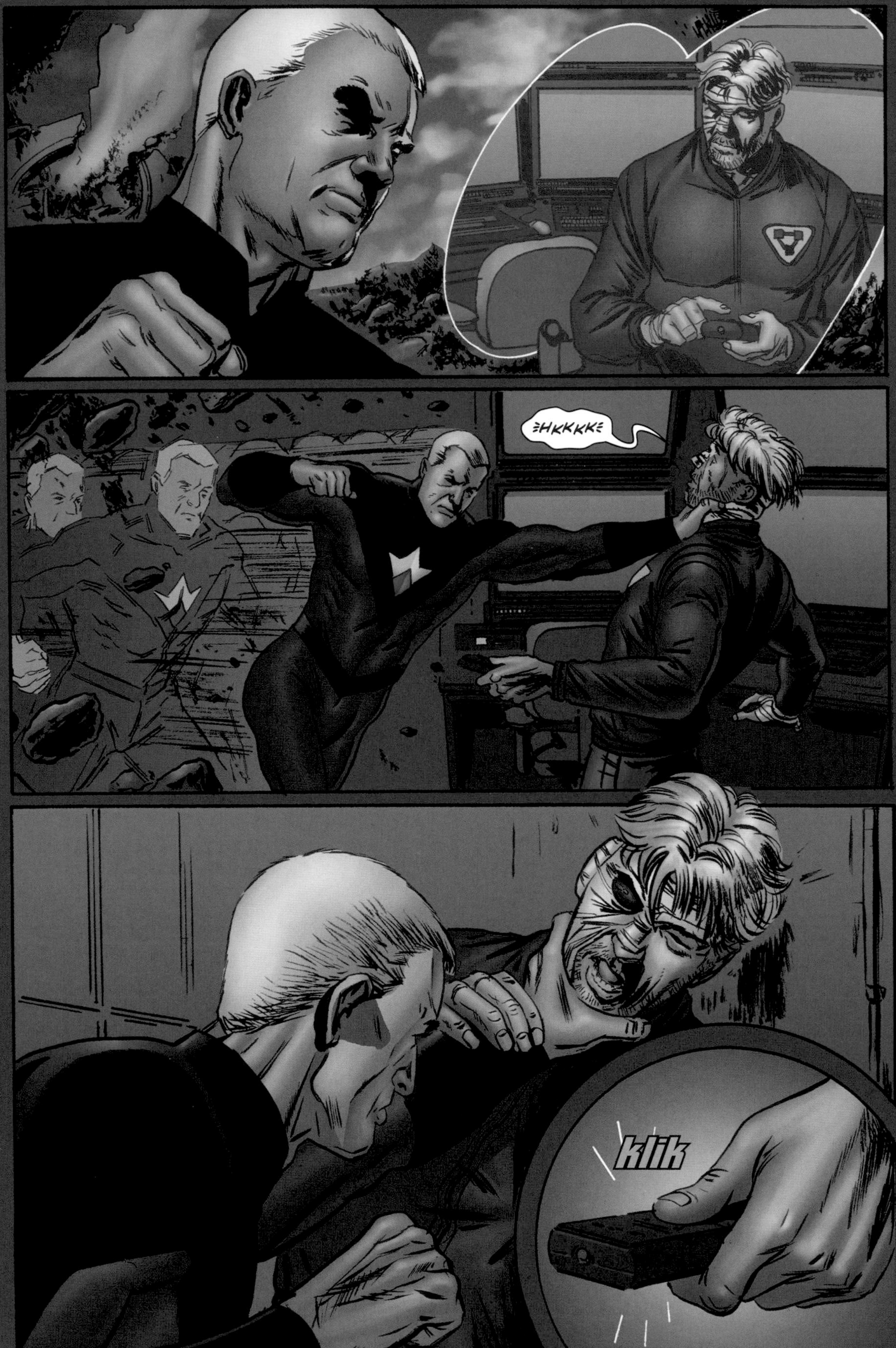
HKKKK
klik

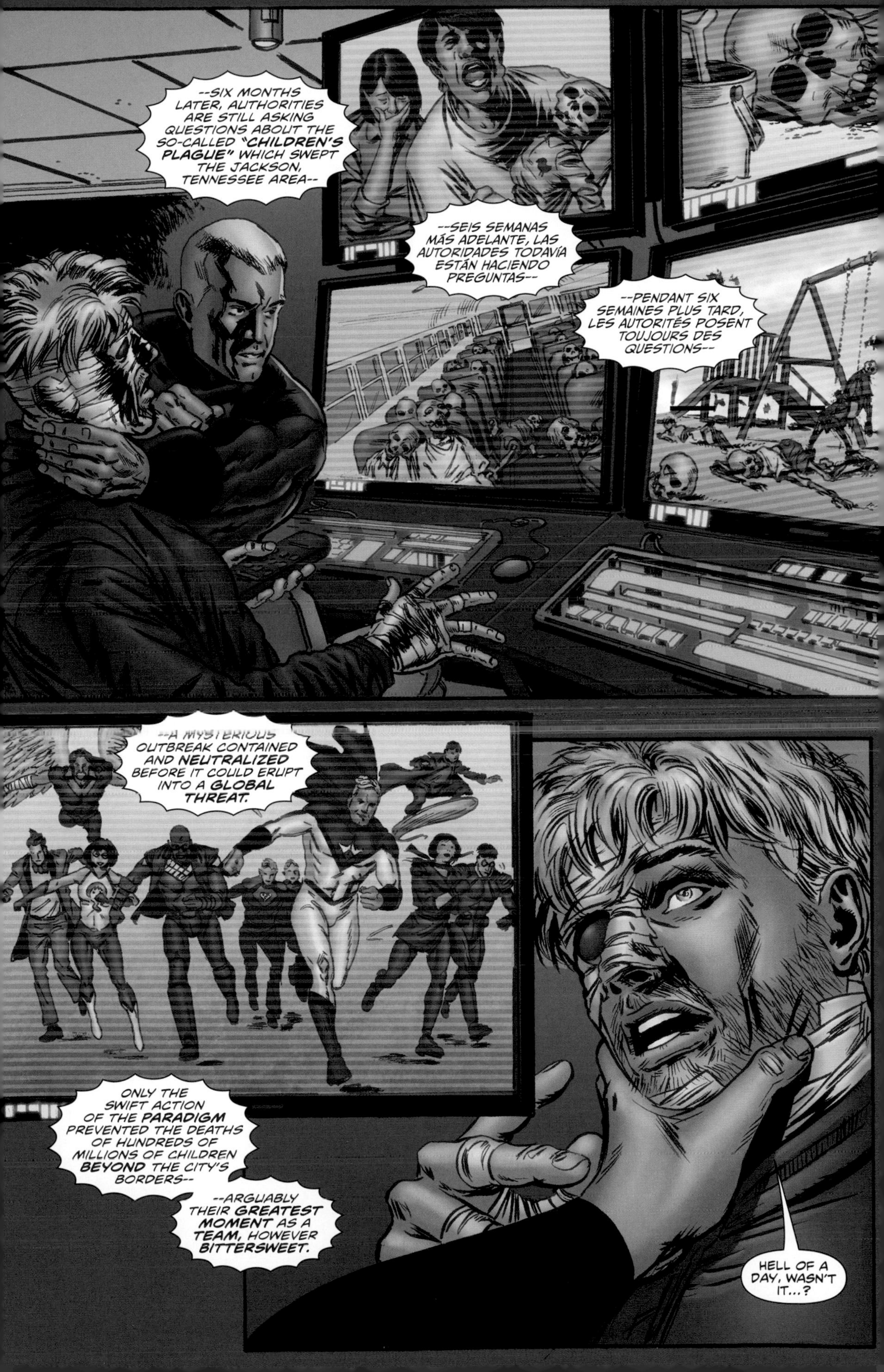
--SIX MONTHS LATER, AUTHORITIES ARE STILL ASKING QUESTIONS ABOUT THE SO-CALLED "CHILDREN'S PLAGUE" WHICH SWEPT THE JACKSON, TENNESSEE AREA--
--SEIS SEMANAS MÁS ADELANTE, LAS AUTORIDADES TODAVÍA ESTÁN HACIENDO PREGUNTAS--
--PENDANT SIX SEMAINES PLUS TARD, LES AUTORITÉS POSENT TOUJOURS DES QUESTIONS--
--A MYSTERIOUS OUTBREAK CONTAINED AND NEUTRALIZED BEFORE IT COULD ERUPT INTO A GLOBAL THREAT.
ONLY THE SWIFT ACTION OF THE PARADIGM PREVENTED THE DEATHS OF HUNDREDS OF MILLIONS OF CHILDREN BEYOND THE CITY'S BORDERS--
--ARGUABLY THEIR GREATEST MOMENT AS A TEAM, HOWEVER BITTERSWEET.
HELL OF A DAY, WASN'T IT...?

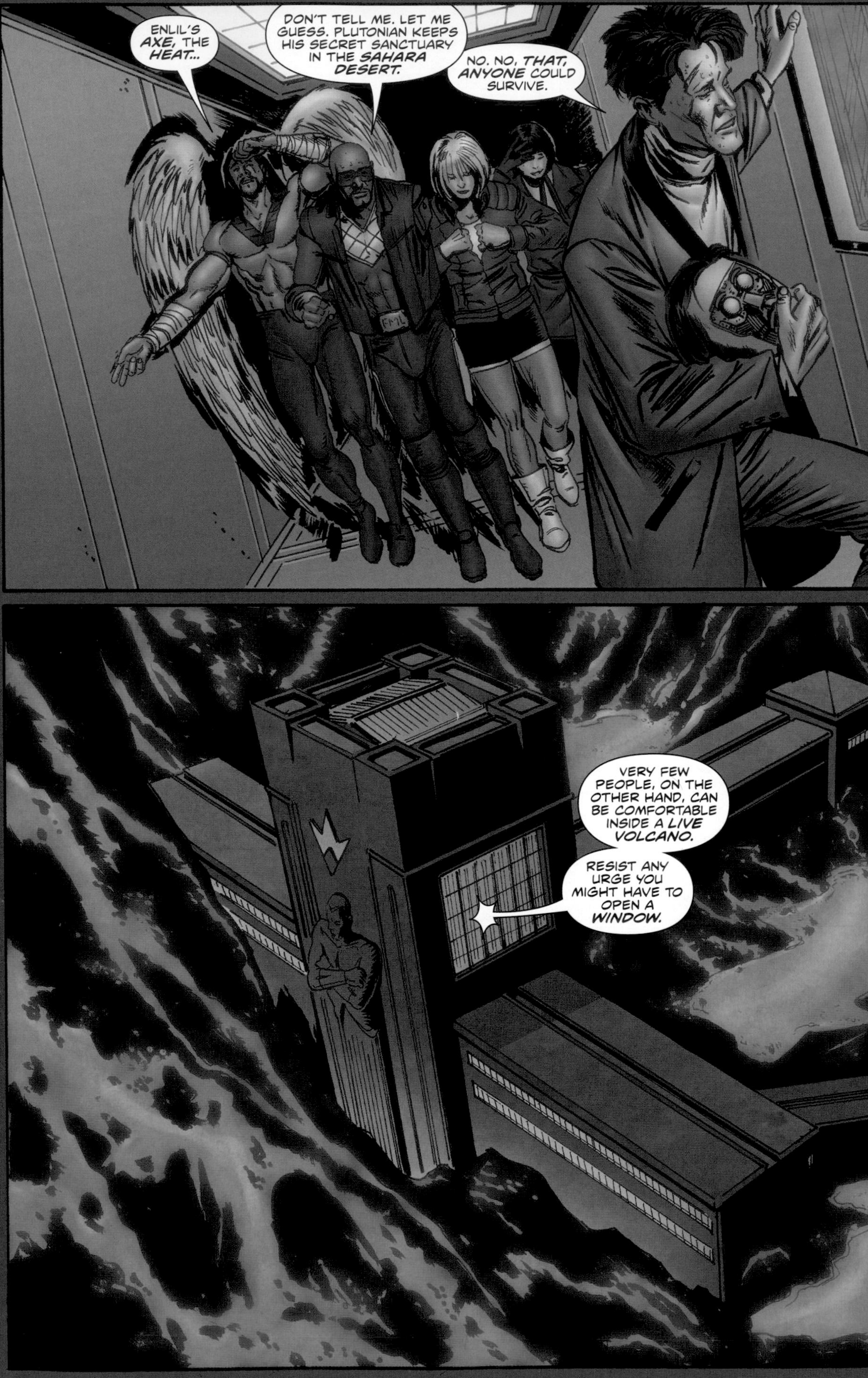
ENLIL'S *AXE*, THE *HEAT*...
DON'T TELL ME. LET ME GUESS. PLUTONIAN KEEPS HIS SECRET SANCTUARY IN THE *SAHARA DESERT*.
NO. NO. *THAT*, *ANYONE* COULD SURVIVE.
VERY FEW PEOPLE, ON THE OTHER HAND, CAN BE COMFORTABLE INSIDE A *LIVE VOLCANO*.
RESIST ANY URGE YOU MIGHT HAVE TO OPEN A *WINDOW*.

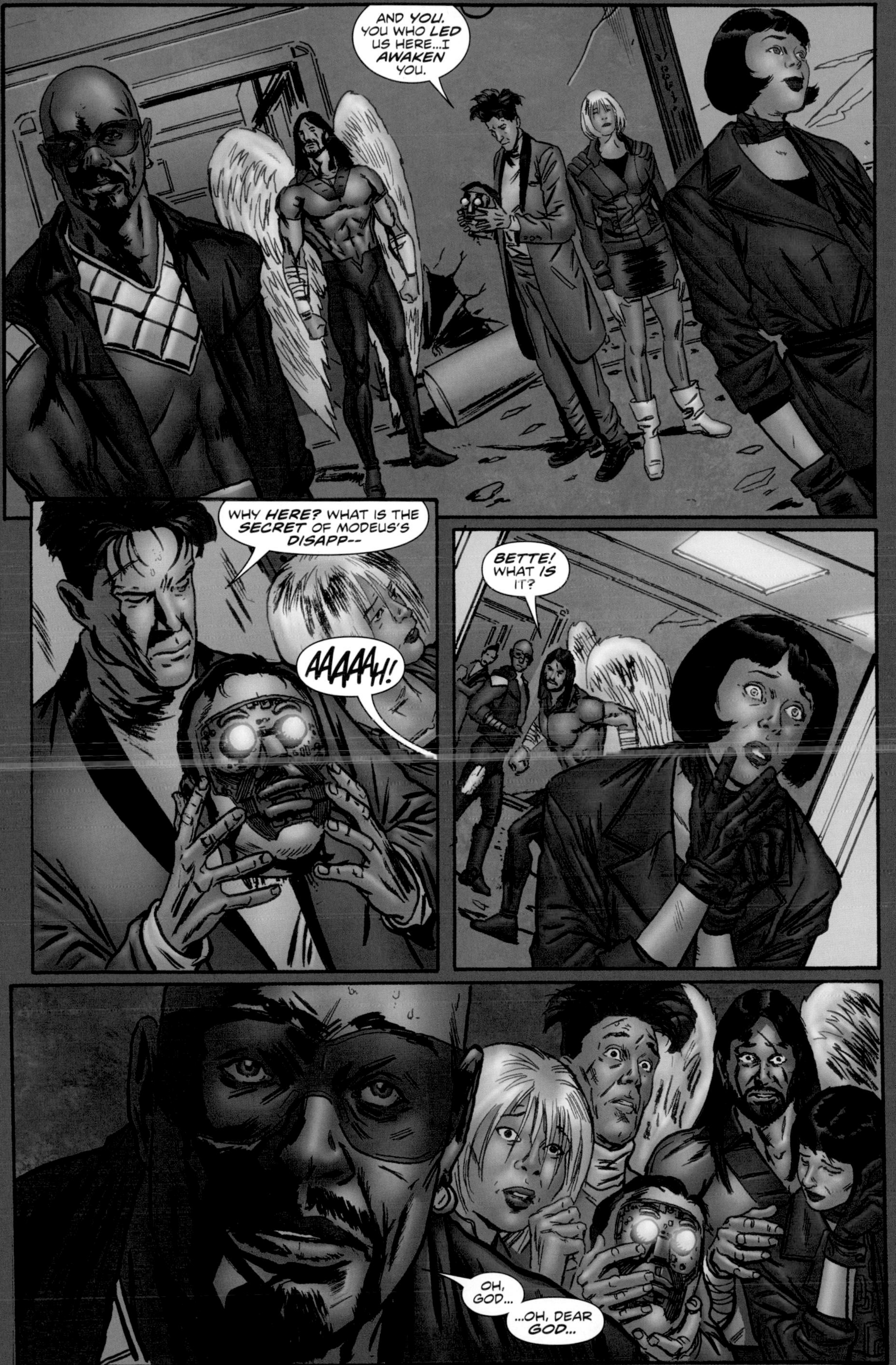
AND YOU. YOU WHO LED US HERE...I AWAKEN YOU.
WHY HERE? WHAT IS THE SECRET OF MODEUS'S DISAPP--
AAAAAH!
BETTE! WHAT IS IT?
OH, GOD...
...OH, DEAR GOD...

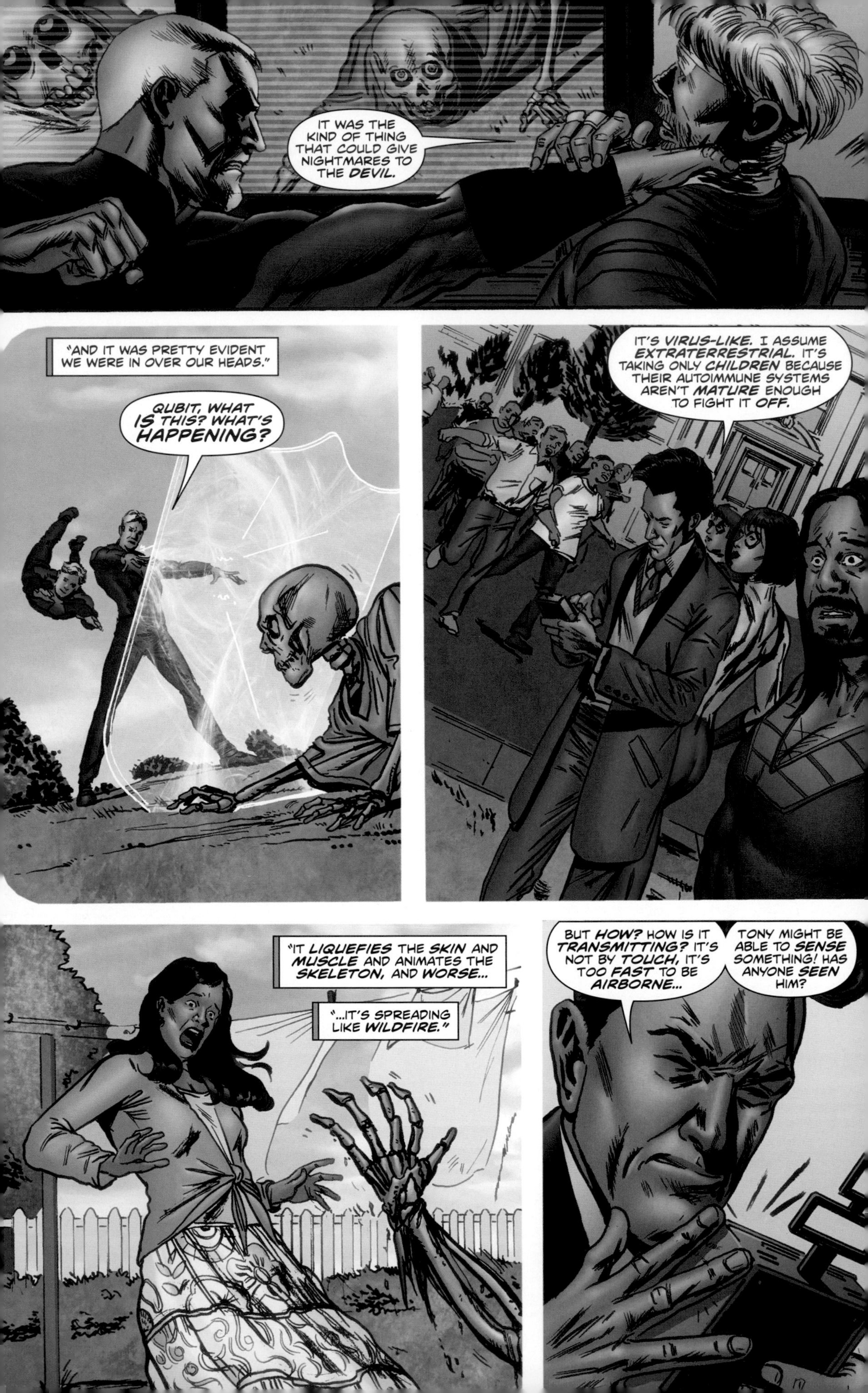
IT WAS THE KIND OF THING THAT COULD GIVE NIGHTMARES TO THE DEVIL.
"AND IT WAS PRETTY EVIDENT WE WERE IN OVER OUR HEADS."
QUBIT, WHAT IS THIS? WHAT'S HAPPENING?
IT'S VIRUS-LIKE. I ASSUME EXTRATERRESTRIAL. IT'S TAKING ONLY CHILDREN BECAUSE THEIR AUTOIMMUNE SYSTEMS AREN'T MATURE ENOUGH TO FIGHT IT OFF.
"IT LIQUEFIES THE SKIN AND MUSCLE AND ANIMATES THE SKELETON, AND WORSE...
"...IT'S SPREADING LIKE WILDFIRE."
BUT HOW? HOW IS IT TRANSMITTING? IT'S NOT BY TOUCH, IT'S TOO FAST TO BE AIRBORNE...
TONY MIGHT BE ABLE TO SENSE SOMETHING! HAS ANYONE SEEN HIM?

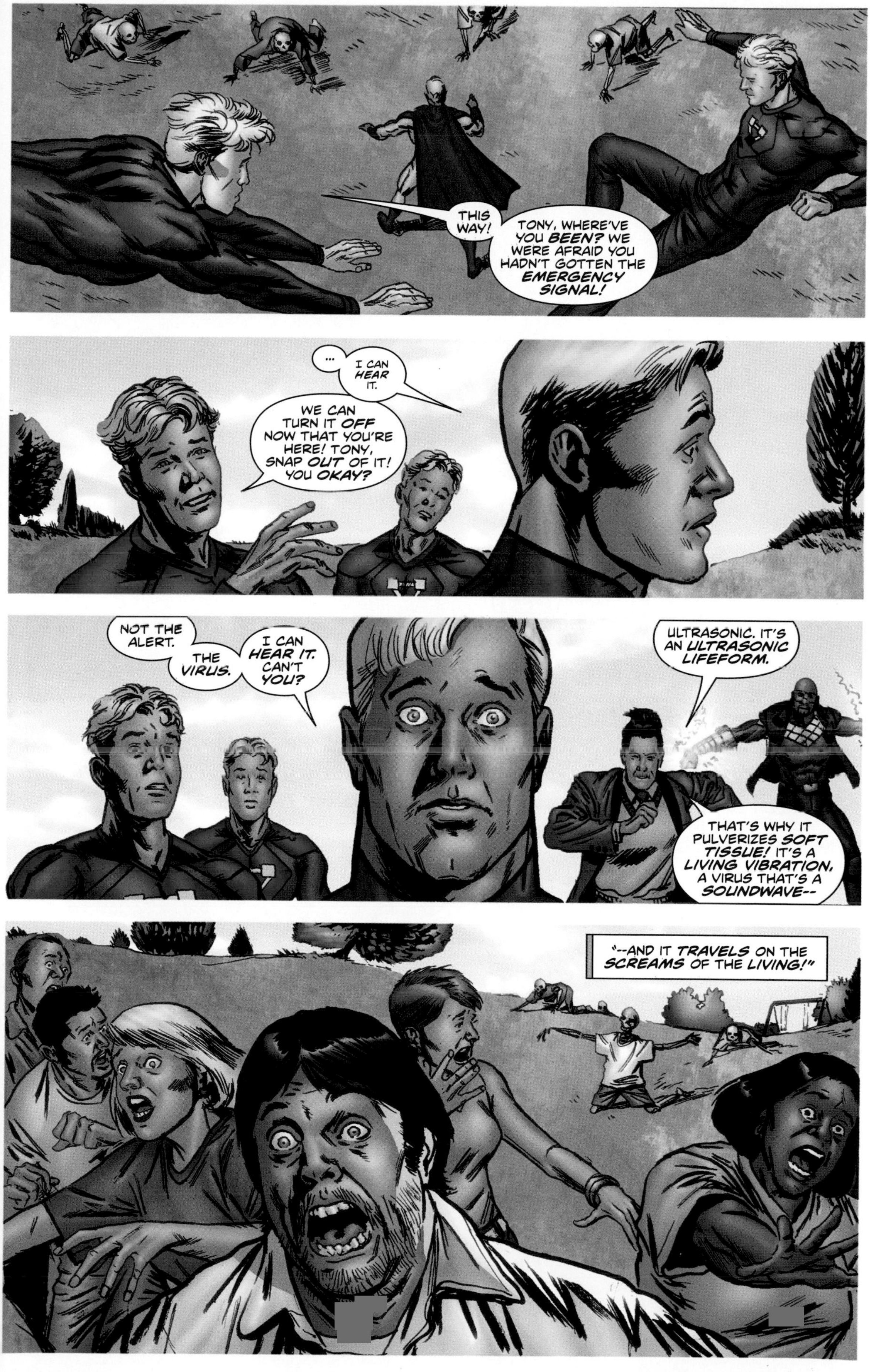
THIS WAY!
TONY, WHERE'VE YOU BEEN? WE WERE AFRAID YOU HADN'T GOTTEN THE EMERGENCY SIGNAL!
... I CAN HEAR IT.
WE CAN TURN IT OFF NOW THAT YOU'RE HERE! TONY, SNAP OUT OF IT! YOU OKAY?
NOT THE ALERT.
THE VIRUS.
I CAN HEAR IT. CAN'T YOU?
ULTRASONIC. IT'S AN ULTRASONIC LIFEFORM.
THAT'S WHY IT PULVERIZES SOFT TISSUE! IT'S A LIVING VIBRATION, A VIRUS THAT'S A SOUNDWAVE--
"--AND IT TRAVELS ON THE SCREAMS OF THE LIVING!"

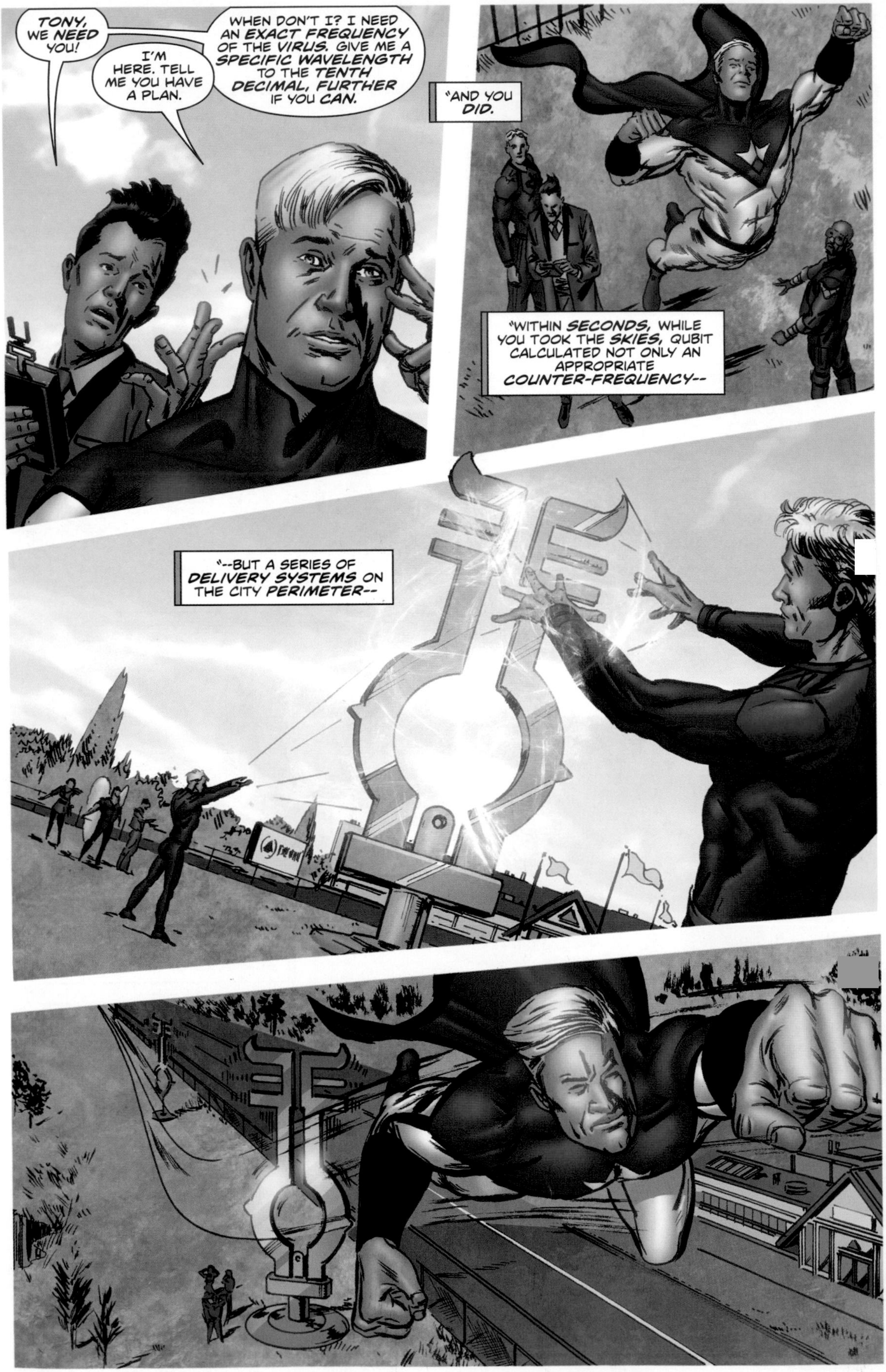
TONY, WE NEED YOU!
I'M HERE. TELL ME YOU HAVE A PLAN.
WHEN DON'T I? I NEED AN EXACT FREQUENCY OF THE VIRUS. GIVE ME A SPECIFIC WAVELENGTH TO THE TENTH DECIMAL, FURTHER IF YOU CAN.
"AND YOU DID.
"WITHIN SECONDS, WHILE YOU TOOK THE SKIES, QUBIT CALCULATED NOT ONLY AN APPROPRIATE COUNTER-FREQUENCY--
"--BUT A SERIES OF DELIVERY SYSTEMS ON THE CITY PERIMETER--

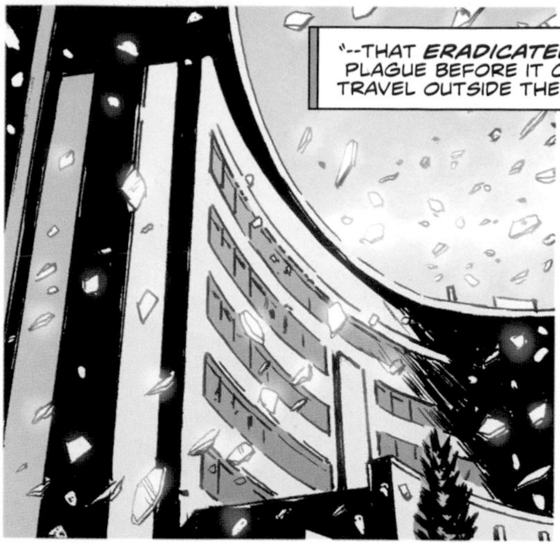
"--THAT *ERADICATED* THE PLAGUE BEFORE IT COULD TRAVEL OUTSIDE THE *CITY*.

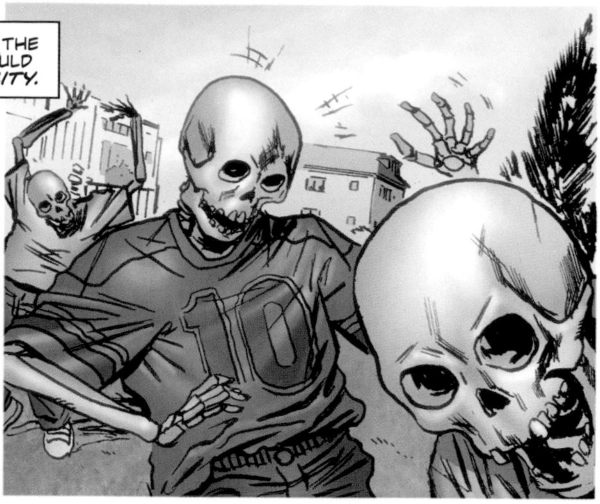

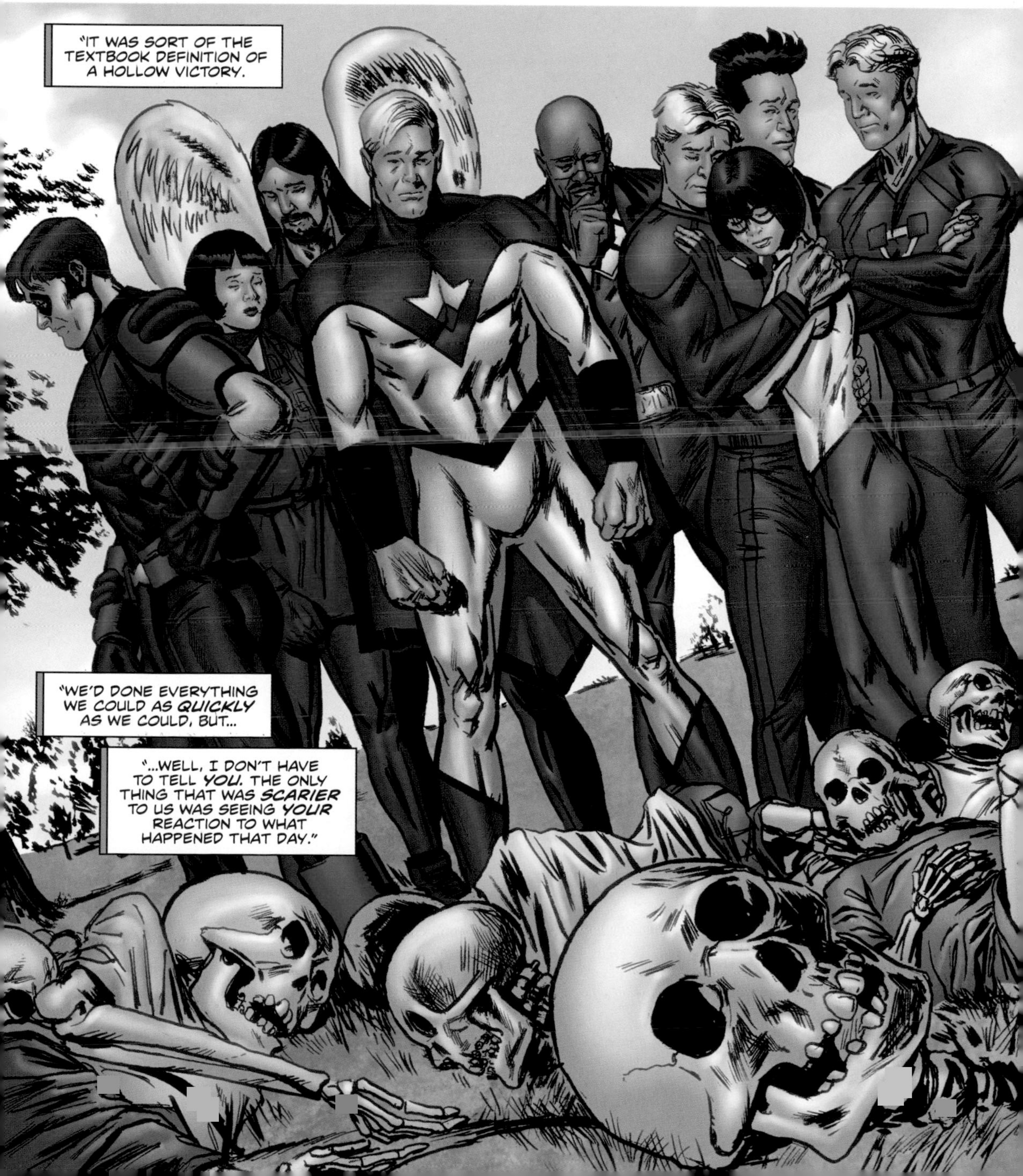
"IT WAS SORT OF THE TEXTBOOK DEFINITION OF A HOLLOW VICTORY.
"WE'D DONE EVERYTHING WE COULD AS *QUICKLY* AS WE COULD, BUT...
"...WELL, I DON'T HAVE TO TELL *YOU*. THE ONLY THING THAT WAS *SCARIER* TO US WAS SEEING *YOUR* REACTION TO WHAT HAPPENED THAT DAY."

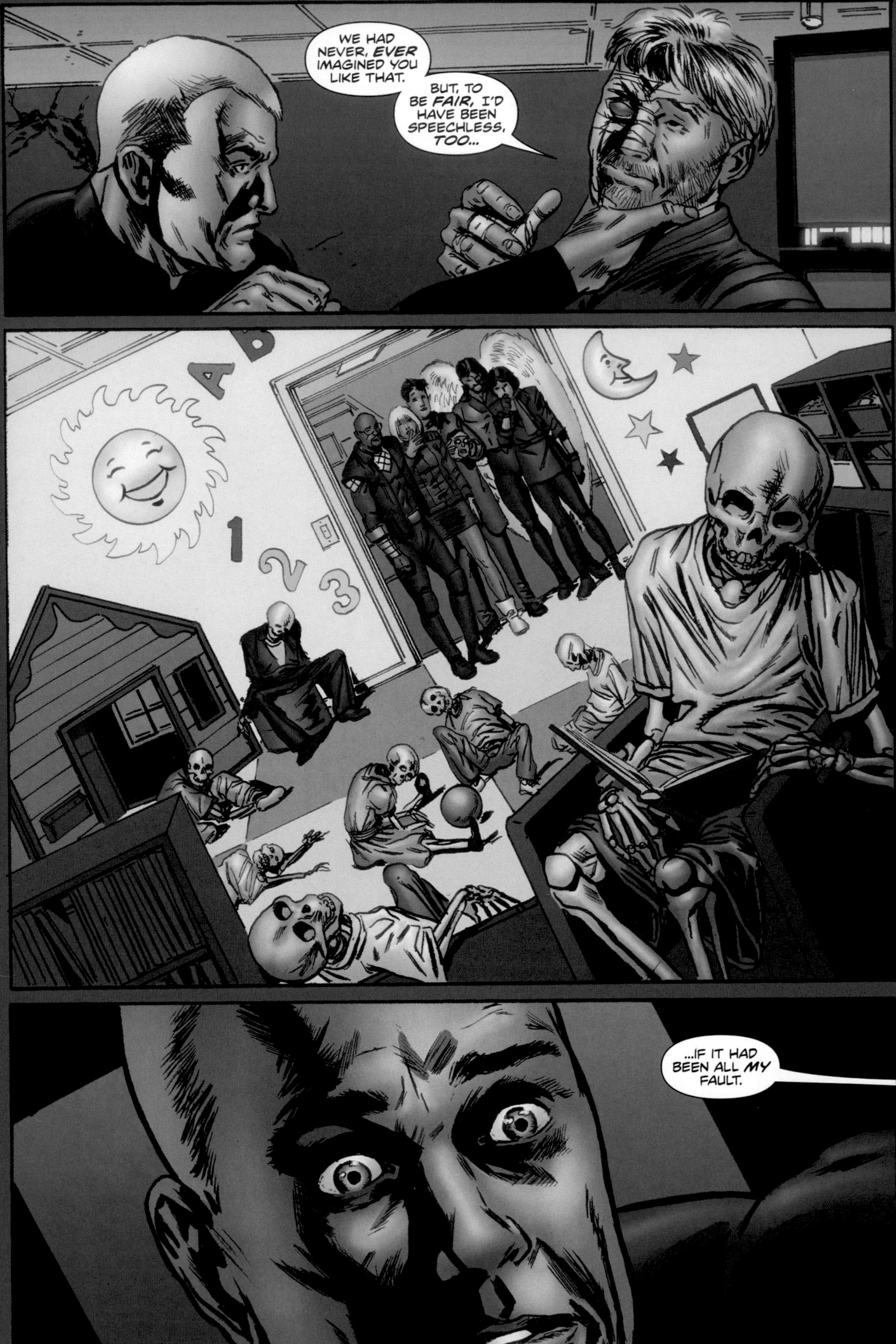
WE HAD NEVER, EVER IMAGINED YOU LIKE THAT.
BUT, TO BE FAIR, I'D HAVE BEEN SPEECHLESS, TOO...
A B
1 2 3
...IF IT HAD BEEN ALL MY FAULT.

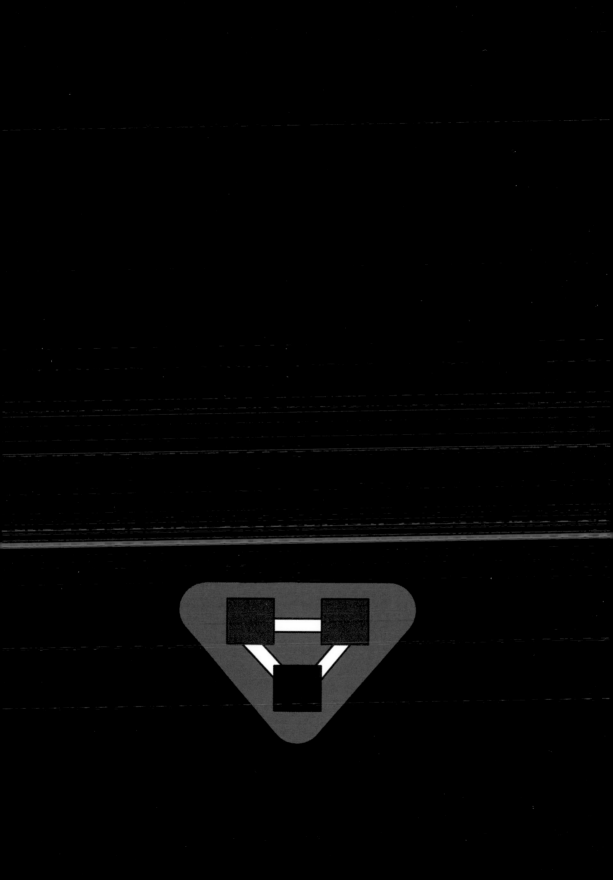

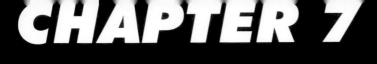

CHAPTER 7

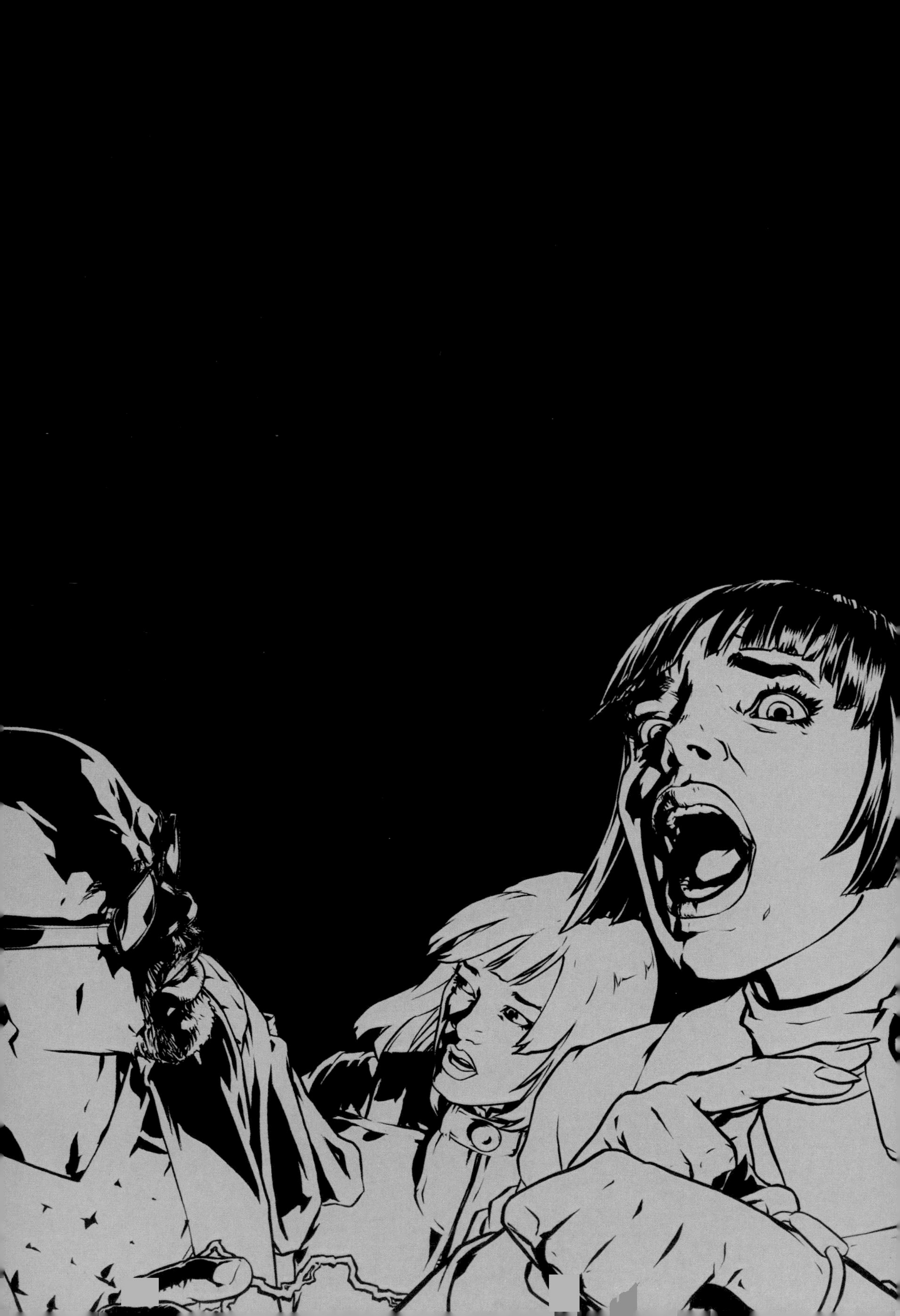

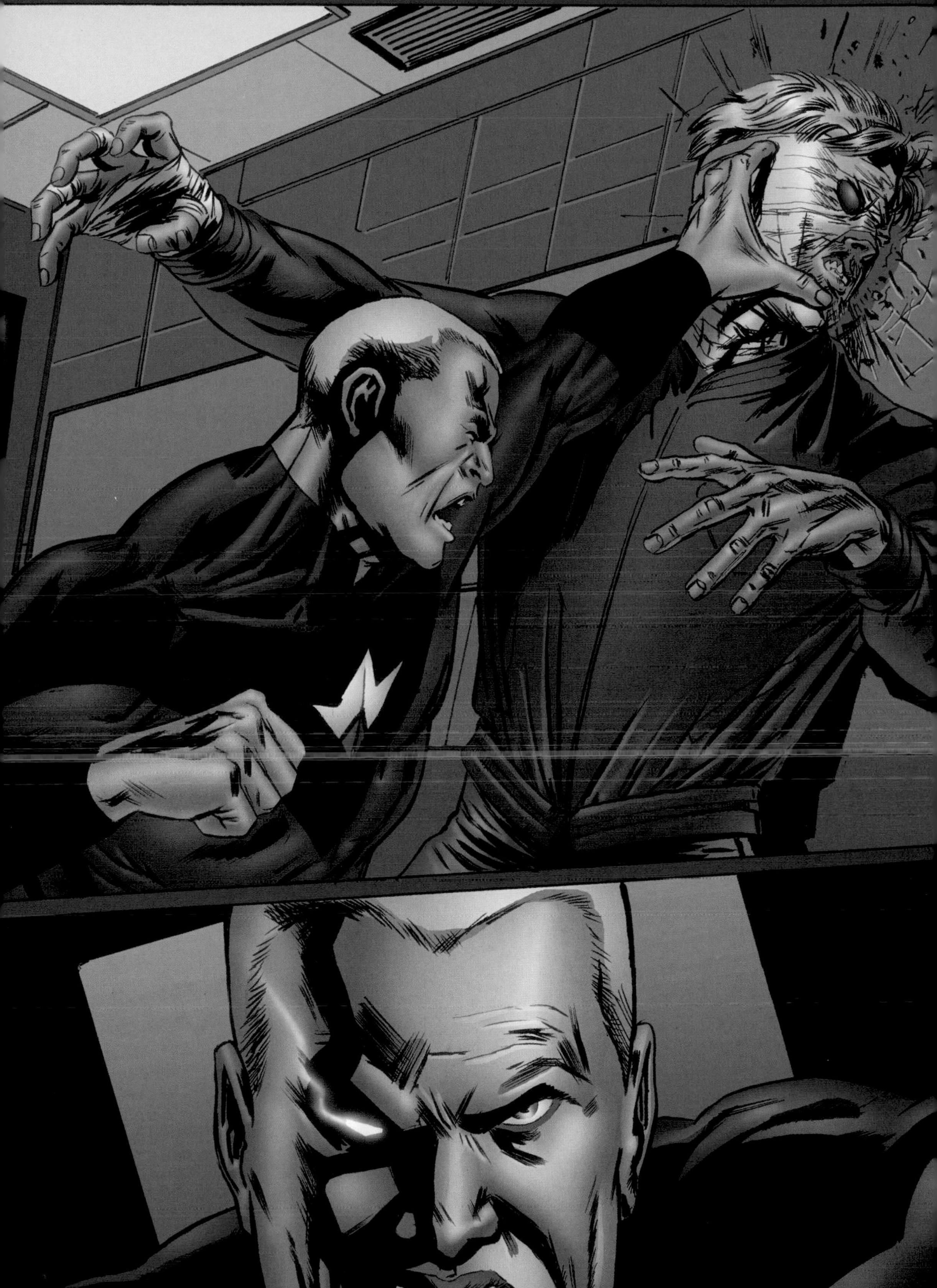

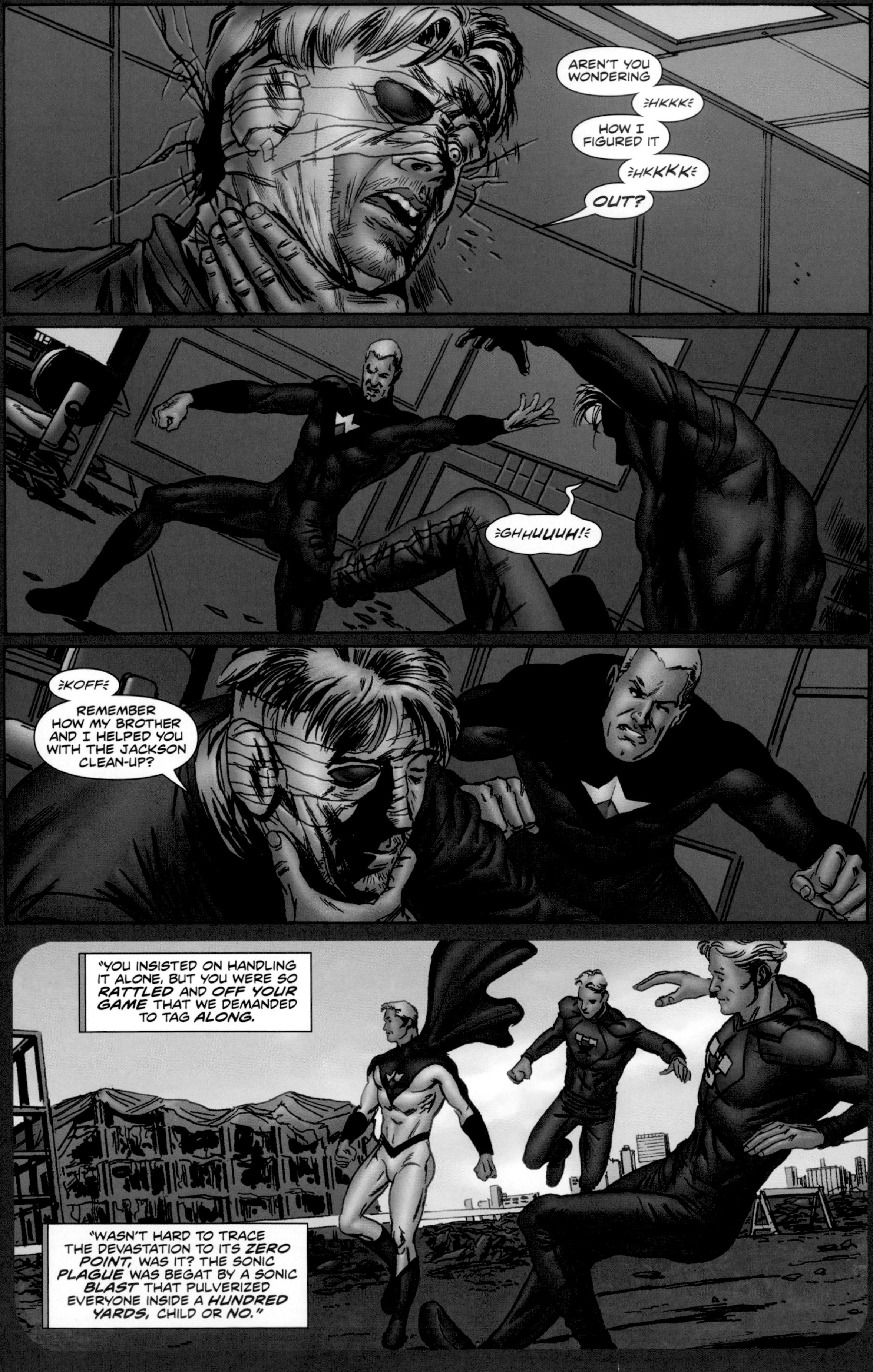

AREN'T YOU WONDERING
HKKK
HOW I FIGURED IT
HKKKK
OUT?
GHHUUUH!
KOFF
REMEMBER HOW MY BROTHER AND I HELPED YOU WITH THE JACKSON CLEAN-UP?
"YOU INSISTED ON HANDLING IT ALONE, BUT YOU WERE SO RATTLED AND OFF YOUR GAME THAT WE DEMANDED TO TAG ALONG.
"WASN'T HARD TO TRACE THE DEVASTATION TO ITS ZERO POINT, WAS IT? THE SONIC PLAGUE WAS BEGAT BY A SONIC BLAST THAT PULVERIZED EVERYONE INSIDE A HUNDRED YARDS, CHILD OR NO."

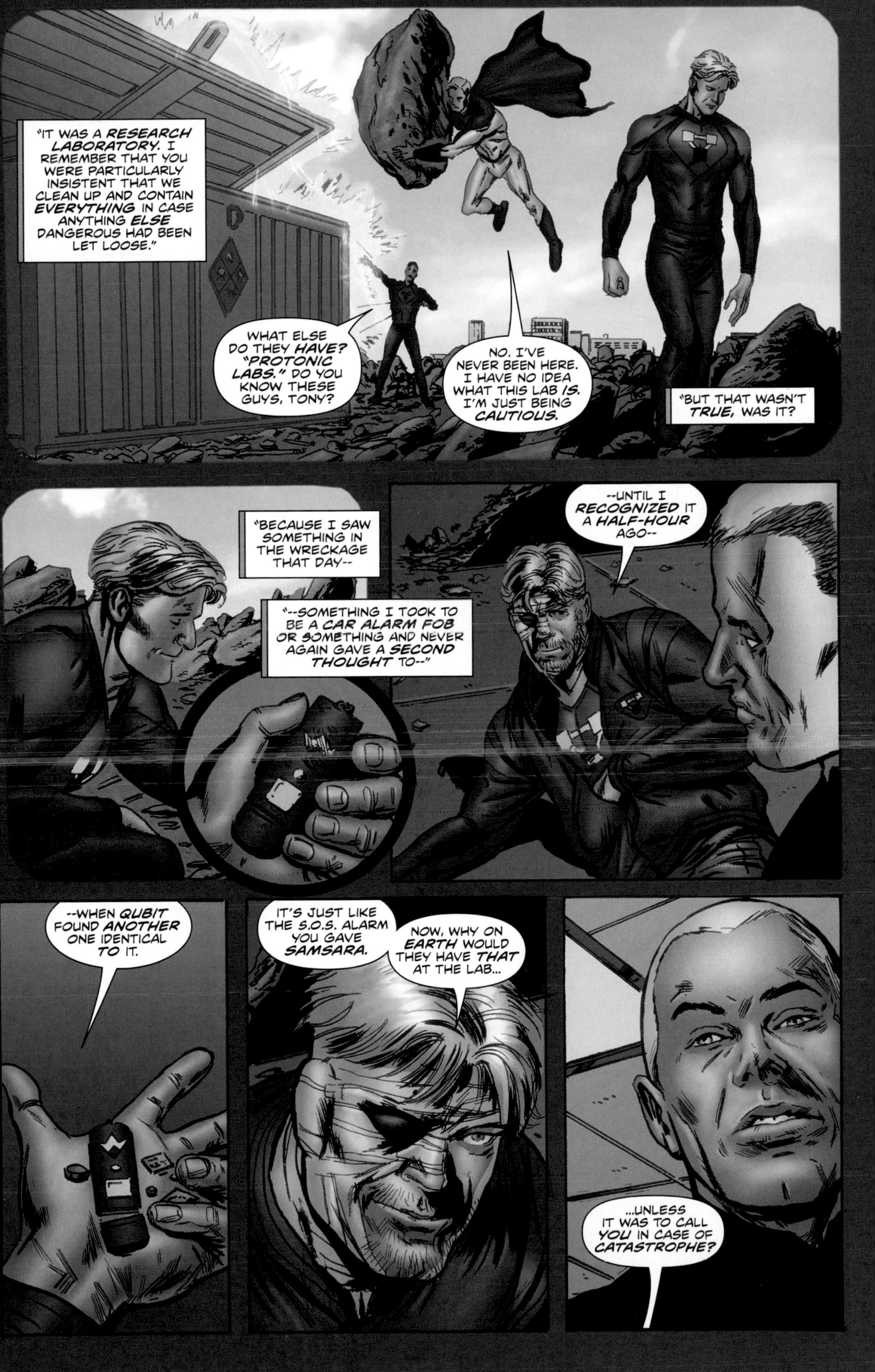
"IT WAS A RESEARCH LABORATORY. I REMEMBER THAT YOU WERE PARTICULARLY INSISTENT THAT WE CLEAN UP AND CONTAIN EVERYTHING IN CASE ANYTHING ELSE DANGEROUS HAD BEEN LET LOOSE."
WHAT ELSE DO THEY HAVE? "PROTONIC LABS." DO YOU KNOW THESE GUYS, TONY?
NO. I'VE NEVER BEEN HERE. I HAVE NO IDEA WHAT THIS LAB IS. I'M JUST BEING CAUTIOUS.
"BUT THAT WASN'T TRUE, WAS IT?
"BECAUSE I SAW SOMETHING IN THE WRECKAGE THAT DAY--
"--SOMETHING I TOOK TO BE A CAR ALARM FOB OR SOMETHING AND NEVER AGAIN GAVE A SECOND THOUGHT TO--"
--UNTIL I RECOGNIZED IT A HALF-HOUR AGO--
--WHEN QUBIT FOUND ANOTHER ONE IDENTICAL TO IT.
IT'S JUST LIKE THE S.O.S. ALARM YOU GAVE SAMSARA.
NOW, WHY ON EARTH WOULD THEY HAVE THAT AT THE LAB...
...UNLESS IT WAS TO CALL YOU IN CASE OF CATASTROPHE?

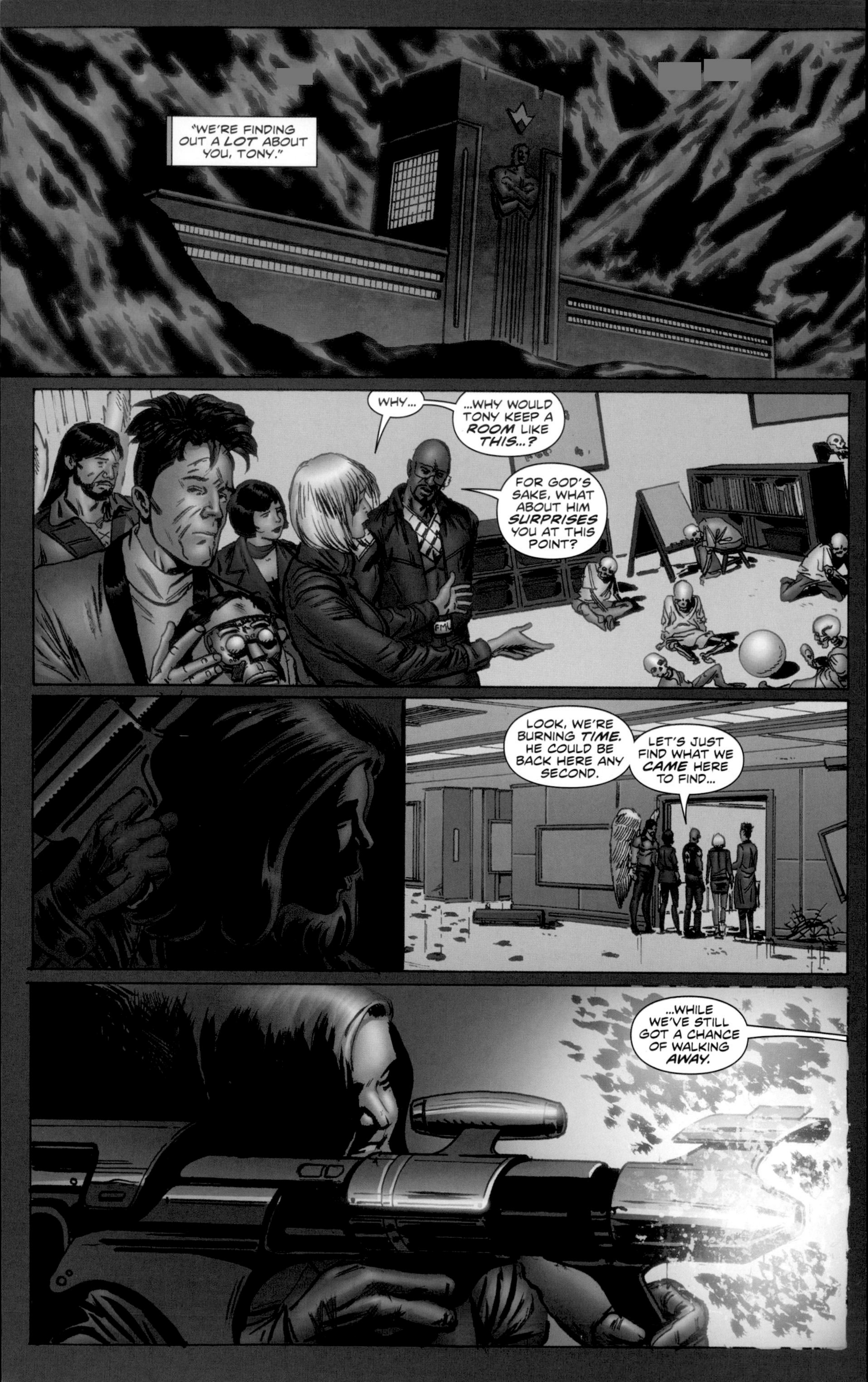
"WE'RE FINDING OUT A LOT ABOUT YOU, TONY."
WHY...
...WHY WOULD TONY KEEP A ROOM LIKE THIS...?
FOR GOD'S SAKE, WHAT ABOUT HIM SURPRISES YOU AT THIS POINT?
LOOK, WE'RE BURNING TIME. HE COULD BE BACK HERE ANY SECOND.
LET'S JUST FIND WHAT WE CAME HERE TO FIND...
...WHILE WE'VE STILL GOT A CHANCE OF WALKING AWAY.

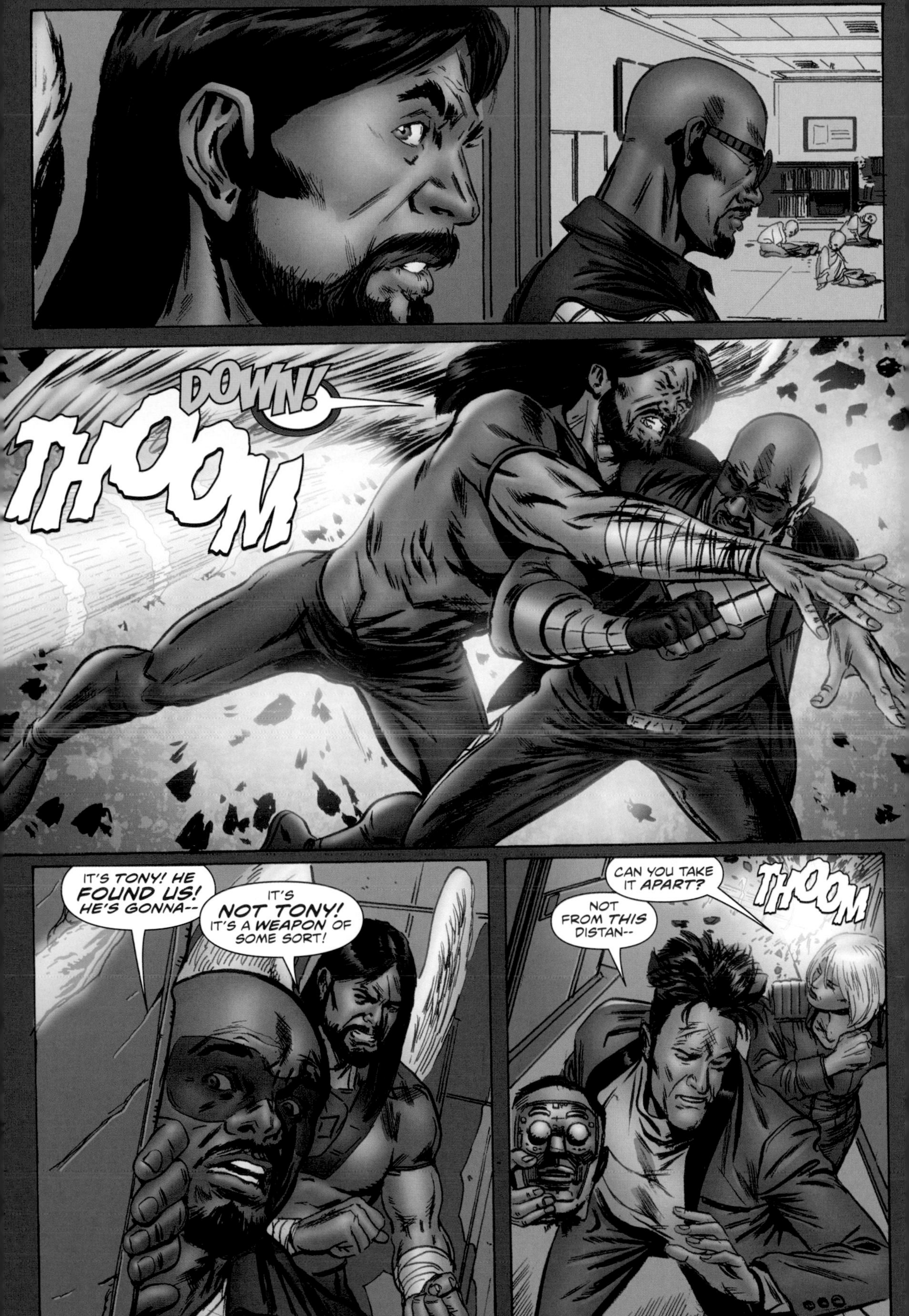
DOWN!
THOOM
IT'S TONY! HE FOUND US! HE'S GONNA--
IT'S NOT TONY! IT'S A WEAPON OF SOME SORT!
CAN YOU TAKE IT APART?
NOT FROM THIS DISTAN--
THOOM

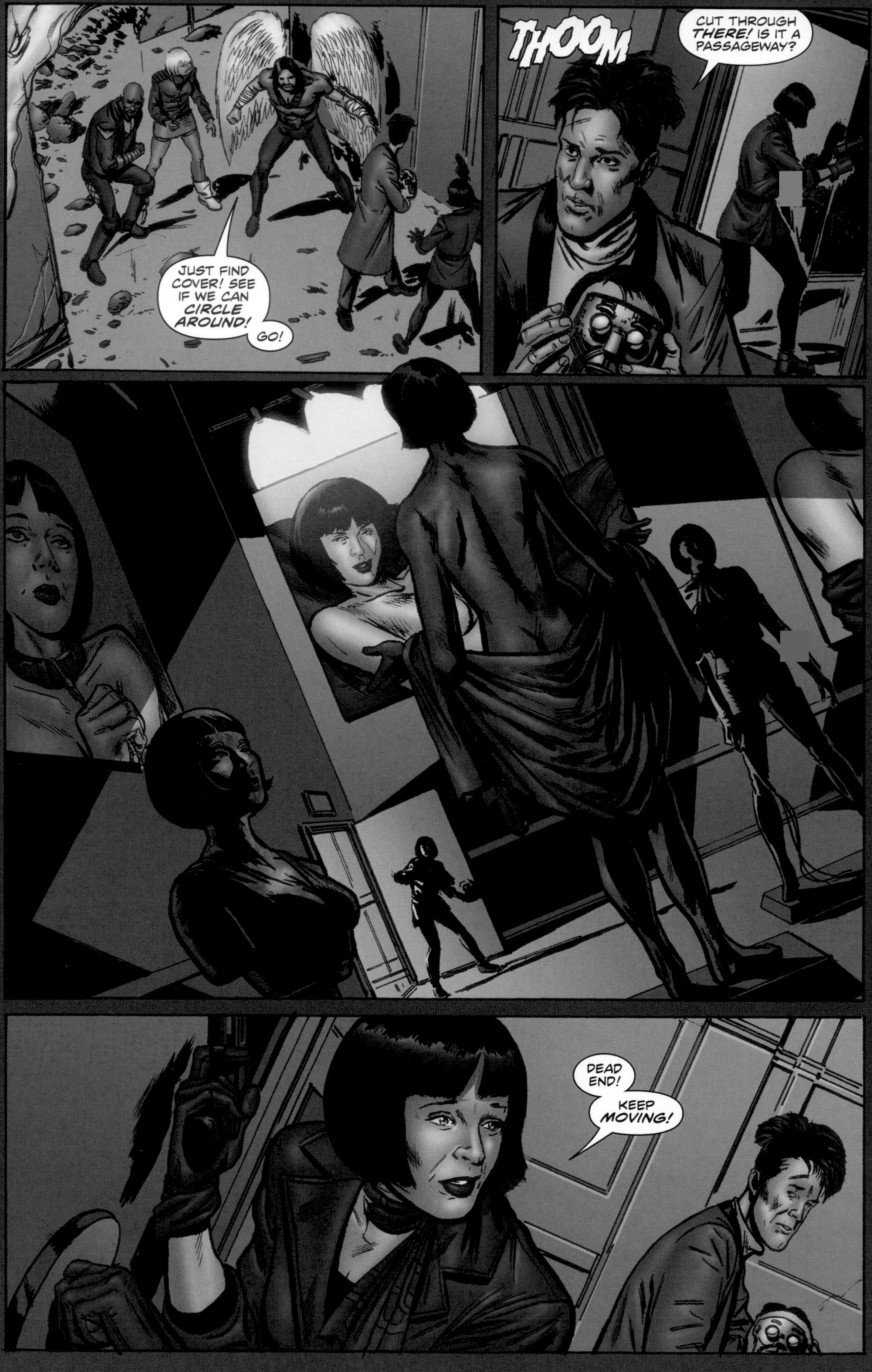
JUST FIND COVER! SEE IF WE CAN CIRCLE AROUND!
GO!
THOOM
CUT THROUGH THERE! IS IT A PASSAGEWAY?
DEAD END!
KEEP MOVING!

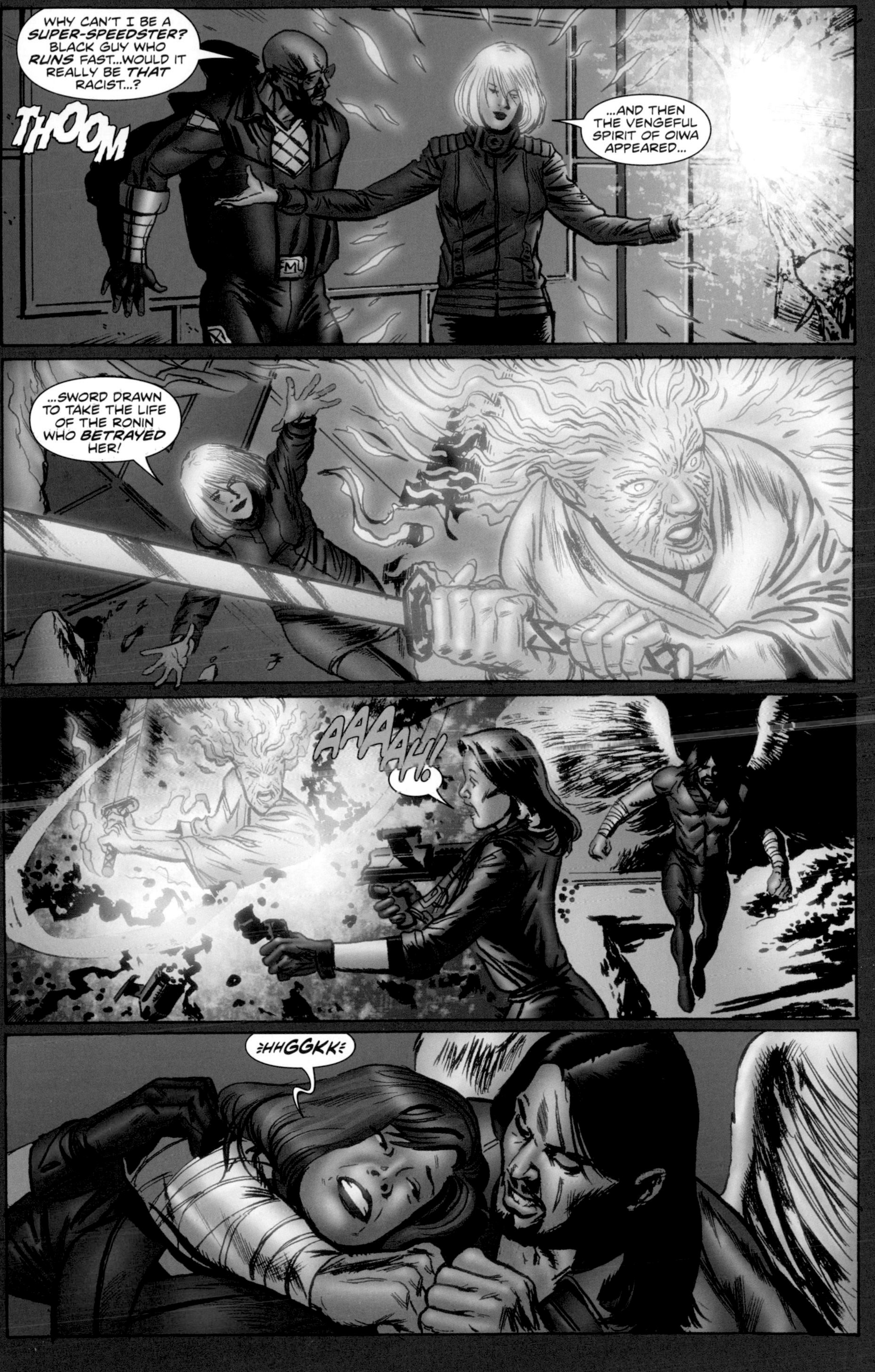
WHY CAN'T I BE A SUPER-SPEEDSTER? BLACK GUY WHO RUNS FAST...WOULD IT REALLY BE THAT RACIST...?
THOOM
...AND THEN THE VENGEFUL SPIRIT OF OIWA APPEARED...
...SWORD DRAWN TO TAKE THE LIFE OF THE RONIN WHO BETRAYED HER!
AAAAH!
HHGGKK

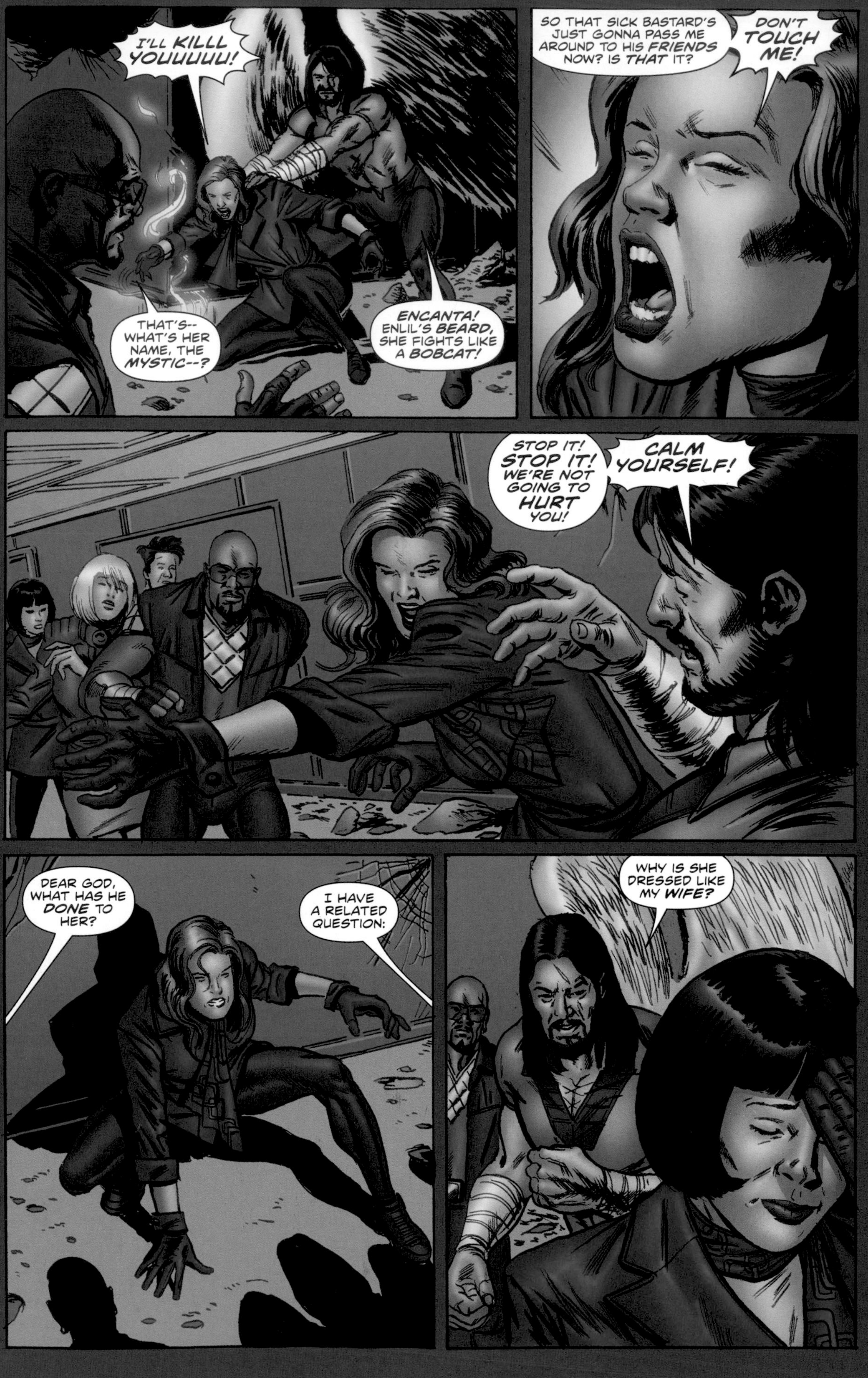
I'LL KILLL YOUUUUU!
THAT'S-- WHAT'S HER NAME, THE MYSTIC--?
ENCANTA! ENLIL'S BEARD, SHE FIGHTS LIKE A BOBCAT!
SO THAT SICK BASTARD'S JUST GONNA PASS ME AROUND TO HIS FRIENDS NOW? IS THAT IT?
DON'T TOUCH ME!
STOP IT! STOP IT! WE'RE NOT GOING TO HURT YOU!
CALM YOURSELF!
DEAR GOD, WHAT HAS HE DONE TO HER?
I HAVE A RELATED QUESTION:
WHY IS SHE DRESSED LIKE MY WIFE?

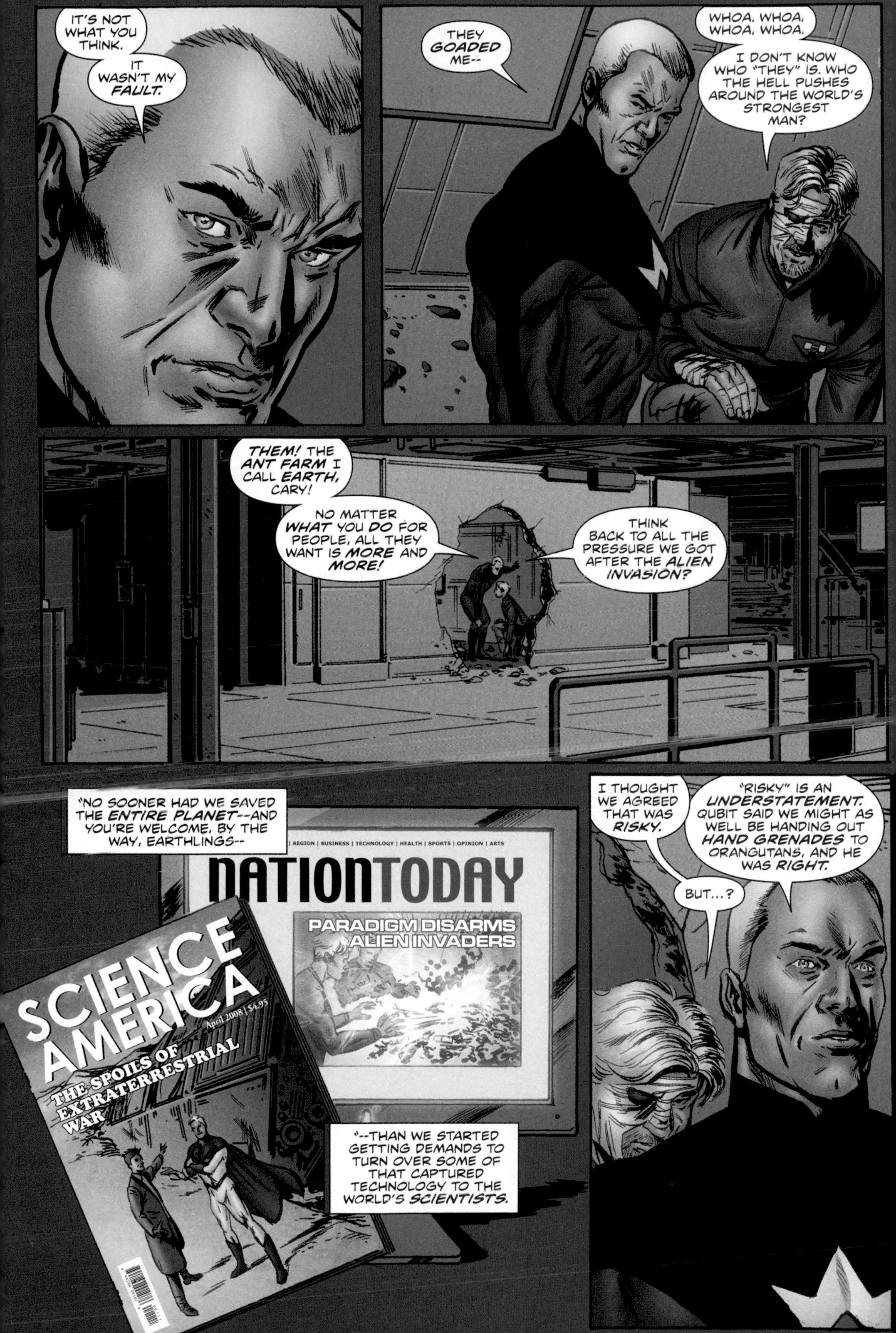
IT'S NOT WHAT YOU THINK.
IT WASN'T MY FAULT.
THEY GOADED ME--
WHOA. WHOA, WHOA, WHOA.
I DON'T KNOW WHO "THEY" IS. WHO THE HELL PUSHES AROUND THE WORLD'S STRONGEST MAN?
THEM! THE ANT FARM I CALL EARTH, CARY!
NO MATTER WHAT YOU DO FOR PEOPLE, ALL THEY WANT IS MORE AND MORE!
THINK BACK TO ALL THE PRESSURE WE GOT AFTER THE ALIEN INVASION?
"NO SOONER HAD WE SAVED THE ENTIRE PLANET--AND YOU'RE WELCOME, BY THE WAY, EARTHLINGS--
REGION | BUSINESS | TECHNOLOGY | HEALTH | SPORTS | OPINION | ARTS
NATIONTODAY
PARADIGM DISARMS ALIEN INVADERS
SCIENCE AMERICA
April 2008 | $4.95
THE SPOILS OF EXTRATERRESTRIAL WAR
"--THAN WE STARTED GETTING DEMANDS TO TURN OVER SOME OF THAT CAPTURED TECHNOLOGY TO THE WORLD'S SCIENTISTS.
I THOUGHT WE AGREED THAT WAS RISKY.
"RISKY" IS AN UNDERSTATEMENT. QUBIT SAID WE MIGHT AS WELL BE HANDING OUT HAND GRENADES TO ORANGUTANS, AND HE WAS RIGHT.
BUT...?

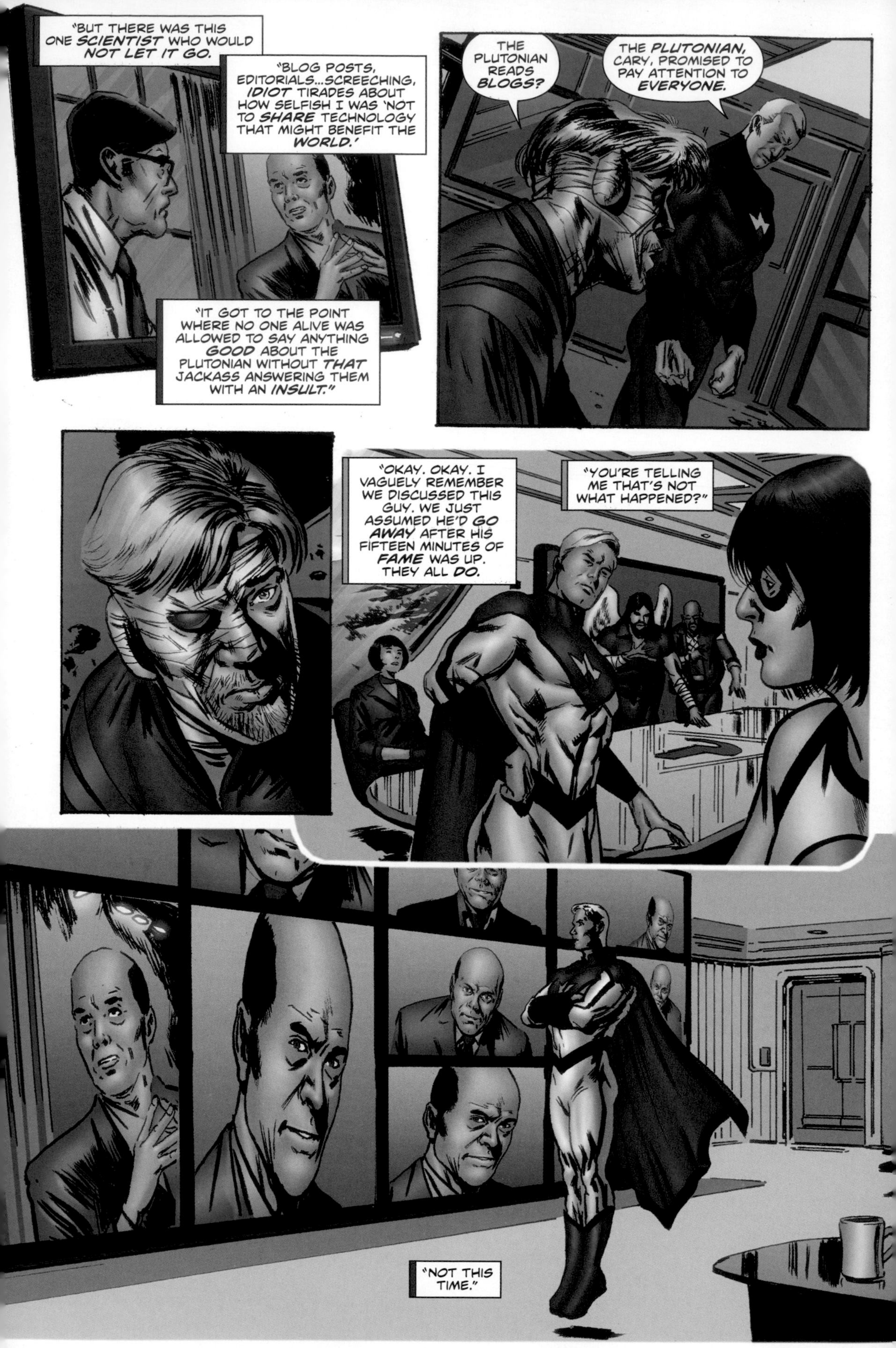
"BUT THERE WAS THIS ONE SCIENTIST WHO WOULD NOT LET IT GO.
"BLOG POSTS, EDITORIALS...SCREECHING, IDIOT TIRADES ABOUT HOW SELFISH I WAS 'NOT TO SHARE TECHNOLOGY THAT MIGHT BENEFIT THE WORLD.'
"IT GOT TO THE POINT WHERE NO ONE ALIVE WAS ALLOWED TO SAY ANYTHING GOOD ABOUT THE PLUTONIAN WITHOUT THAT JACKASS ANSWERING THEM WITH AN INSULT."
THE PLUTONIAN READS BLOGS?
THE PLUTONIAN, CARY, PROMISED TO PAY ATTENTION TO EVERYONE.
"OKAY. OKAY. I VAGUELY REMEMBER WE DISCUSSED THIS GUY. WE JUST ASSUMED HE'D GO AWAY AFTER HIS FIFTEEN MINUTES OF FAME WAS UP. THEY ALL DO.
"YOU'RE TELLING ME THAT'S NOT WHAT HAPPENED?"
"NOT THIS TIME."

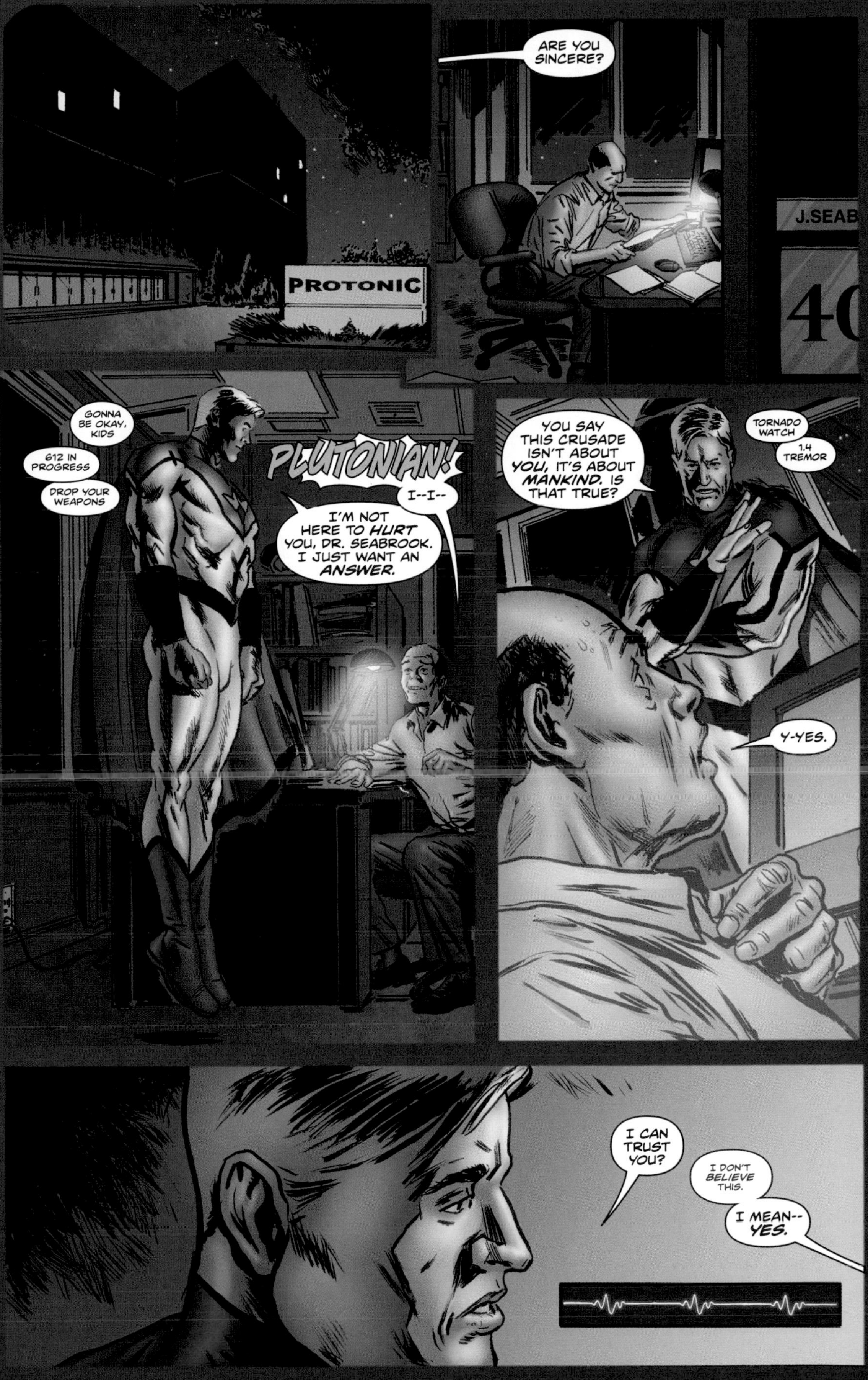
PROTONIC
ARE YOU SINCERE?
J.SEAB
40
GONNA BE OKAY, KIDS
612 IN PROGRESS
DROP YOUR WEAPONS
PLUTONIAN!
I--I--
I'M NOT HERE TO HURT YOU, DR. SEABROOK. I JUST WANT AN ANSWER.
YOU SAY THIS CRUSADE ISN'T ABOUT YOU, IT'S ABOUT MANKIND. IS THAT TRUE?
TORNADO WATCH
1.4 TREMOR
Y-YES.
I CAN TRUST YOU?
I DON'T BELIEVE THIS.
I MEAN-- YES.

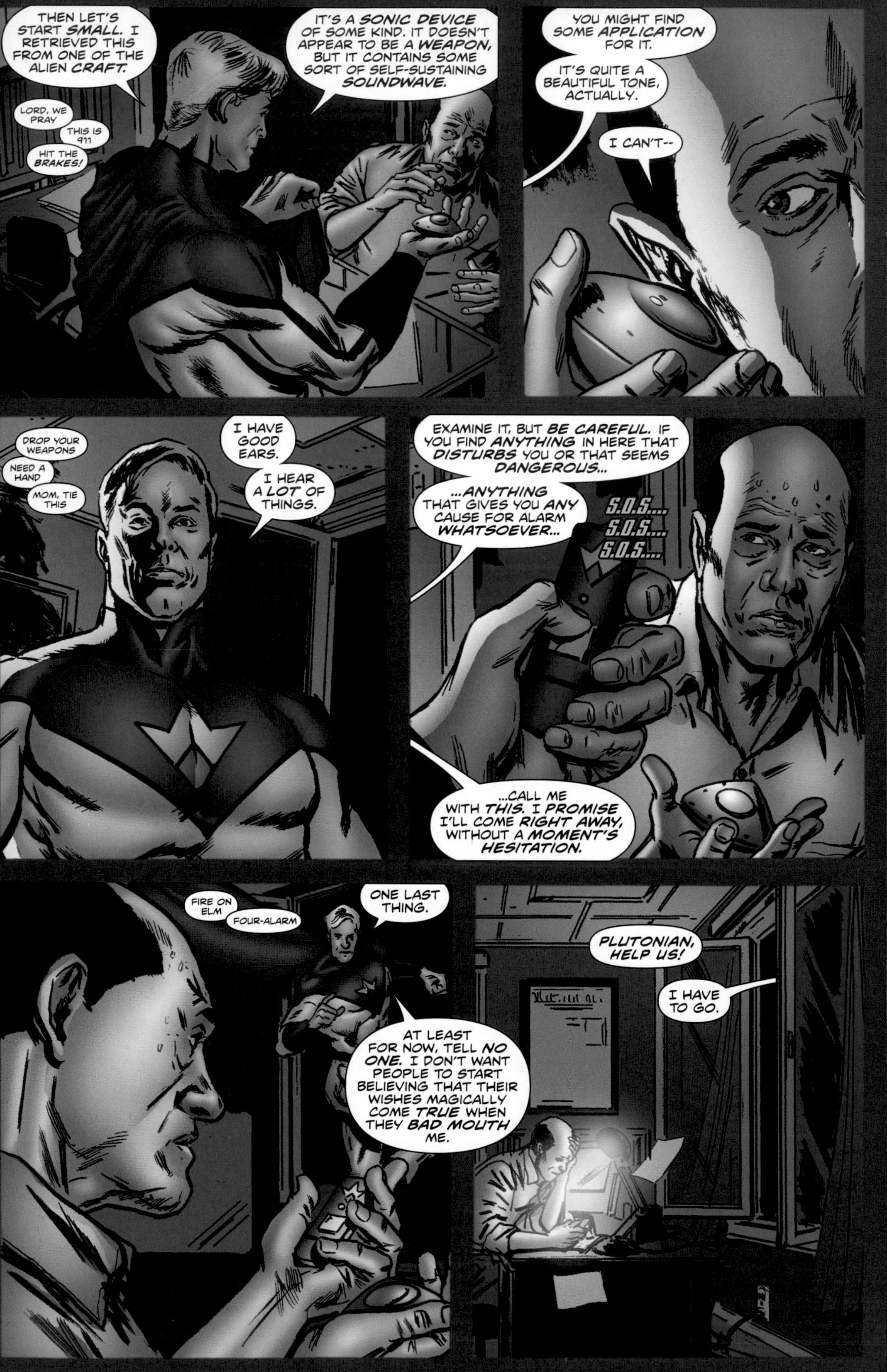
THEN LET'S START SMALL. I RETRIEVED THIS FROM ONE OF THE ALIEN CRAFT.
LORD, WE PRAY
THIS IS 911
HIT THE BRAKES!
IT'S A SONIC DEVICE OF SOME KIND. IT DOESN'T APPEAR TO BE A WEAPON, BUT IT CONTAINS SOME SORT OF SELF-SUSTAINING SOUNDWAVE.
YOU MIGHT FIND SOME APPLICATION FOR IT.
IT'S QUITE A BEAUTIFUL TONE, ACTUALLY.
I CAN'T--
DROP YOUR WEAPONS
NEED A HAND
MOM, TIE THIS
I HAVE GOOD EARS.
I HEAR A LOT OF THINGS.
EXAMINE IT, BUT BE CAREFUL. IF YOU FIND ANYTHING IN HERE THAT DISTURBS YOU OR THAT SEEMS DANGEROUS...
...ANYTHING THAT GIVES YOU ANY CAUSE FOR ALARM WHATSOEVER...
S.O.S.... S.O.S.... S.O.S....
...CALL ME WITH THIS. I PROMISE I'LL COME RIGHT AWAY, WITHOUT A MOMENT'S HESITATION.
FIRE ON ELM
FOUR-ALARM
ONE LAST THING.
AT LEAST FOR NOW, TELL NO ONE. I DON'T WANT PEOPLE TO START BELIEVING THAT THEIR WISHES MAGICALLY COME TRUE WHEN THEY BAD MOUTH ME.
PLUTONIAN, HELP US!
I HAVE TO GO.

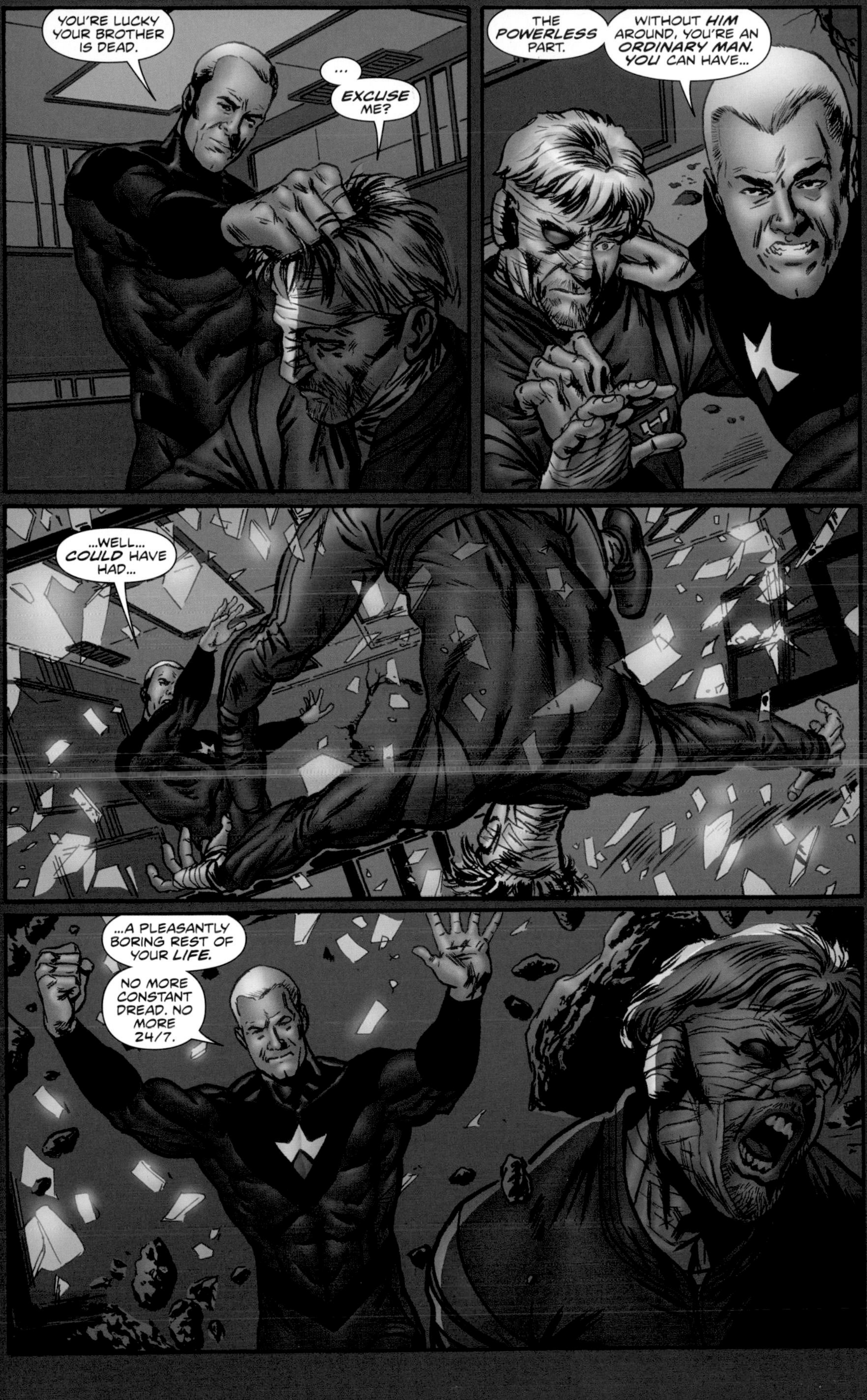
YOU'RE LUCKY YOUR BROTHER IS DEAD.
... EXCUSE ME?
THE POWERLESS PART.
WITHOUT HIM AROUND, YOU'RE AN ORDINARY MAN. YOU CAN HAVE...
...WELL... COULD HAVE HAD...
...A PLEASANTLY BORING REST OF YOUR LIFE.
NO MORE CONSTANT DREAD. NO MORE 24/7.

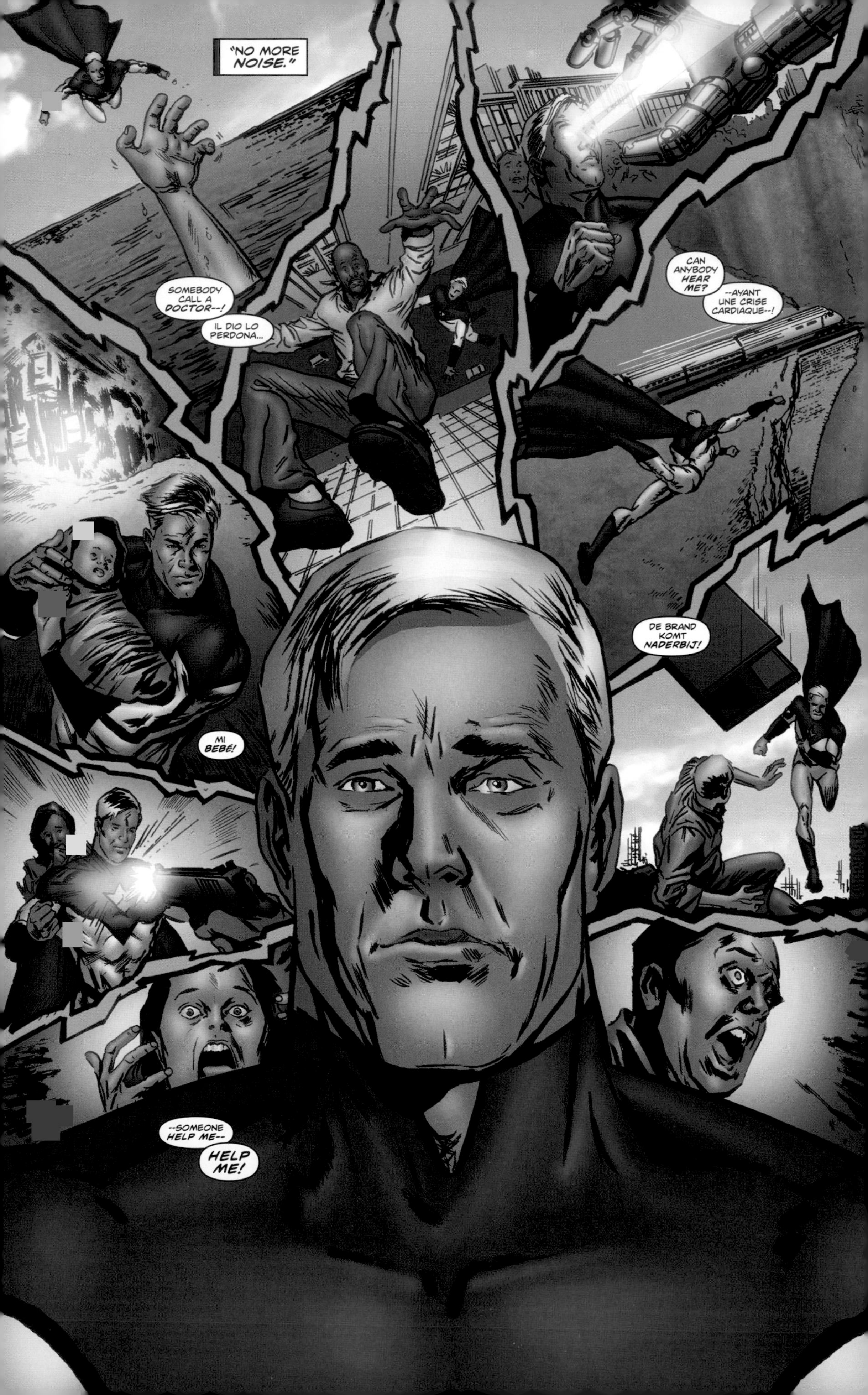
"NO MORE NOISE."
SOMEBODY CALL A DOCTOR--!
IL DIO LO PERDONA...
CAN ANYBODY HEAR ME?
--AYANT UNE CRISE CARDIAQUE--!
DE BRAND KOMT NADERBIJ!
MI BEBÉ!
--SOMEONE HELP ME--
HELP ME!

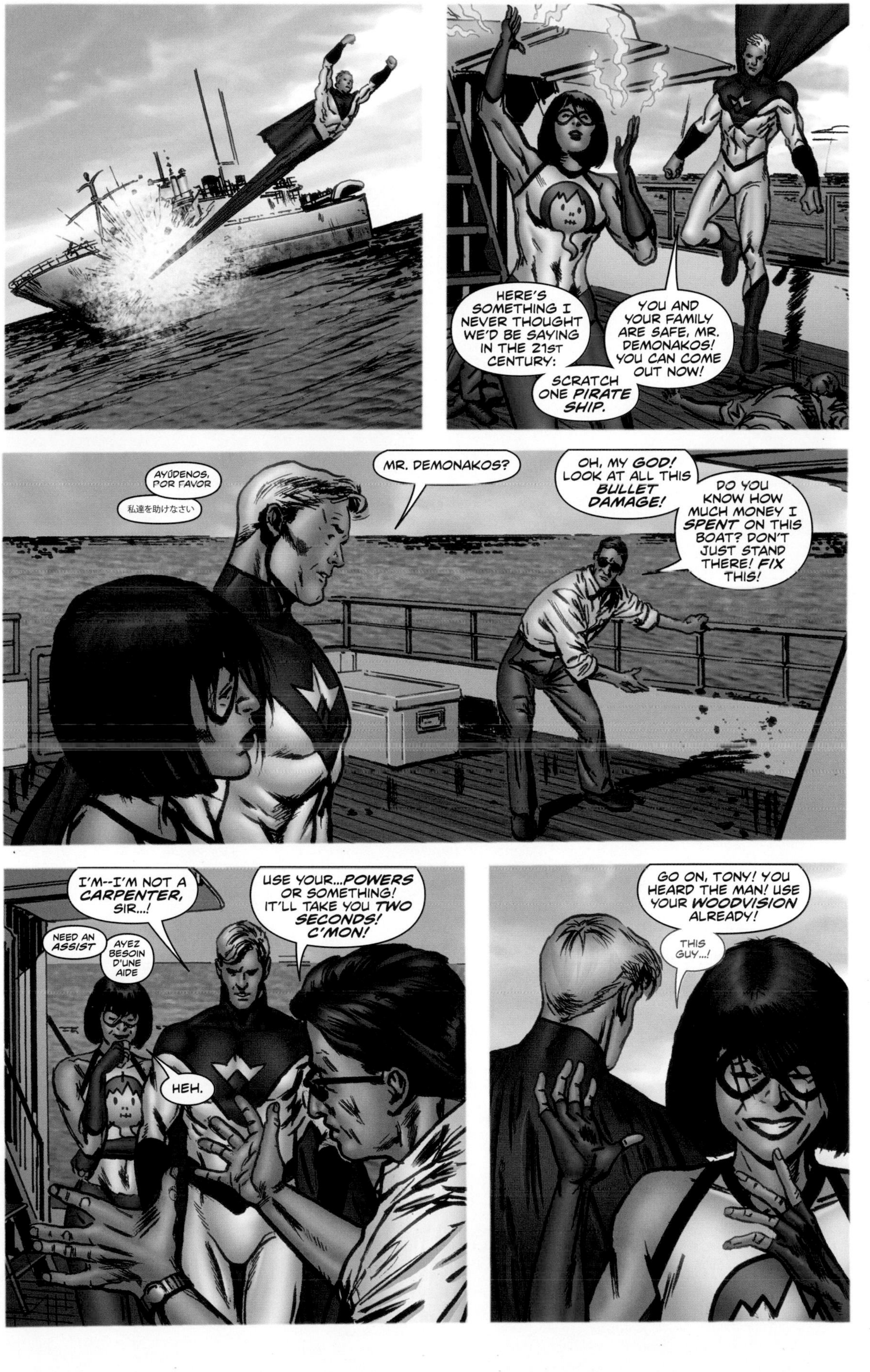
HERE'S SOMETHING I NEVER THOUGHT WE'D BE SAYING IN THE 21ST CENTURY:
SCRATCH ONE PIRATE SHIP.
YOU AND YOUR FAMILY ARE SAFE, MR. DEMONAKOS! YOU CAN COME OUT NOW!
AYÚDENOS, POR FAVOR
私達を助けなさい
MR. DEMONAKOS?
OH, MY GOD! LOOK AT ALL THIS BULLET DAMAGE!
DO YOU KNOW HOW MUCH MONEY I SPENT ON THIS BOAT? DON'T JUST STAND THERE! FIX THIS!
I'M--I'M NOT A CARPENTER, SIR...!
NEED AN ASSIST
AYEZ BESOIN D'UNE AIDE
USE YOUR...POWERS OR SOMETHING! IT'LL TAKE YOU TWO SECONDS! C'MON!
HEH.
GO ON, TONY! YOU HEARD THE MAN! USE YOUR WOODVISION ALREADY!
THIS GUY...!

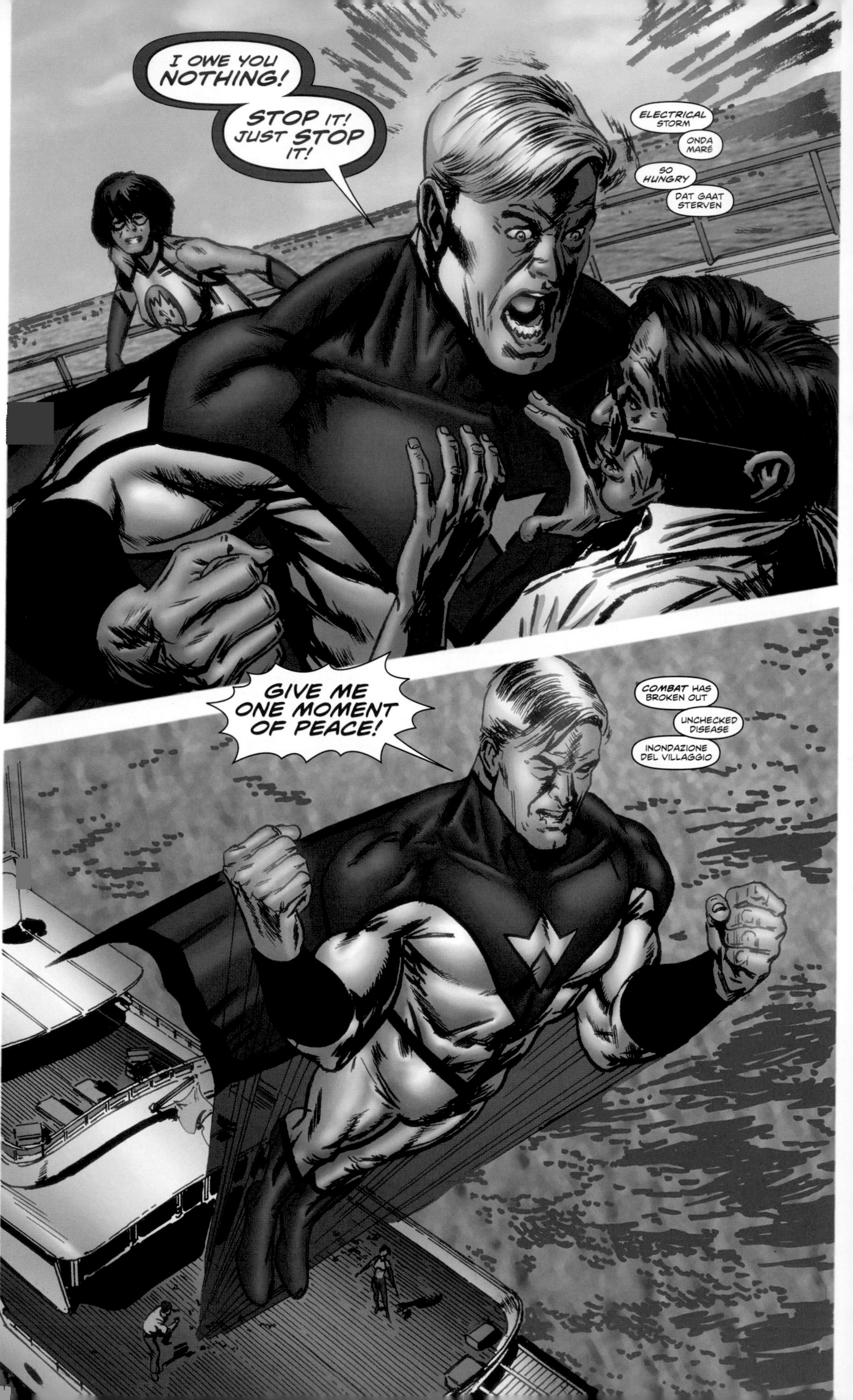
I OWE YOU NOTHING!
STOP IT! JUST STOP IT!
ELECTRICAL STORM
ONDA MARÉ
SO HUNGRY
DAT GAAT STERVEN
GIVE ME ONE MOMENT OF PEACE!
COMBAT HAS BROKEN OUT
UNCHECKED DISEASE
INONDAZIONE DEL VILLAGGIO

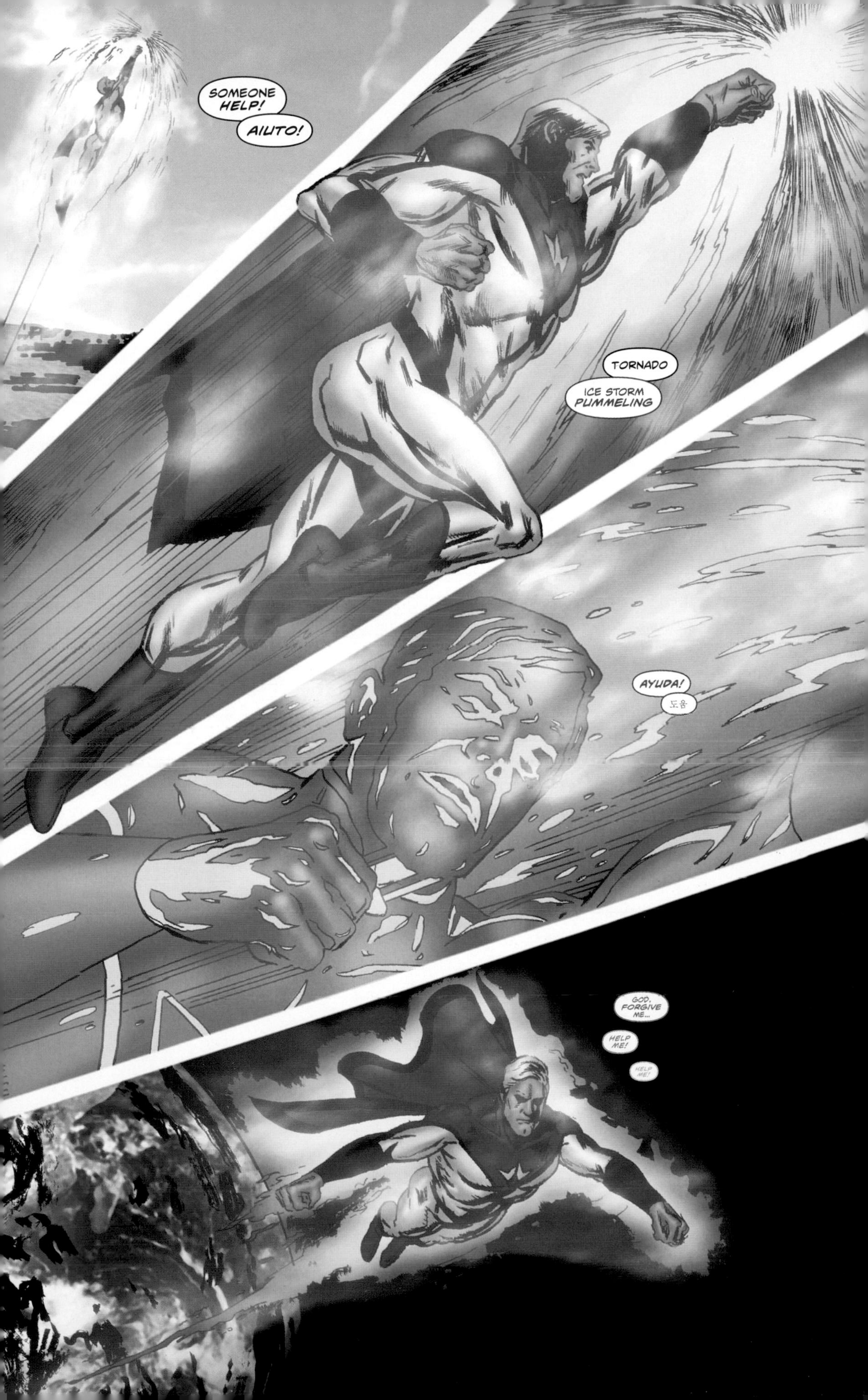
SOMEONE HELP!
AIUTO!
TORNADO
ICE STORM PUMMELING
AYUDA!
도움
GOD, FORGIVE ME...
HELP ME!
HELP ME!

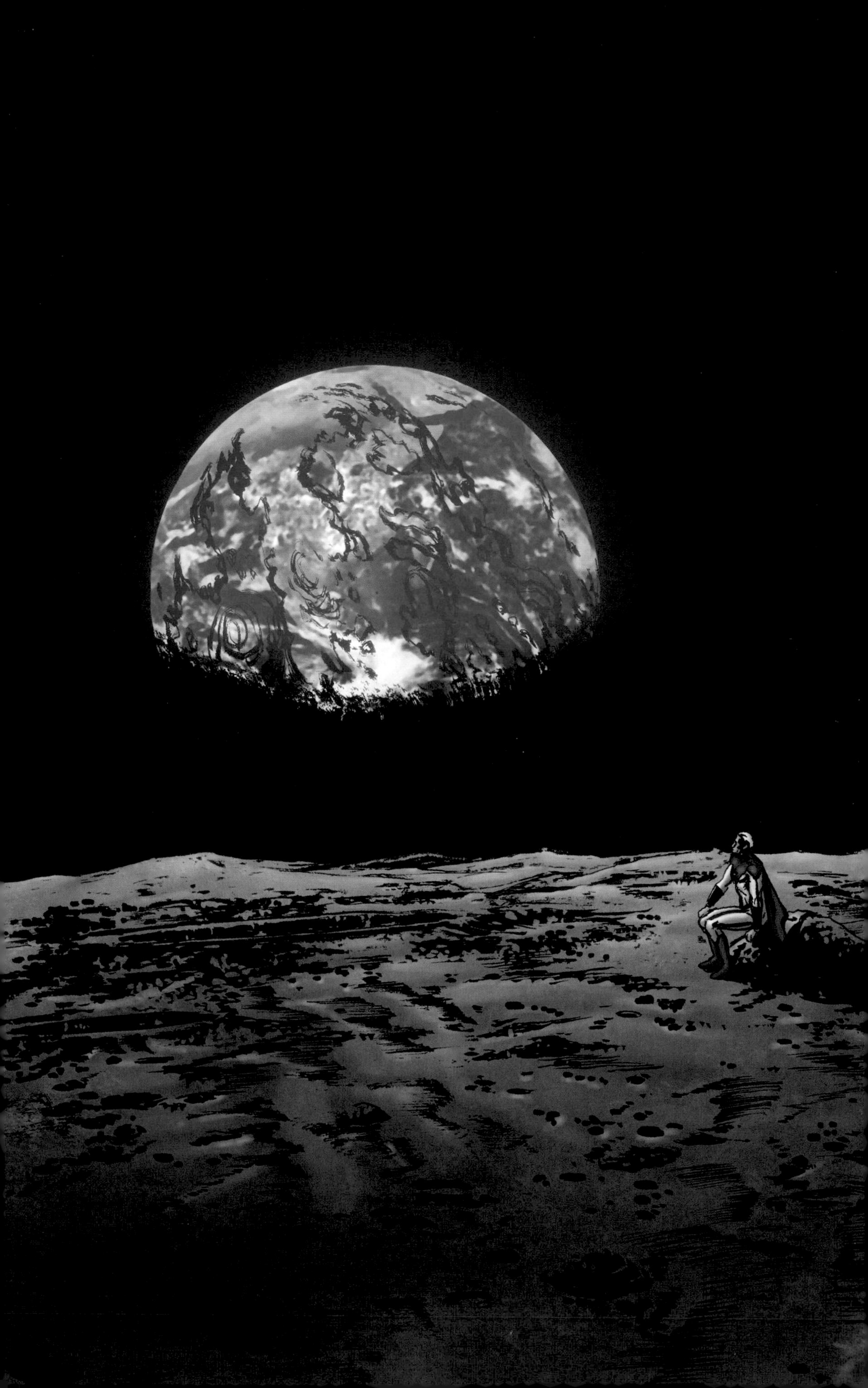

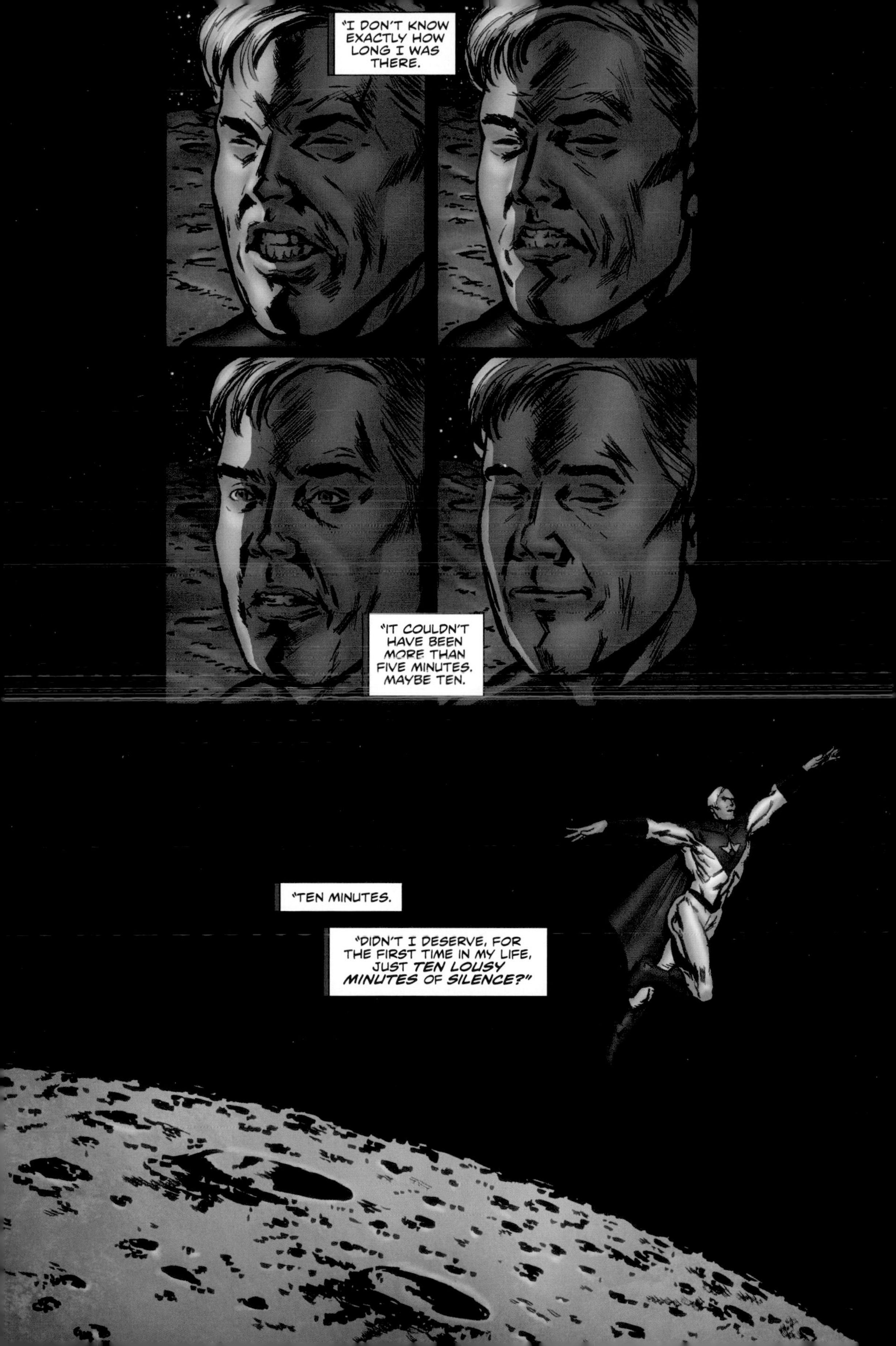

"I DON'T KNOW EXACTLY HOW LONG I WAS THERE.
"IT COULDN'T HAVE BEEN MORE THAN FIVE MINUTES. MAYBE TEN.
"TEN MINUTES.
"DIDN'T I DESERVE, FOR THE FIRST TIME IN MY LIFE, JUST TEN LOUSY MINUTES OF SILENCE?"

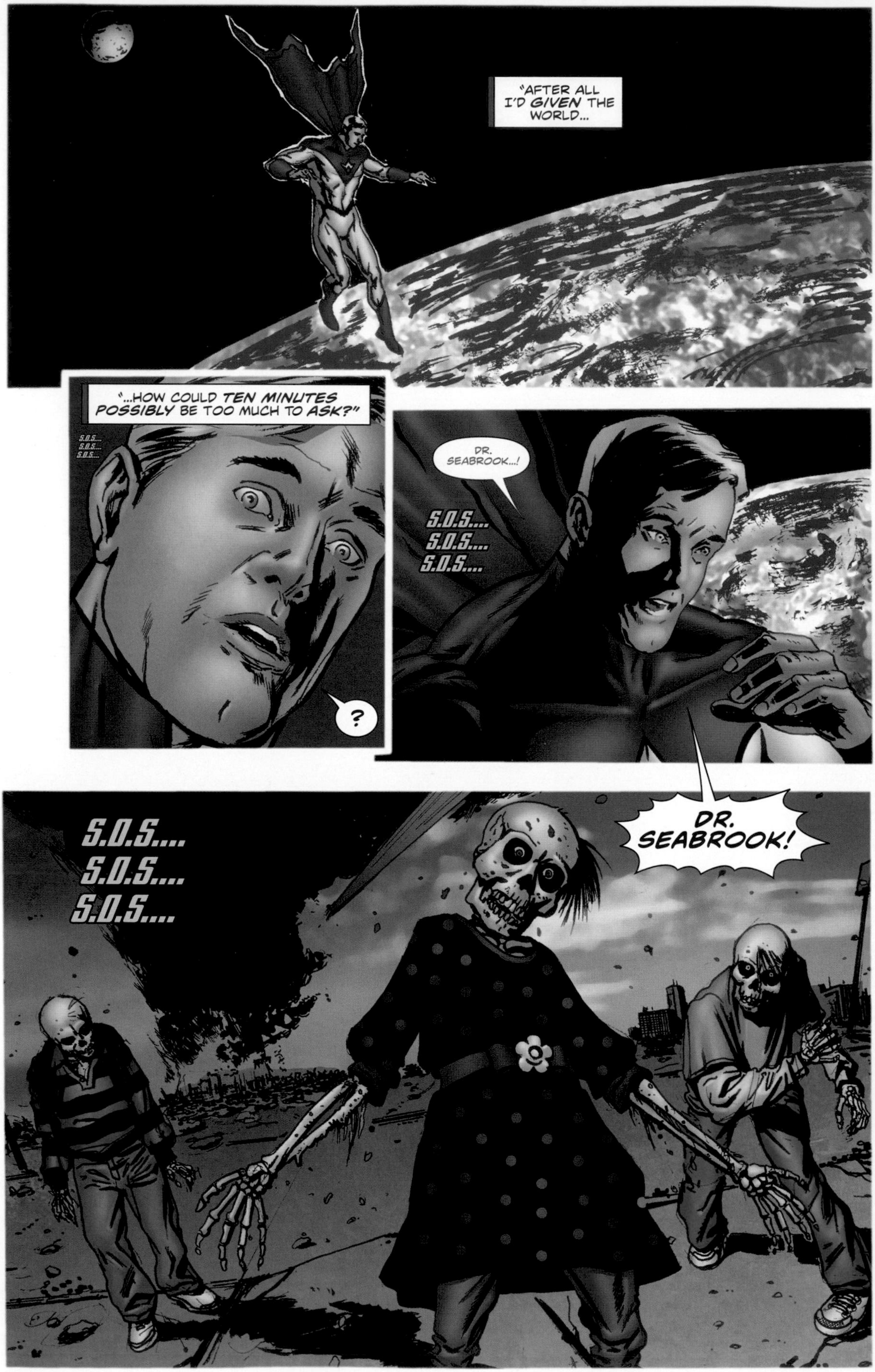
"AFTER ALL I'D GIVEN THE WORLD...
"...HOW COULD TEN MINUTES POSSIBLY BE TOO MUCH TO ASK?"
S.O.S... S.O.S... S.O.S...
?
DR. SEABROOK...!
S.O.S.... S.O.S.... S.O.S....
S.O.S.... S.O.S.... S.O.S....
DR. SEABROOK!

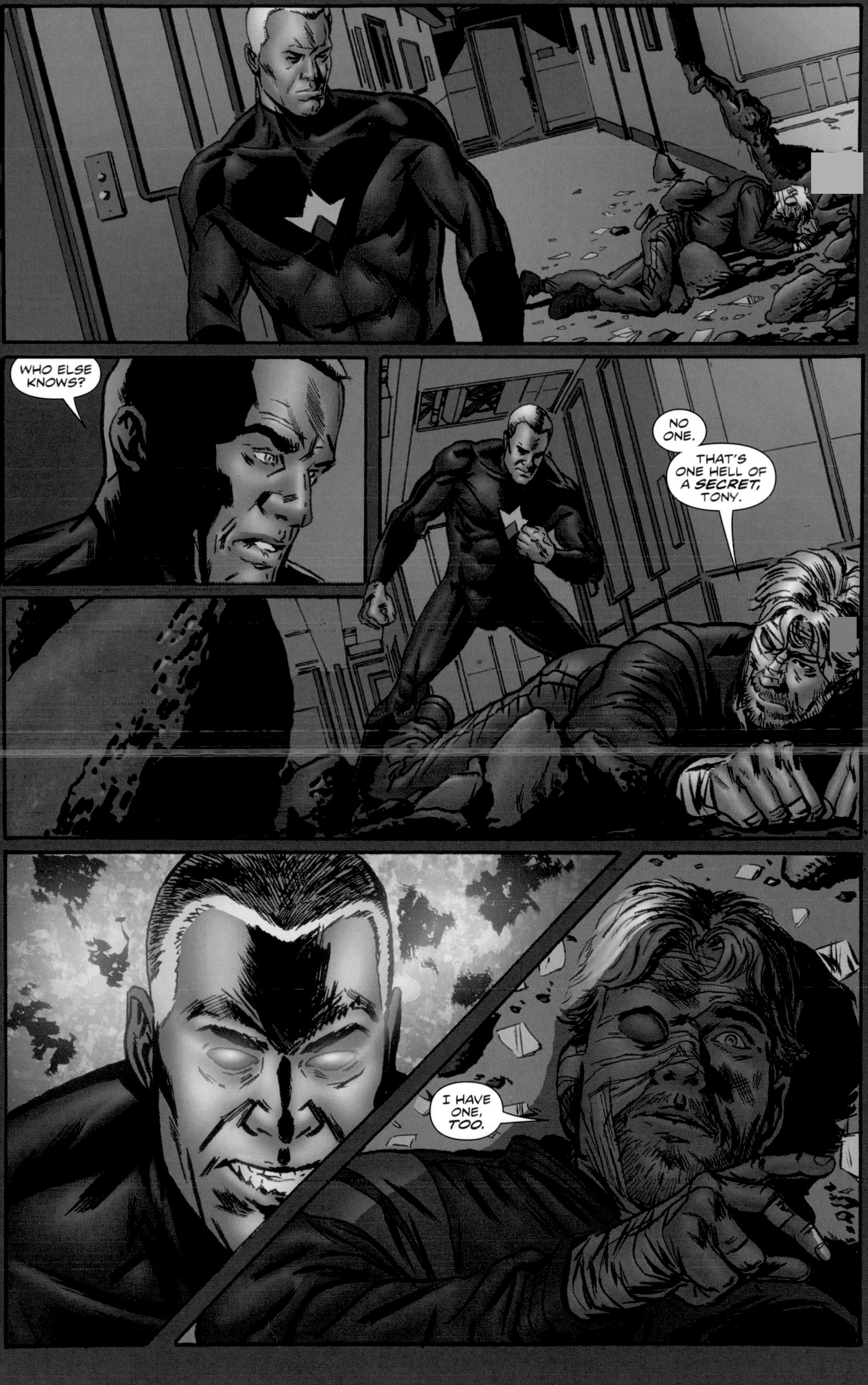
WHO ELSE KNOWS?
NO ONE.
THAT'S ONE HELL OF A *SECRET,* TONY.
I HAVE ONE, *TOO.*

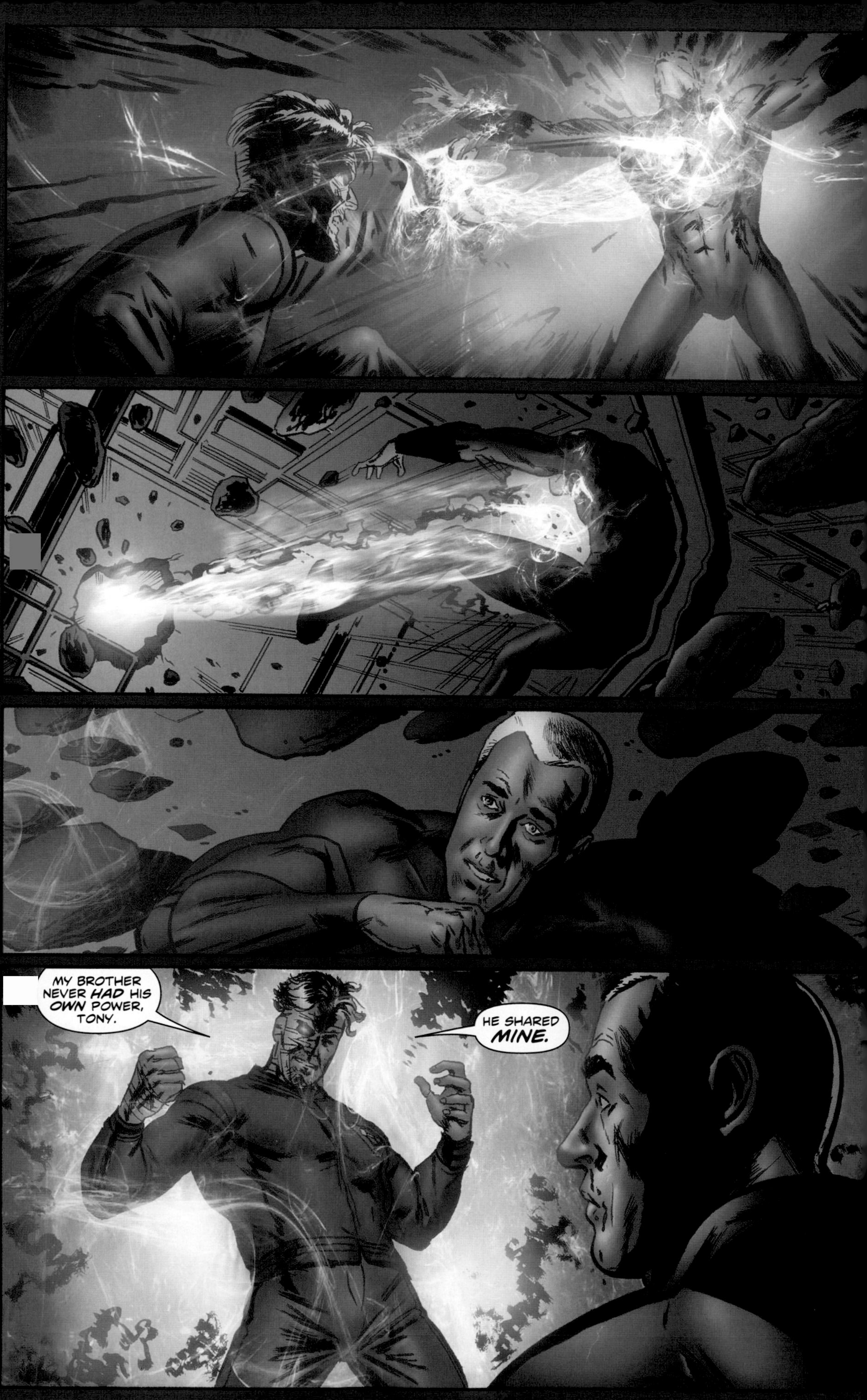
MY BROTHER NEVER HAD HIS OWN POWER, TONY.
HE SHARED MINE.

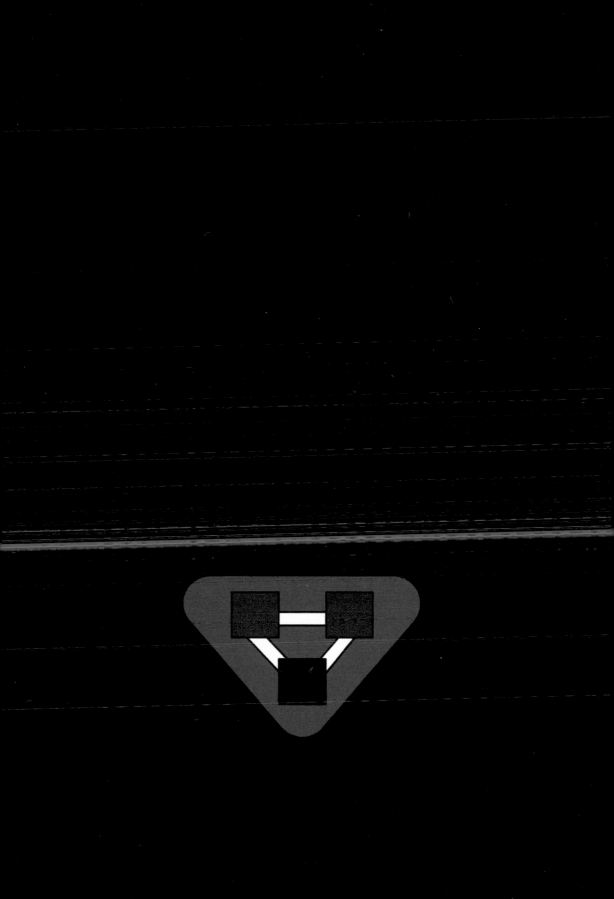

CHAPTER 8

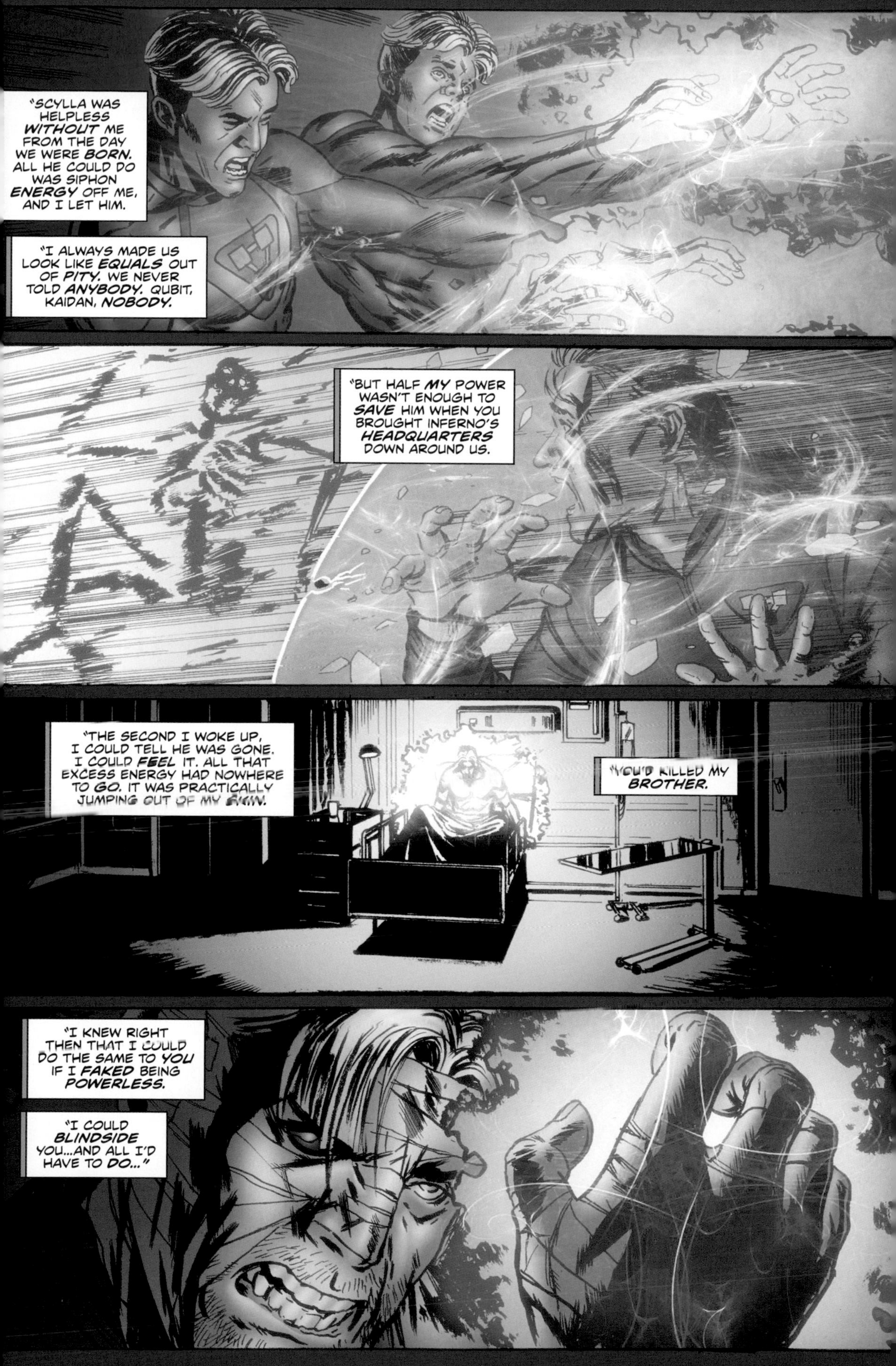
"SCYLLA WAS HELPLESS WITHOUT ME FROM THE DAY WE WERE BORN. ALL HE COULD DO WAS SIPHON ENERGY OFF ME, AND I LET HIM.
"I ALWAYS MADE US LOOK LIKE EQUALS OUT OF PITY. WE NEVER TOLD ANYBODY. QUBIT, KAIDAN, NOBODY.
"BUT HALF MY POWER WASN'T ENOUGH TO SAVE HIM WHEN YOU BROUGHT INFERNO'S HEADQUARTERS DOWN AROUND US.
"THE SECOND I WOKE UP, I COULD TELL HE WAS GONE. I COULD FEEL IT. ALL THAT EXCESS ENERGY HAD NOWHERE TO GO. IT WAS PRACTICALLY JUMPING OUT OF MY SKIN.
"YOU'D KILLED MY BROTHER.
"I KNEW RIGHT THEN THAT I COULD DO THE SAME TO YOU IF I FAKED BEING POWERLESS.
"I COULD BLINDSIDE YOU...AND ALL I'D HAVE TO DO..."

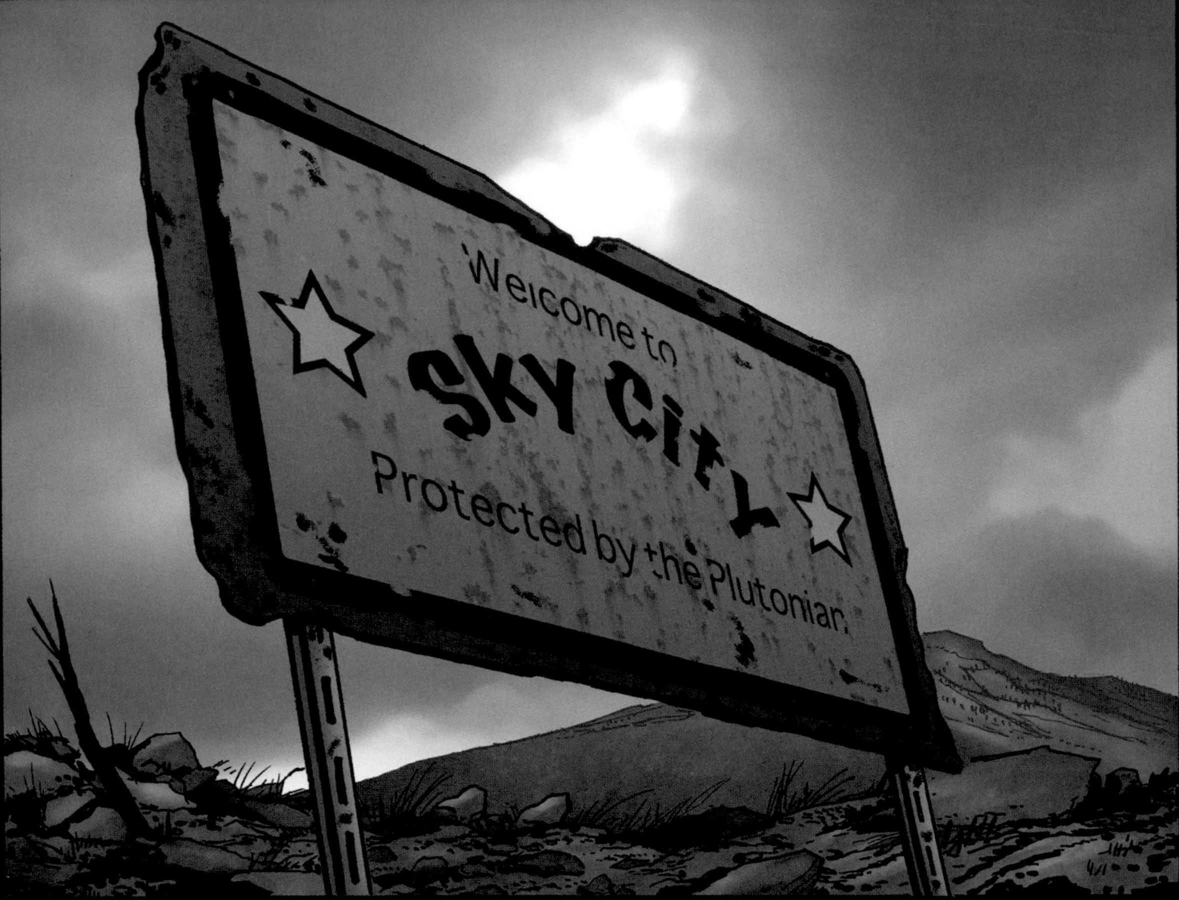
Welcome to
SKY CITY
Protected by the Plutoniar.

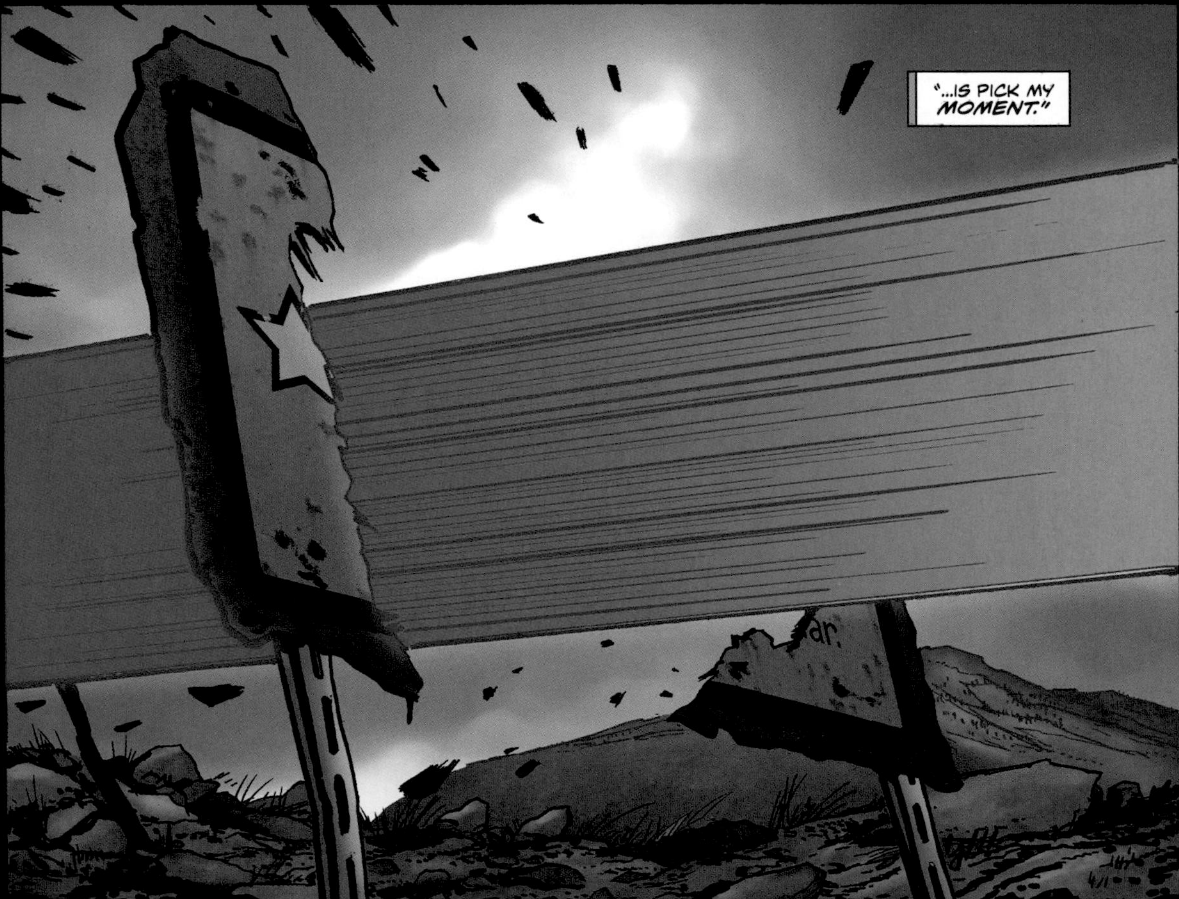
"...IS PICK MY *MOMENT.*"

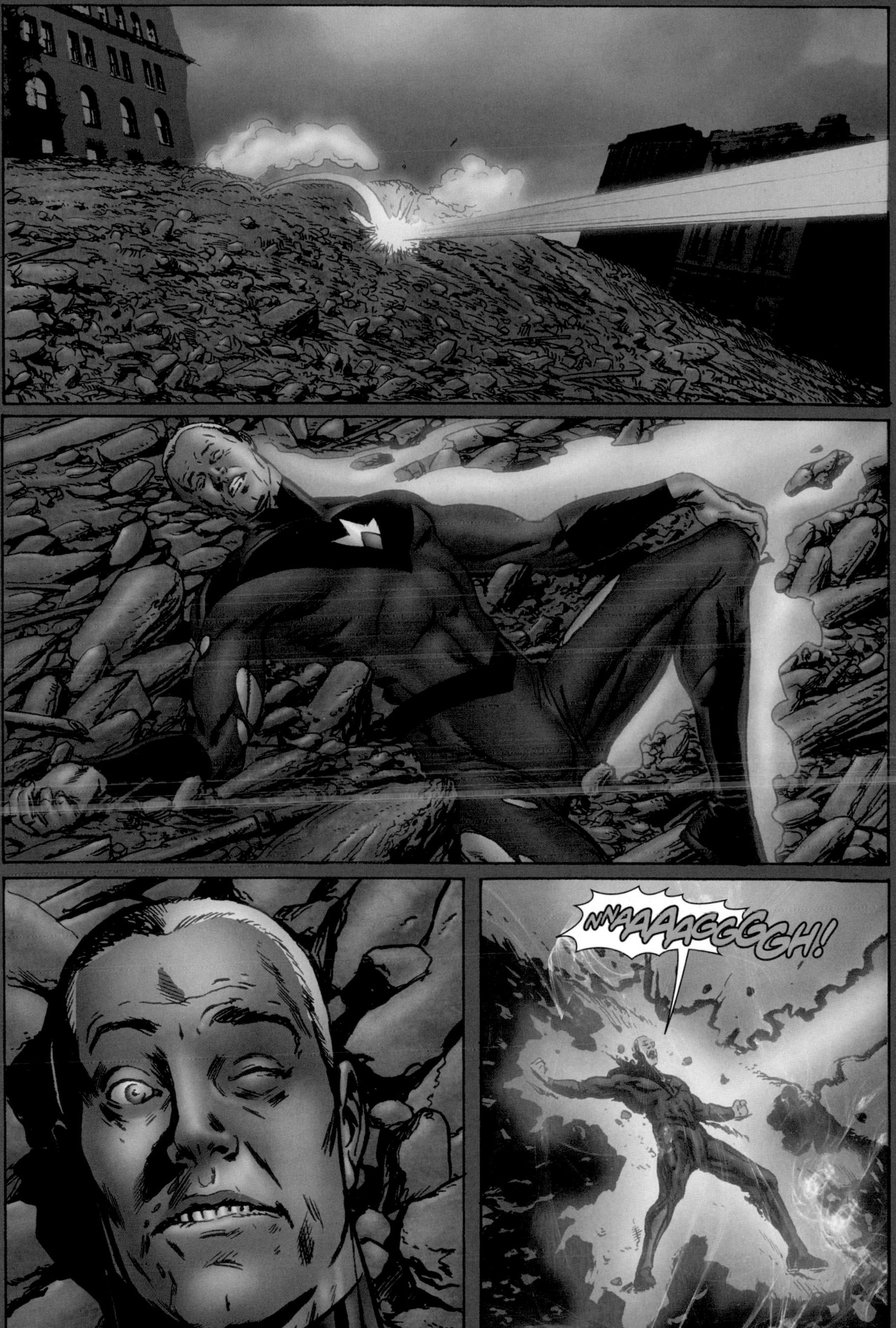
NNAAAAGGGGH!

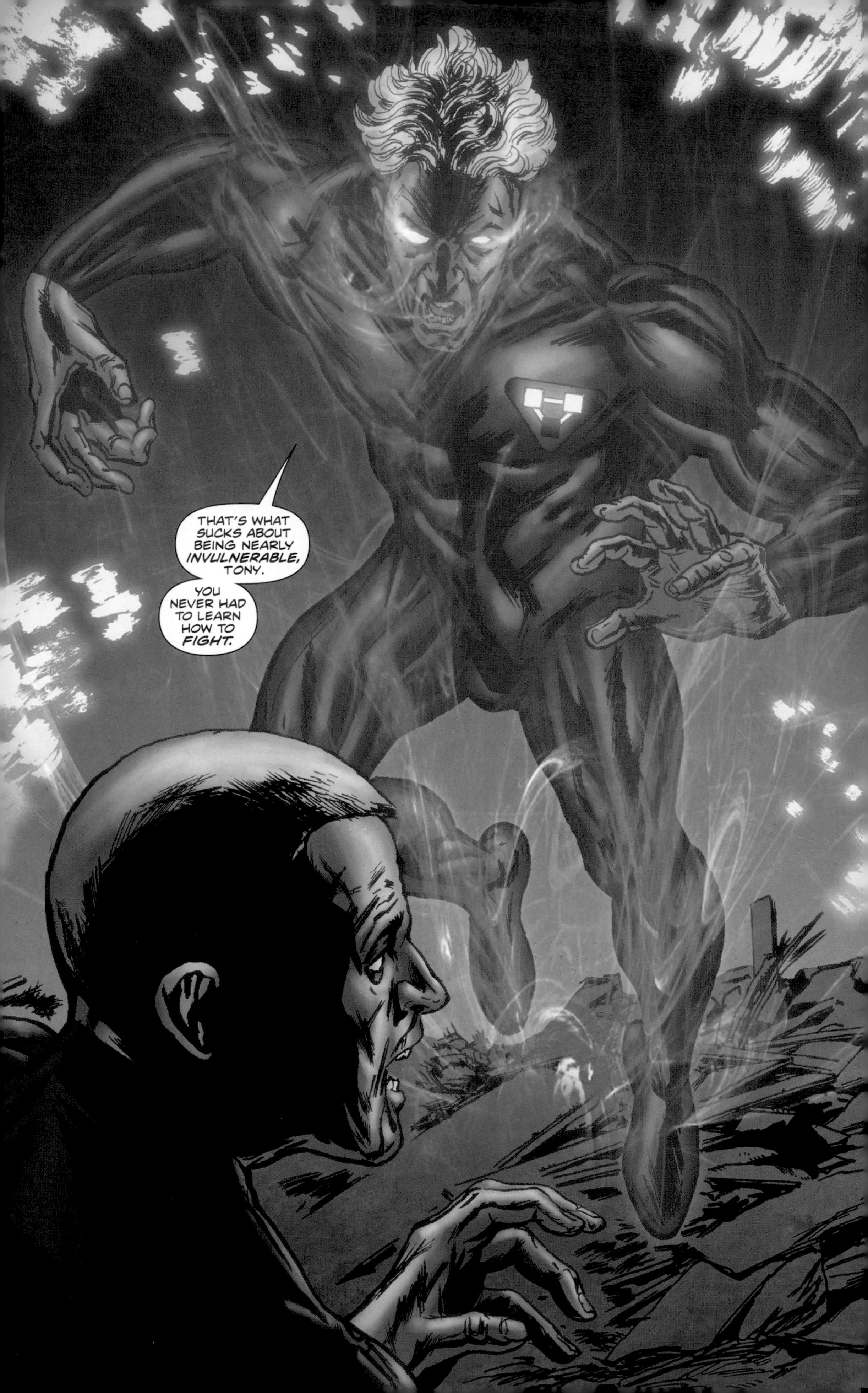
THAT'S WHAT SUCKS ABOUT BEING NEARLY *INVULNERABLE,* TONY.
YOU NEVER HAD TO LEARN HOW TO *FIGHT.*

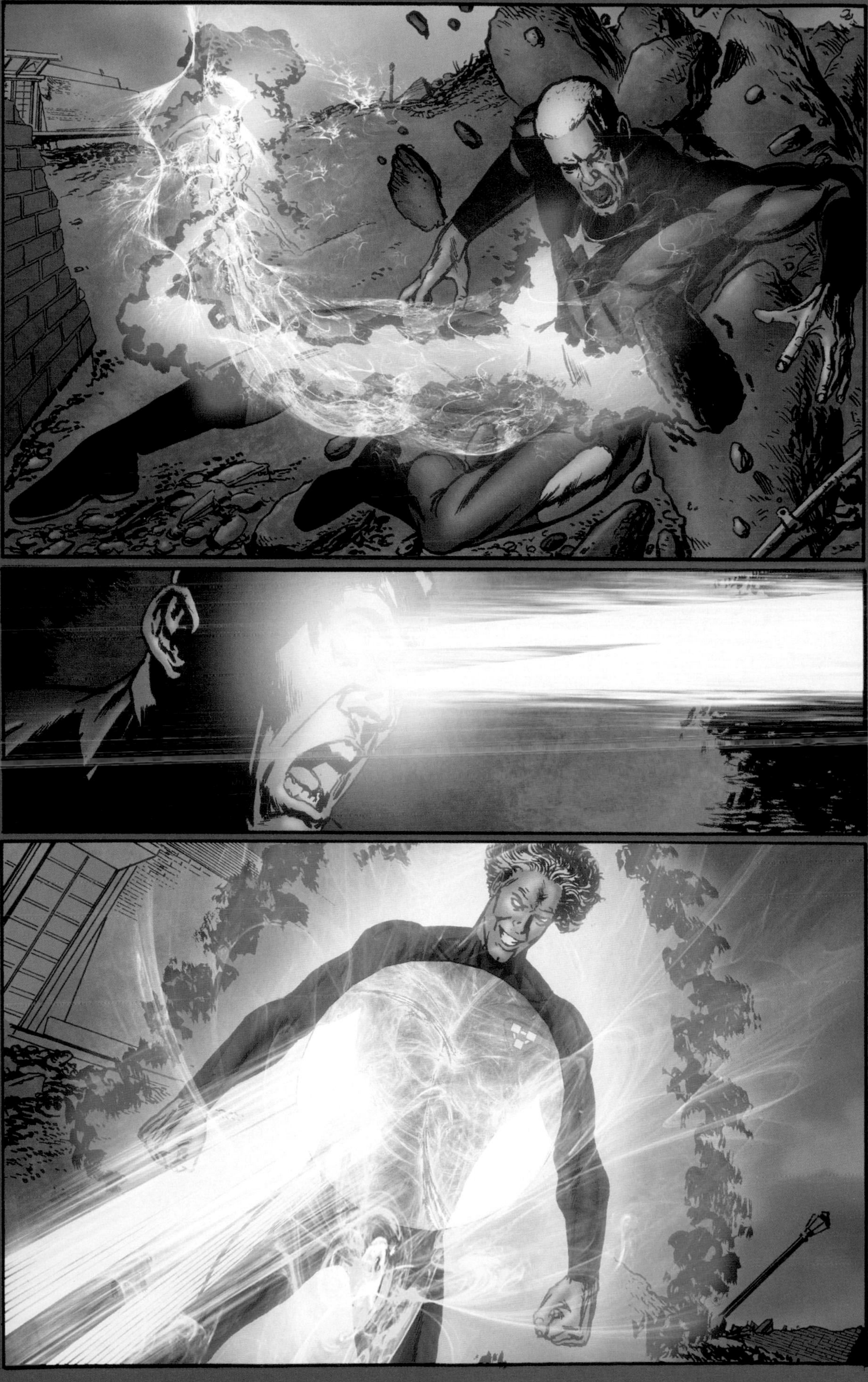

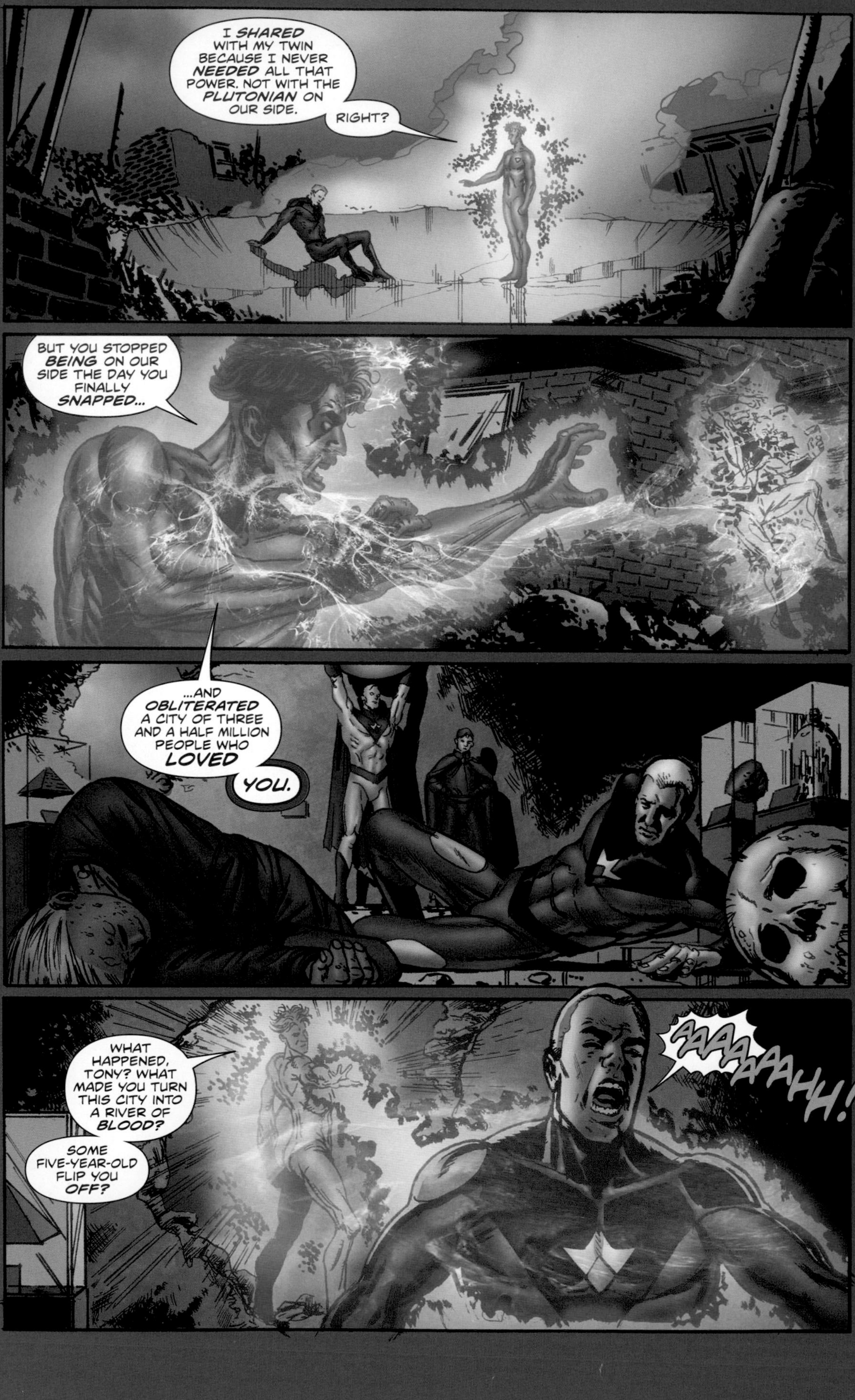
I SHARED WITH MY TWIN BECAUSE I NEVER NEEDED ALL THAT POWER. NOT WITH THE PLUTONIAN ON OUR SIDE.
RIGHT?
BUT YOU STOPPED BEING ON OUR SIDE THE DAY YOU FINALLY SNAPPED...
...AND OBLITERATED A CITY OF THREE AND A HALF MILLION PEOPLE WHO LOVED
YOU.
WHAT HAPPENED, TONY? WHAT MADE YOU TURN THIS CITY INTO A RIVER OF BLOOD?
SOME FIVE-YEAR-OLD FLIP YOU OFF?
AAAAAAAHH!

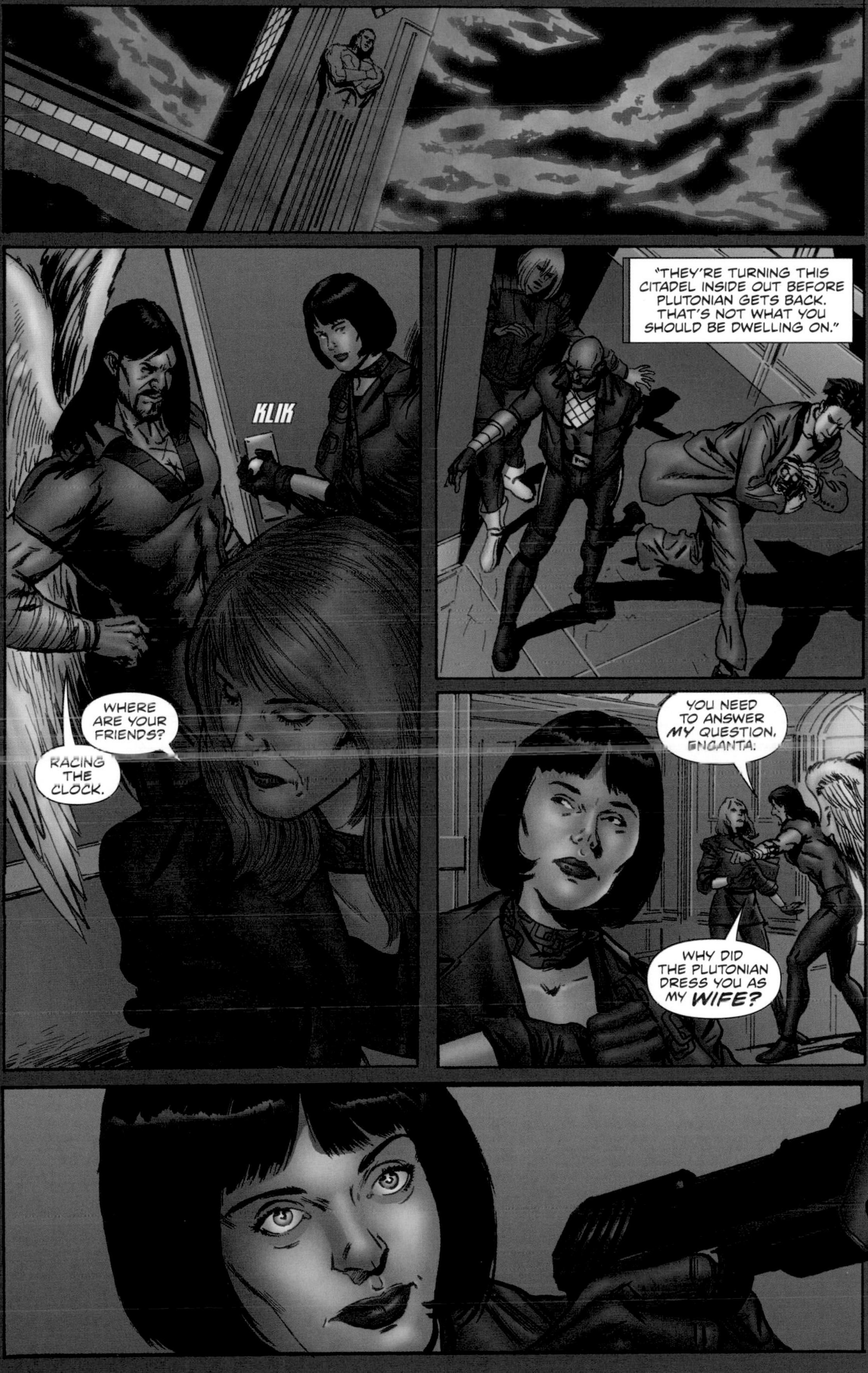
KLIK
"THEY'RE TURNING THIS CITADEL INSIDE OUT BEFORE PLUTONIAN GETS BACK. THAT'S NOT WHAT YOU SHOULD BE DWELLING ON."
WHERE ARE YOUR FRIENDS?
RACING THE CLOCK.
YOU NEED TO ANSWER MY QUESTION, ENCANTA:
WHY DID THE PLUTONIAN DRESS YOU AS MY WIFE?

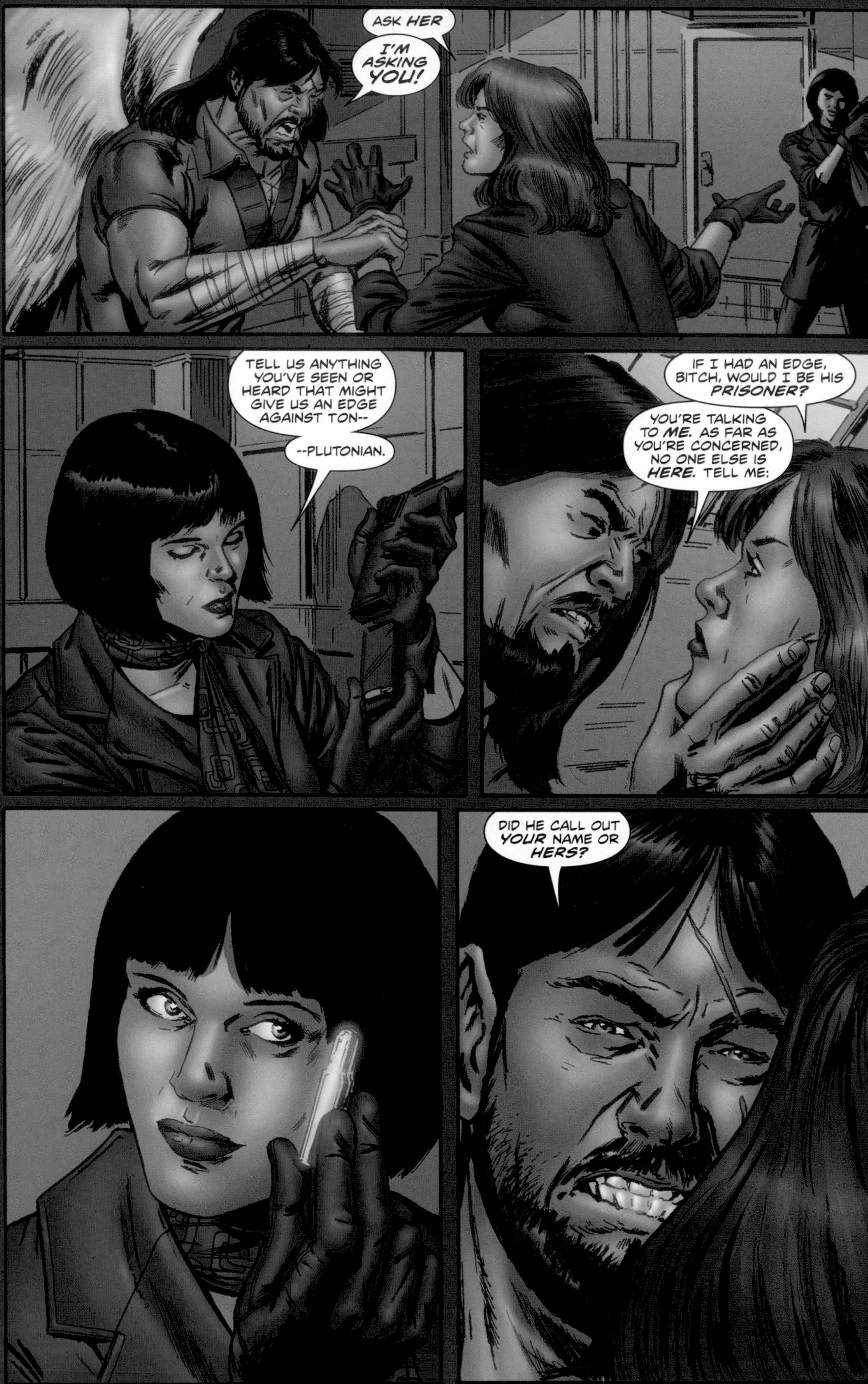
ASK HER
I'M ASKING YOU!
TELL US ANYTHING YOU'VE SEEN OR HEARD THAT MIGHT GIVE US AN EDGE AGAINST TON--
--PLUTONIAN.
IF I HAD AN EDGE, BITCH, WOULD I BE HIS PRISONER?
YOU'RE TALKING TO ME. AS FAR AS YOU'RE CONCERNED, NO ONE ELSE IS HERE. TELL ME:
DID HE CALL OUT YOUR NAME OR HERS?

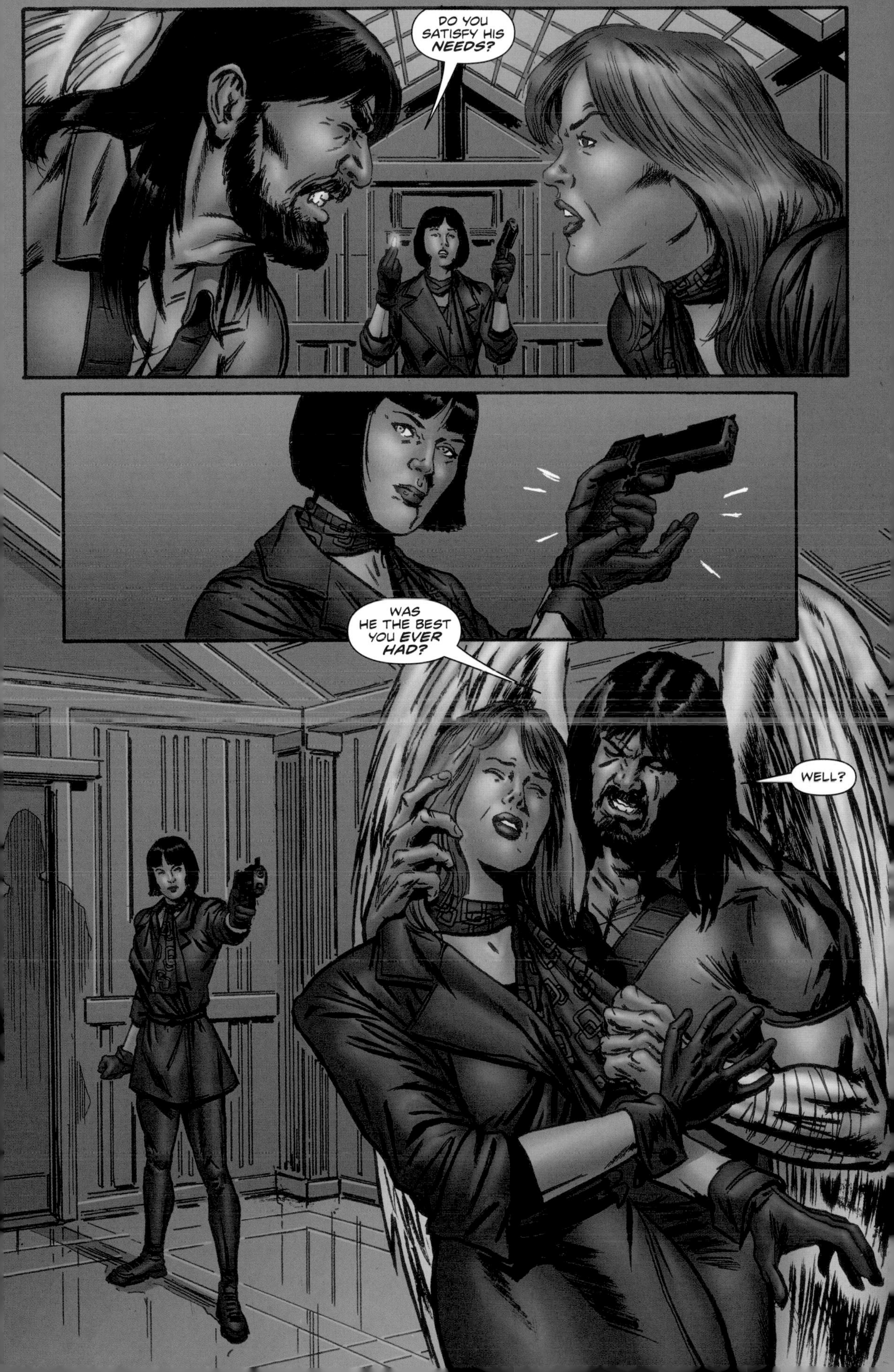
DO YOU SATISFY HIS NEEDS?
WAS HE THE BEST YOU EVER HAD?
WELL?

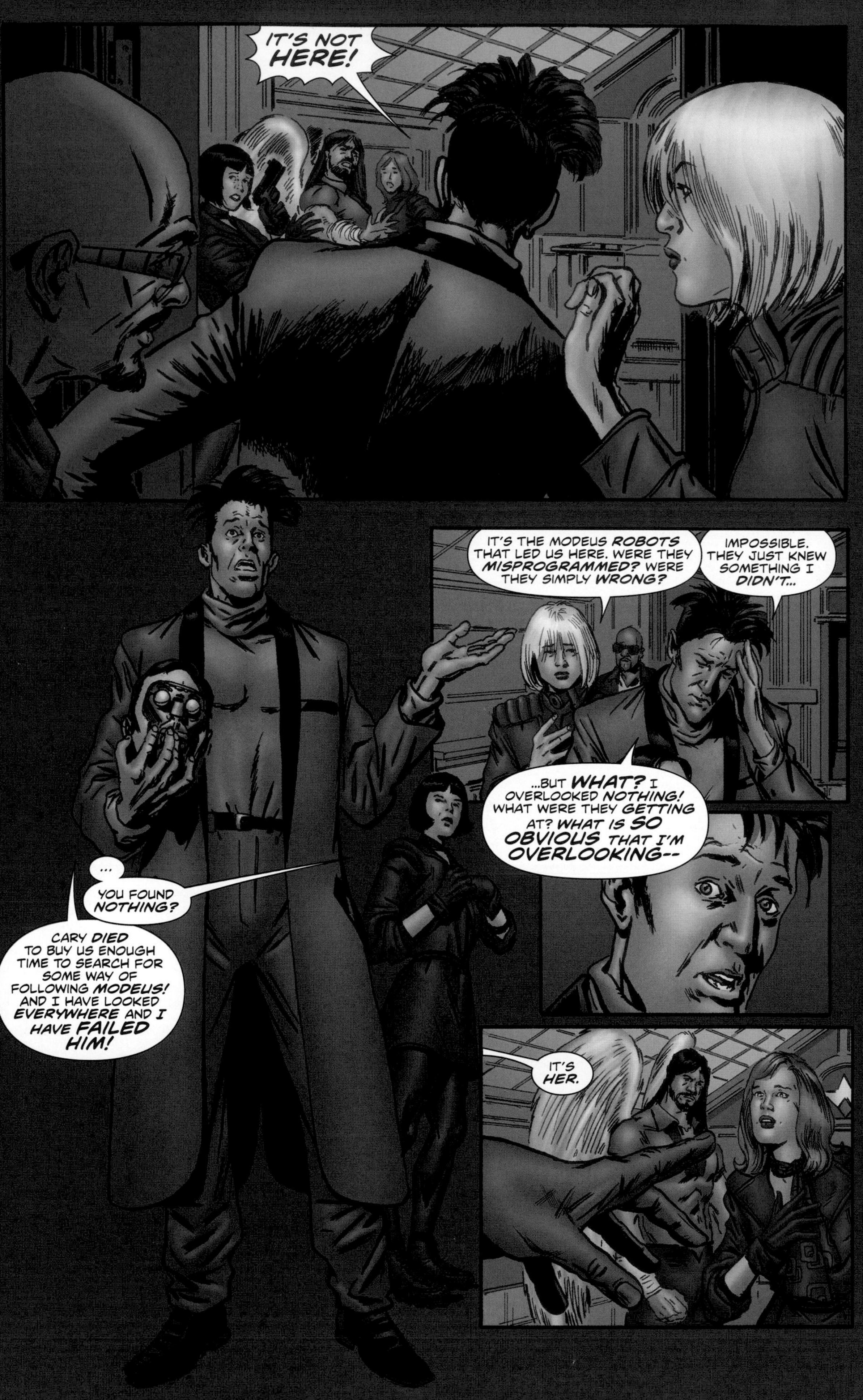
IT'S NOT HERE!
...
YOU FOUND NOTHING?
CARY DIED TO BUY US ENOUGH TIME TO SEARCH FOR SOME WAY OF FOLLOWING MODEUS! AND I HAVE LOOKED EVERYWHERE AND I HAVE FAILED HIM!
IT'S THE MODEUS ROBOTS THAT LED US HERE. WERE THEY MISPROGRAMMED? WERE THEY SIMPLY WRONG?
IMPOSSIBLE. THEY JUST KNEW SOMETHING I DIDN'T...
...BUT WHAT? I OVERLOOKED NOTHING! WHAT WERE THEY GETTING AT? WHAT IS SO OBVIOUS THAT I'M OVERLOOKING--
IT'S HER.

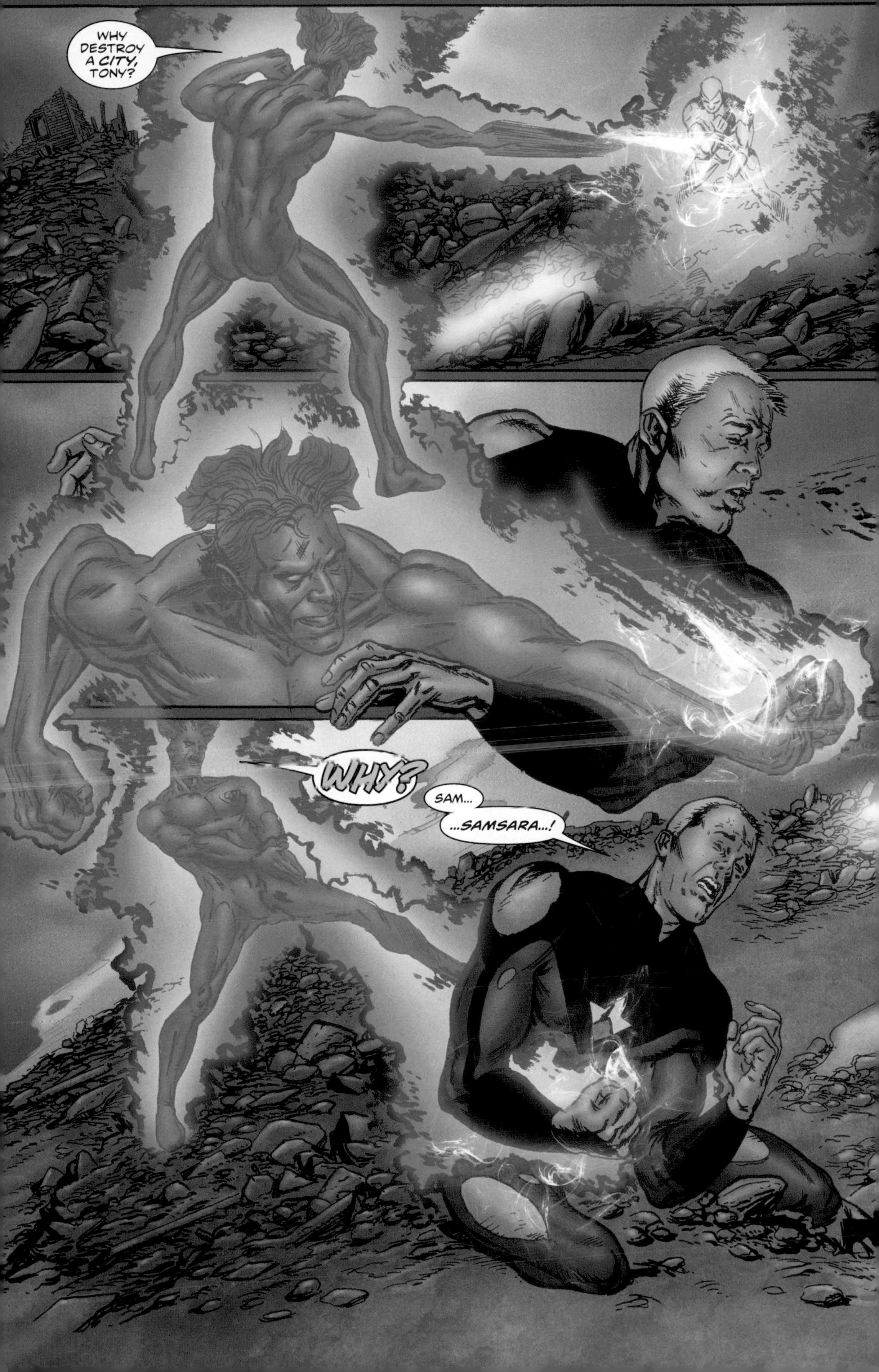
WHY DESTROY A CITY, TONY?
WHY?
SAM...
...SAMSARA...!

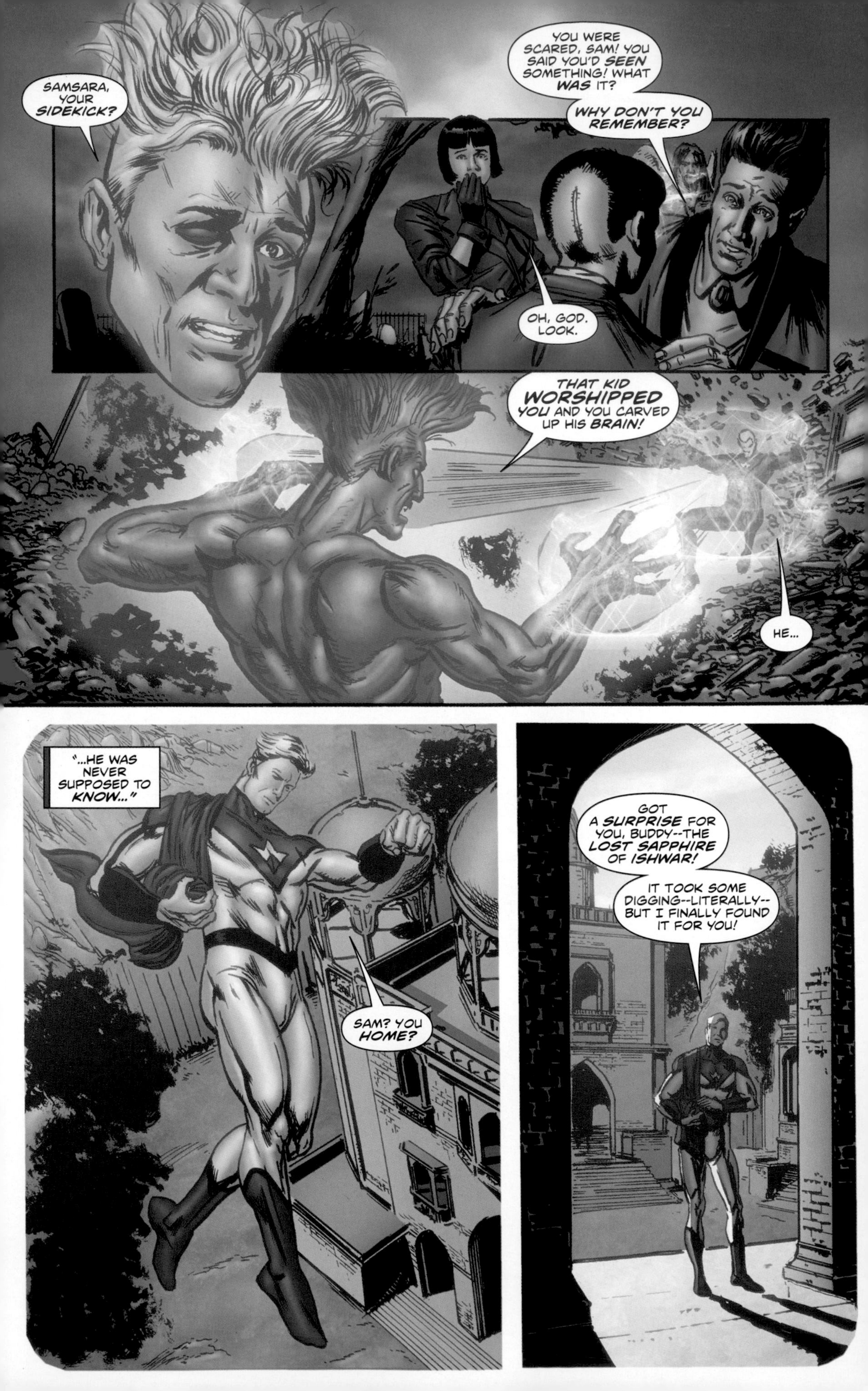

SAMSARA, YOUR SIDEKICK?
YOU WERE SCARED, SAM! YOU SAID YOU'D SEEN SOMETHING! WHAT WAS IT?
WHY DON'T YOU REMEMBER?
OH, GOD. LOOK.
THAT KID WORSHIPPED YOU AND YOU CARVED UP HIS BRAIN!
HE...
"...HE WAS NEVER SUPPOSED TO KNOW..."
SAM? YOU HOME?
GOT A SURPRISE FOR YOU, BUDDY--THE LOST SAPPHIRE OF ISHWAR!
IT TOOK SOME DIGGING--LITERALLY--BUT I FINALLY FOUND IT FOR YOU!

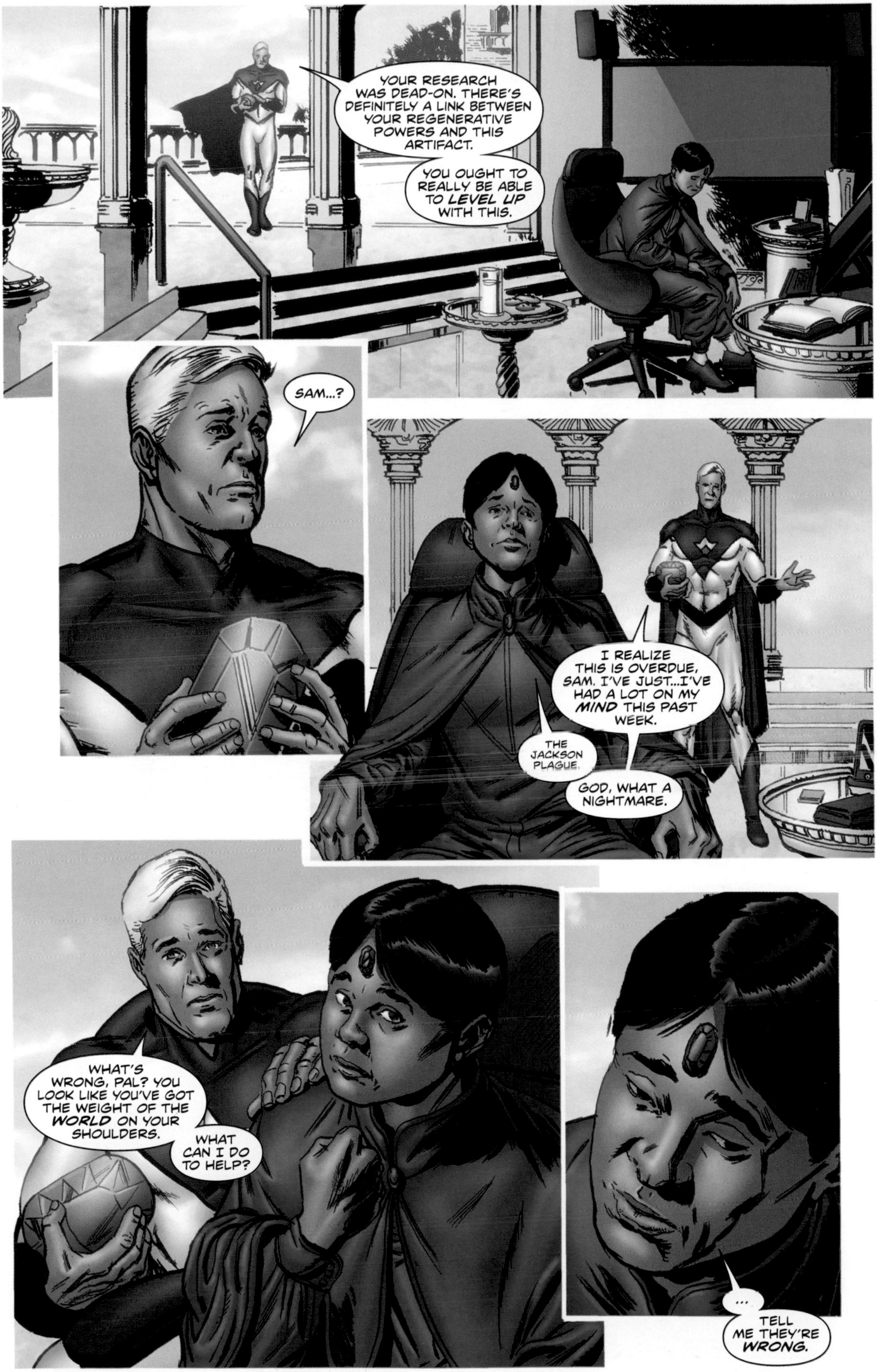
YOUR RESEARCH WAS DEAD-ON. THERE'S DEFINITELY A LINK BETWEEN YOUR REGENERATIVE POWERS AND THIS ARTIFACT.
YOU OUGHT TO REALLY BE ABLE TO *LEVEL UP* WITH THIS.
SAM...?
I REALIZE THIS IS OVERDUE, SAM. I'VE JUST...I'VE HAD A LOT ON MY *MIND* THIS PAST WEEK.
THE JACKSON PLAGUE.
GOD, WHAT A NIGHTMARE.
WHAT'S WRONG, PAL? YOU LOOK LIKE YOU'VE GOT THE WEIGHT OF THE *WORLD* ON YOUR SHOULDERS.
WHAT CAN I DO TO HELP?
...
TELL ME THEY'RE *WRONG.*

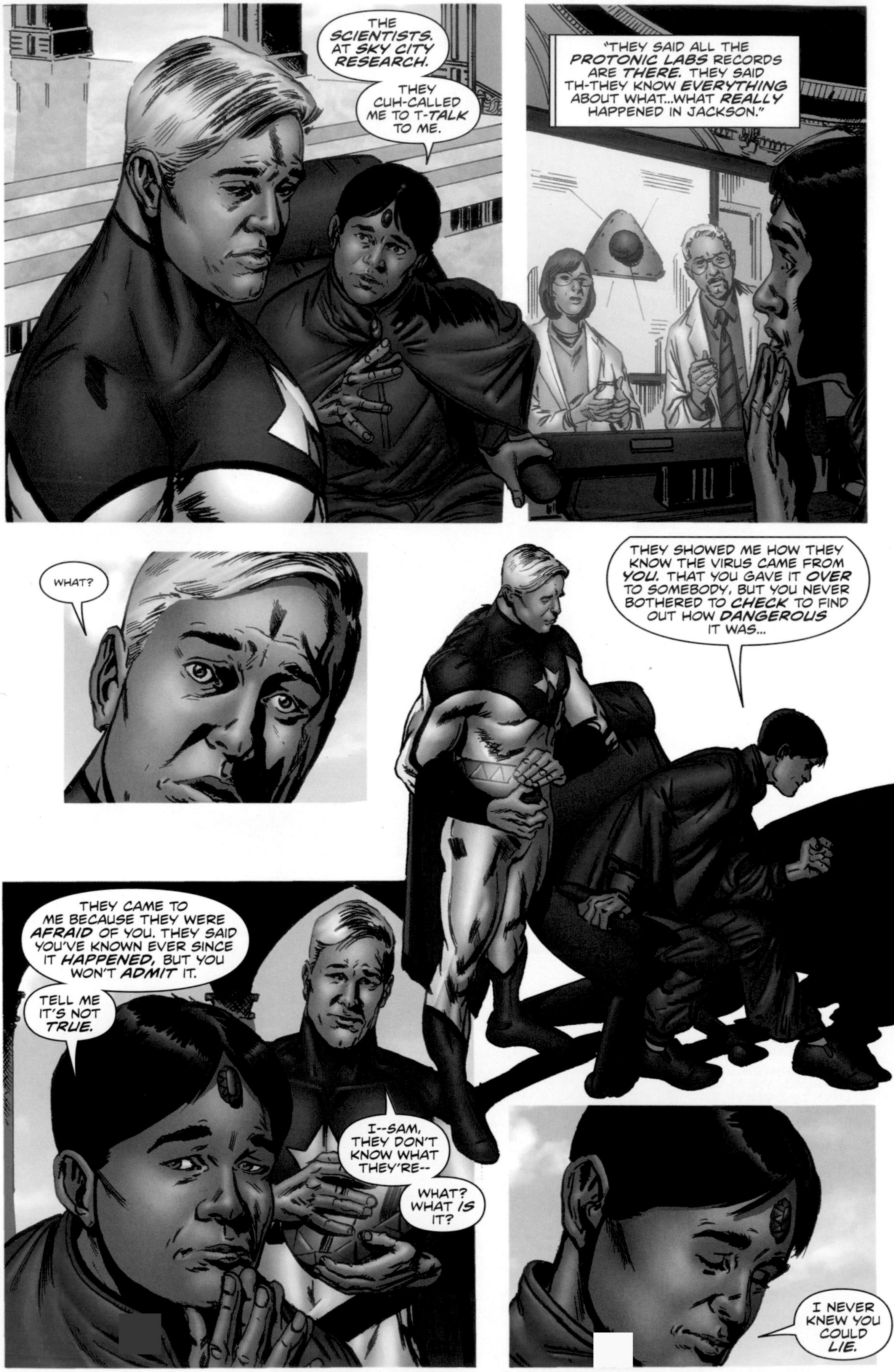

THE SCIENTISTS. AT SKY CITY RESEARCH.
THEY CUH-CALLED ME TO T-TALK TO ME.
"THEY SAID ALL THE PROTONIC LABS RECORDS ARE THERE. THEY SAID TH-THEY KNOW EVERYTHING ABOUT WHAT...WHAT REALLY HAPPENED IN JACKSON."
WHAT?
THEY SHOWED ME HOW THEY KNOW THE VIRUS CAME FROM YOU. THAT YOU GAVE IT OVER TO SOMEBODY, BUT YOU NEVER BOTHERED TO CHECK TO FIND OUT HOW DANGEROUS IT WAS...
THEY CAME TO ME BECAUSE THEY WERE AFRAID OF YOU. THEY SAID YOU'VE KNOWN EVER SINCE IT HAPPENED, BUT YOU WON'T ADMIT IT.
TELL ME IT'S NOT TRUE.
I--SAM, THEY DON'T KNOW WHAT THEY'RE--
WHAT? WHAT IS IT?
I NEVER KNEW YOU COULD LIE.

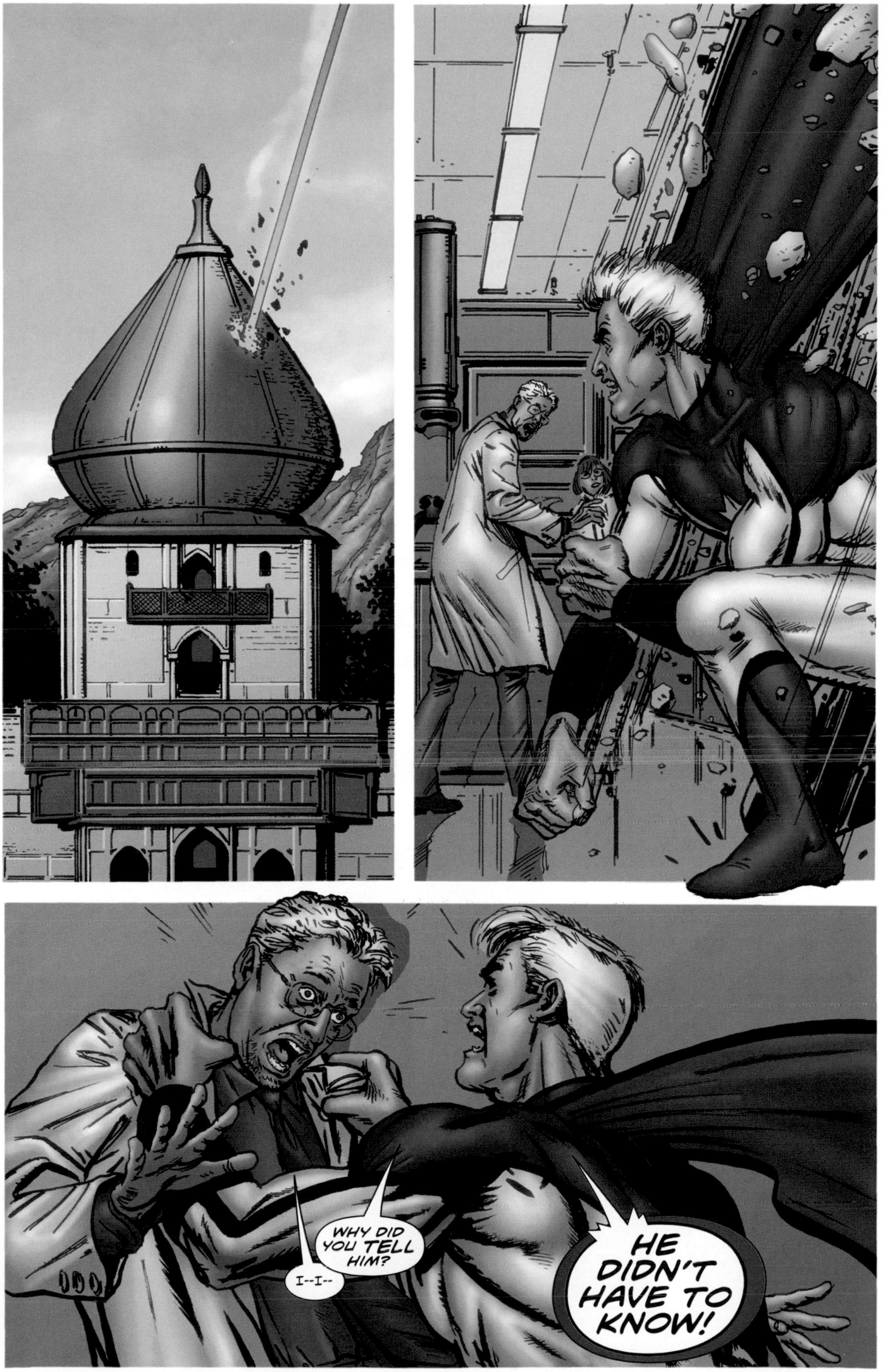
WHY DID YOU TELL HIM?
I--I--
HE DIDN'T HAVE TO KNOW!

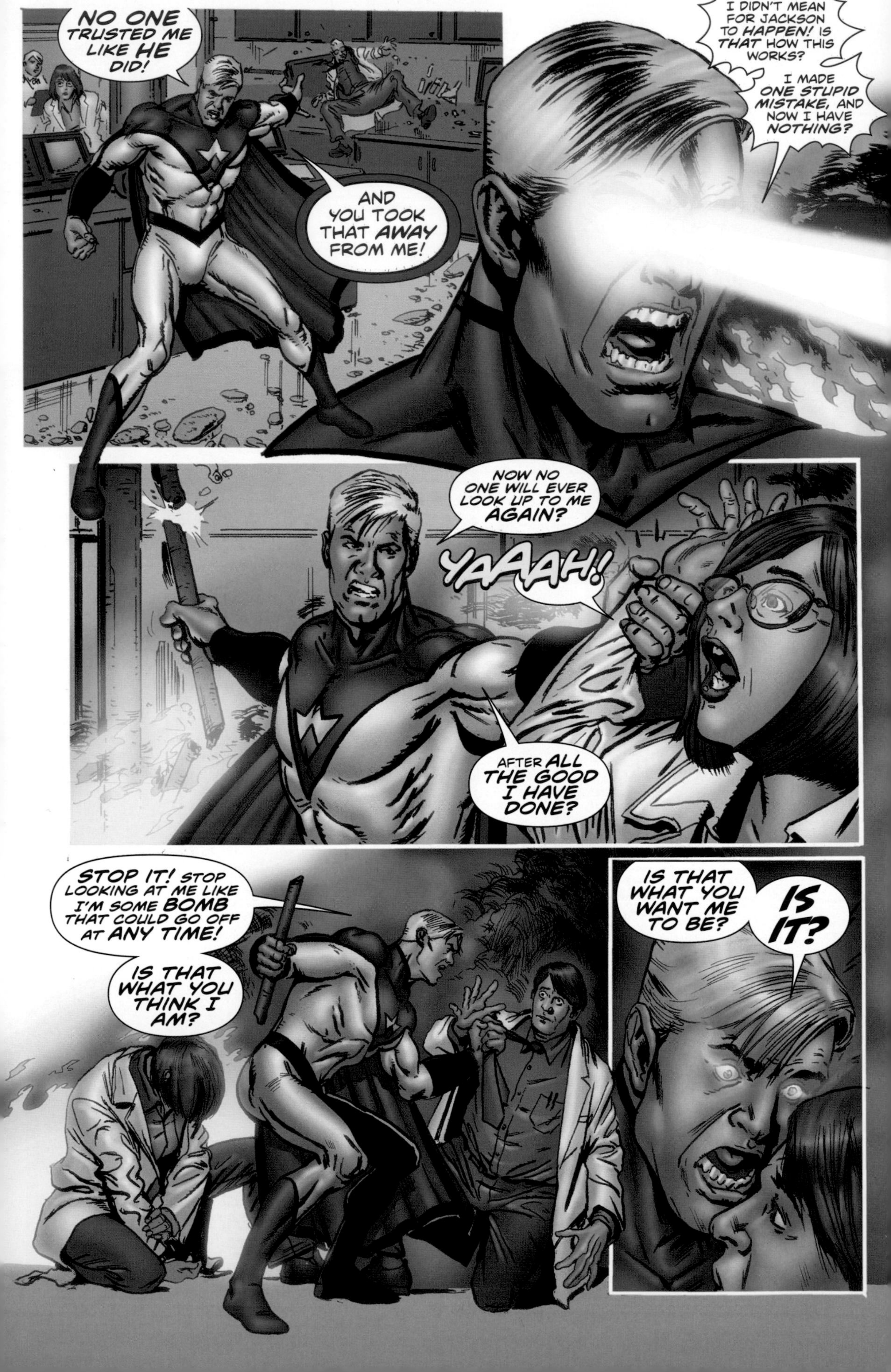
NO ONE TRUSTED ME LIKE HE DID!
AND YOU TOOK THAT AWAY FROM ME!
I DIDN'T MEAN FOR JACKSON TO HAPPEN! IS THAT HOW THIS WORKS?
I MADE ONE STUPID MISTAKE, AND NOW I HAVE NOTHING?
NOW NO ONE WILL EVER LOOK UP TO ME AGAIN?
YAAAH!
AFTER ALL THE GOOD I HAVE DONE?
STOP IT! STOP LOOKING AT ME LIKE I'M SOME BOMB THAT COULD GO OFF AT ANY TIME!
IS THAT WHAT YOU THINK I AM?
IS THAT WHAT YOU WANT ME TO BE?
IS IT?

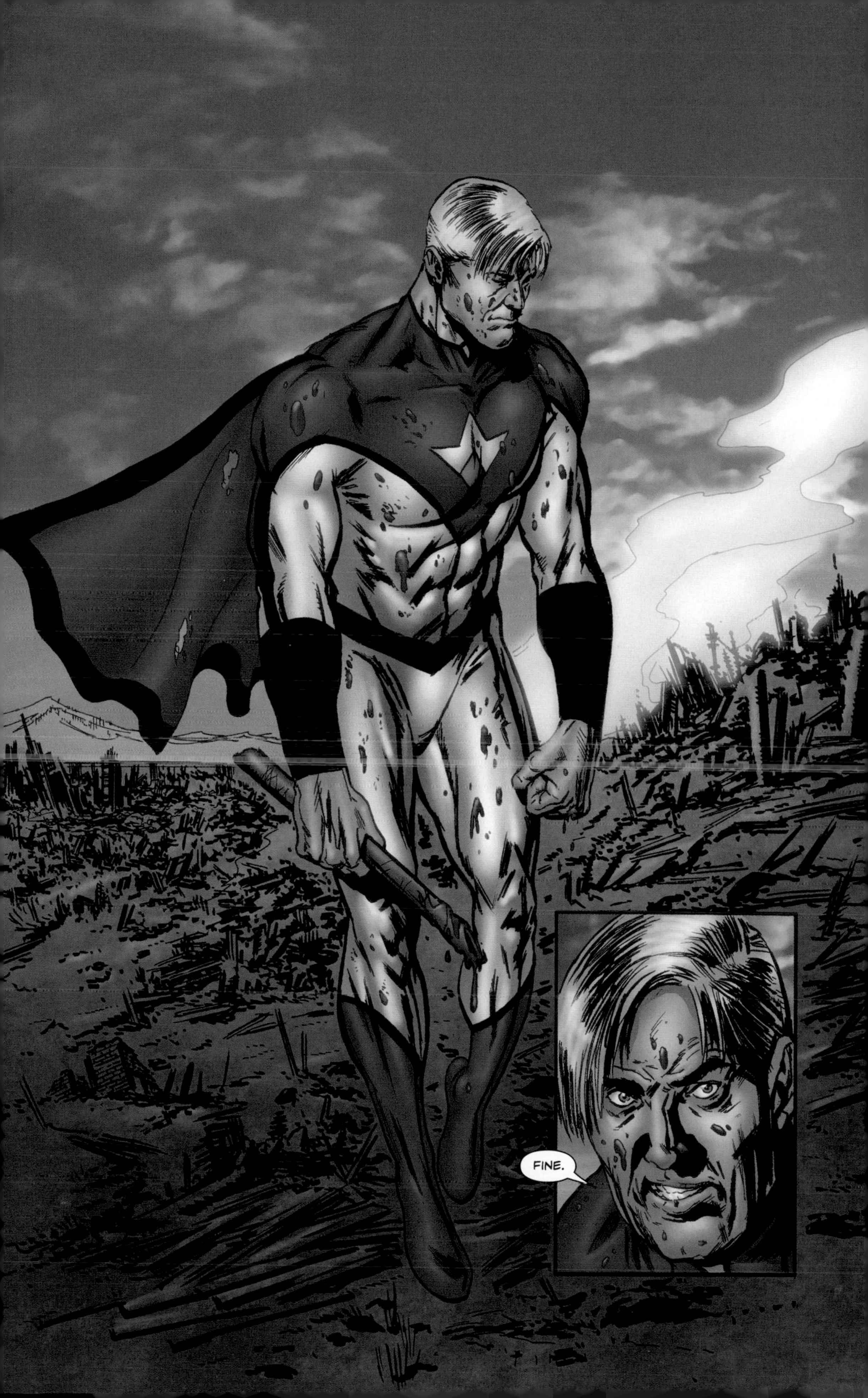
FINE.

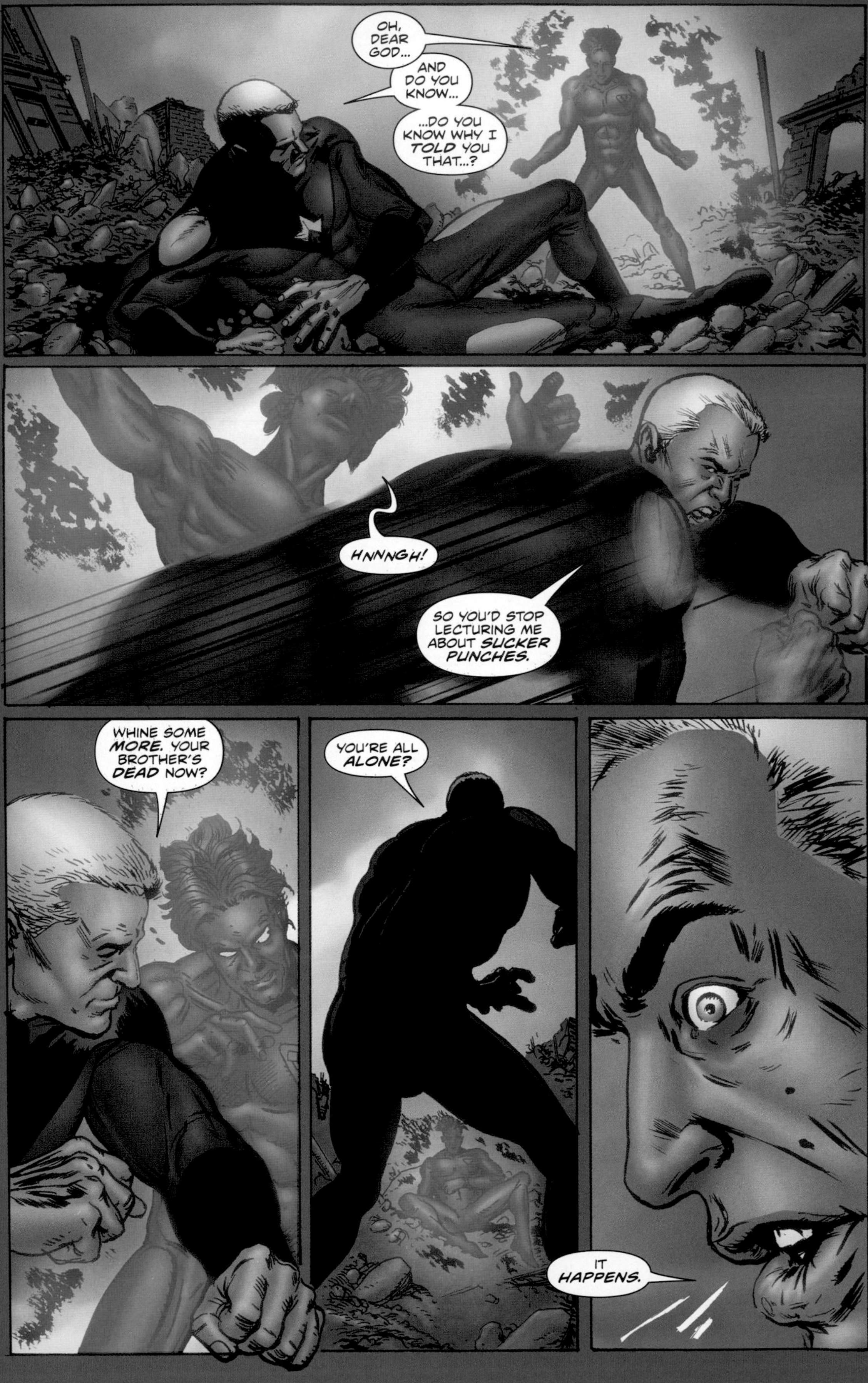
OH, DEAR GOD...
AND DO YOU KNOW...
...DO YOU KNOW WHY I TOLD YOU THAT...?
HNNNGH!
SO YOU'D STOP LECTURING ME ABOUT SUCKER PUNCHES.
WHINE SOME MORE. YOUR BROTHER'S DEAD NOW?
YOU'RE ALL ALONE?
IT HAPPENS.

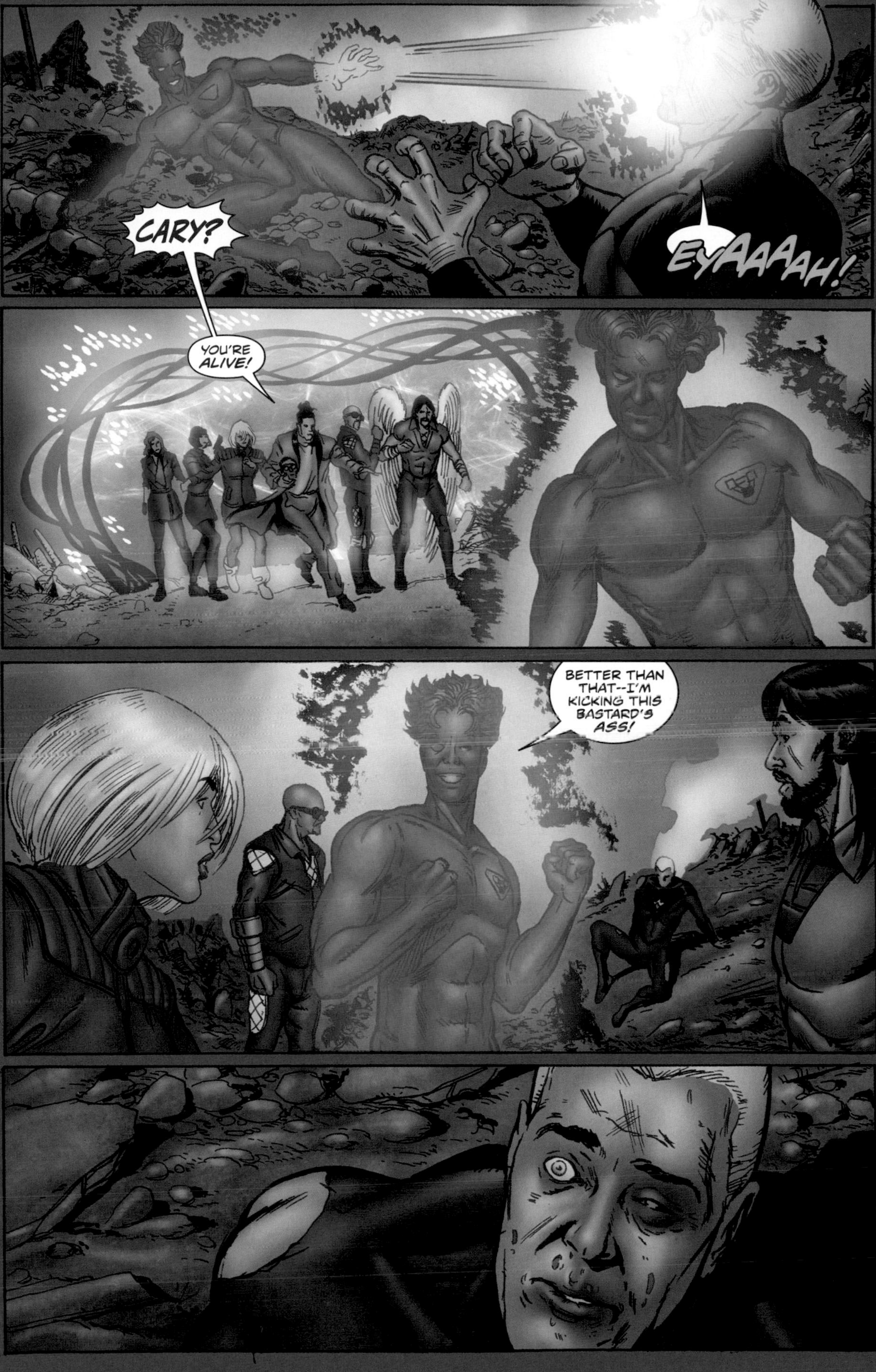
CARY?
EYAAAAH!
YOU'RE ALIVE!
BETTER THAN THAT--I'M KICKING THIS BASTARD'S ASS!

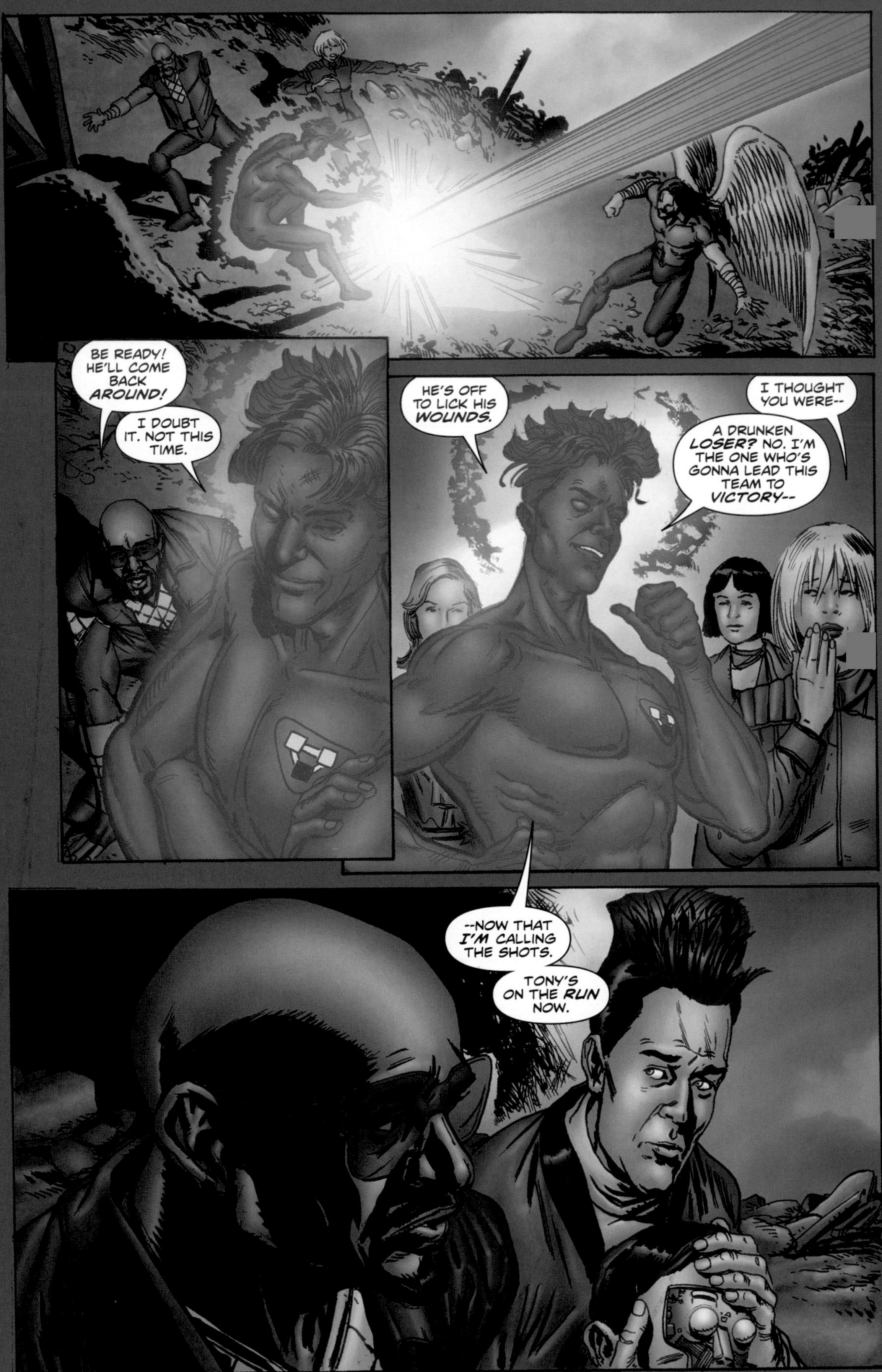
BE READY! HE'LL COME BACK AROUND!
I DOUBT IT. NOT THIS TIME.
HE'S OFF TO LICK HIS WOUNDS.
I THOUGHT YOU WERE--
A DRUNKEN LOSER? NO. I'M THE ONE WHO'S GONNA LEAD THIS TEAM TO VICTORY--
--NOW THAT I'M CALLING THE SHOTS.
TONY'S ON THE RUN NOW.

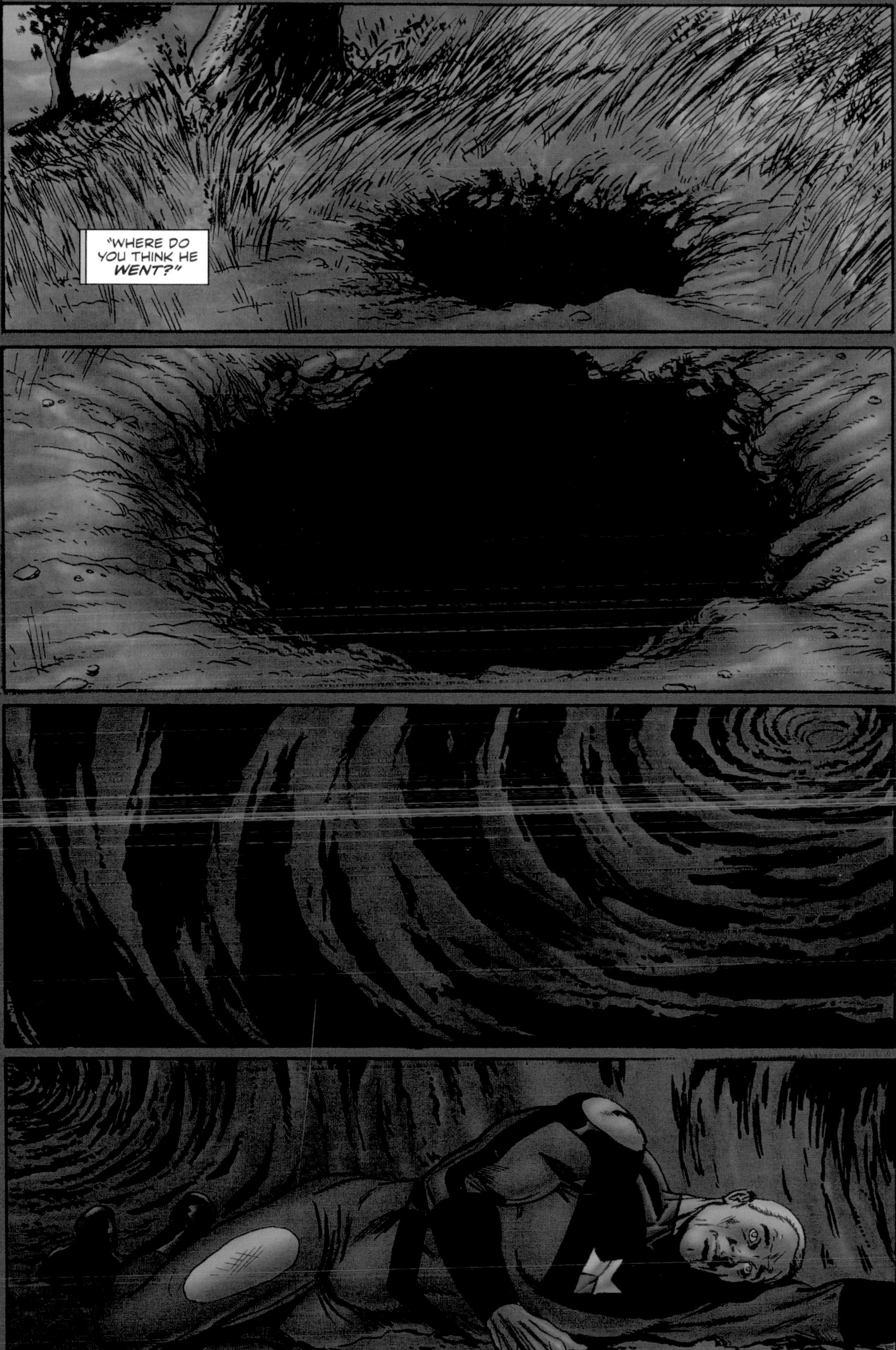
"WHERE DO YOU THINK HE WENT?"

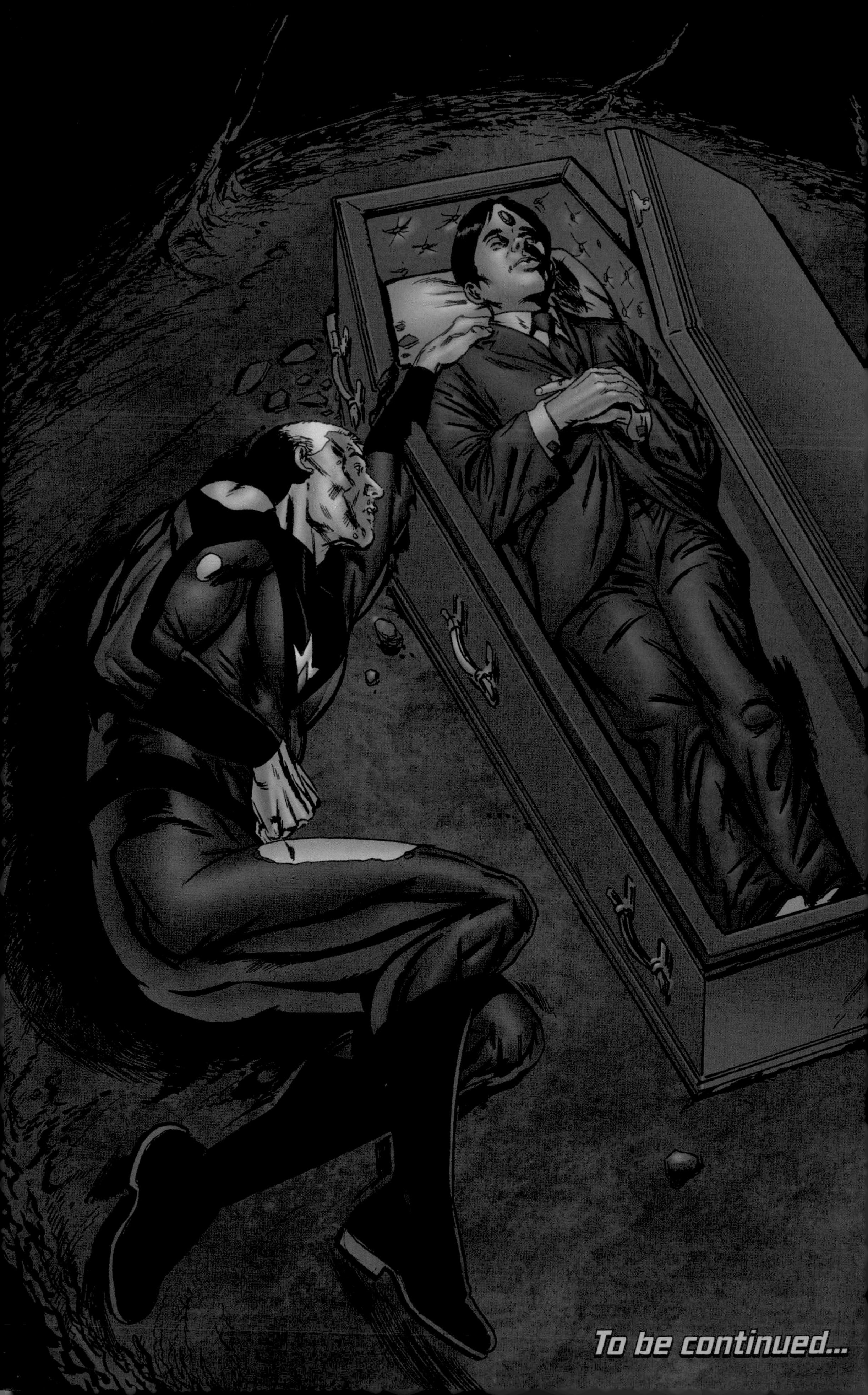
To be continued...

COVER
GALLERY

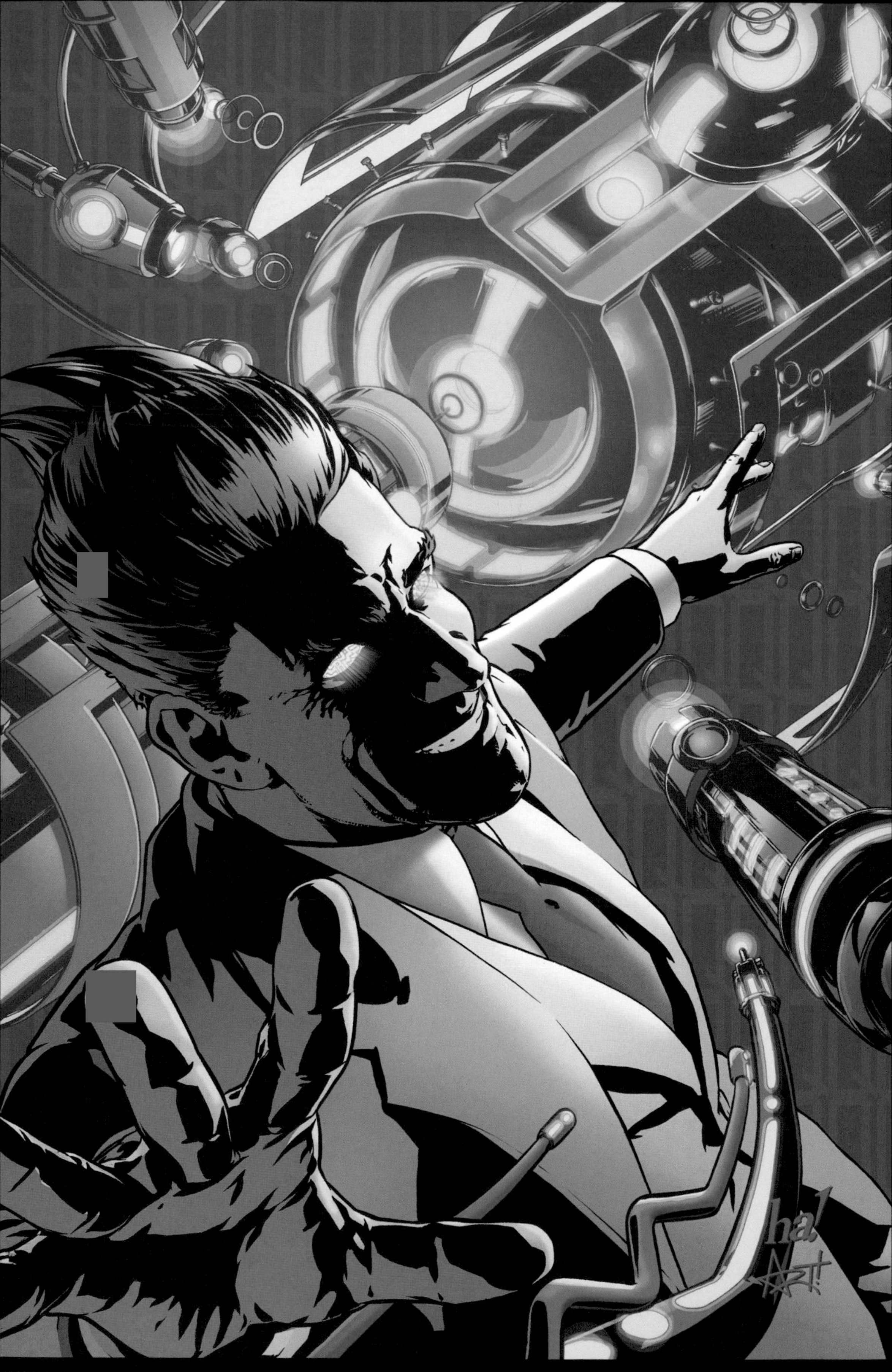
ha!
ART!

COVER 5A
GENE HA / COLORS BY ART LYON

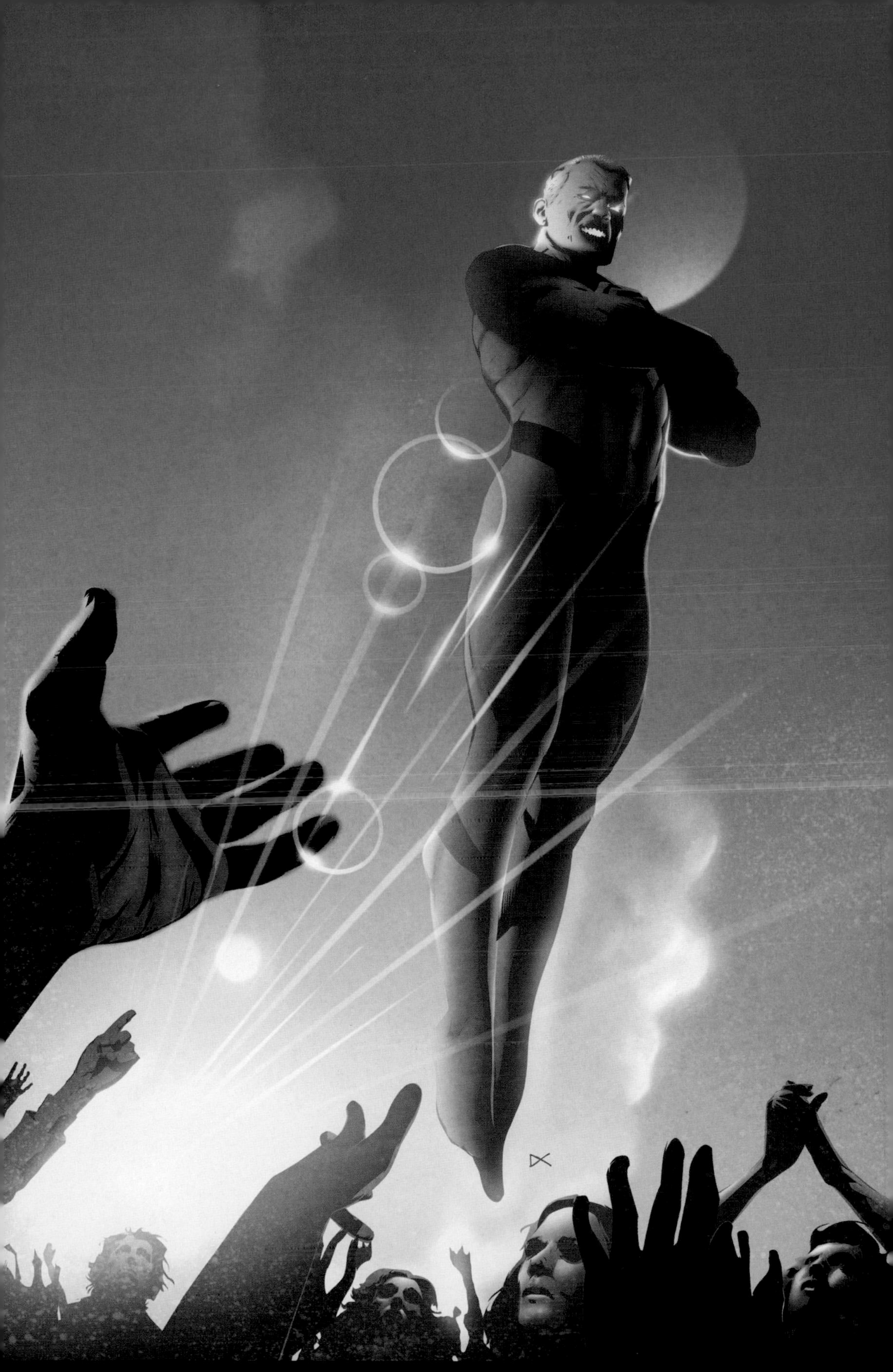

COVER 5B
DENNIS CALERO

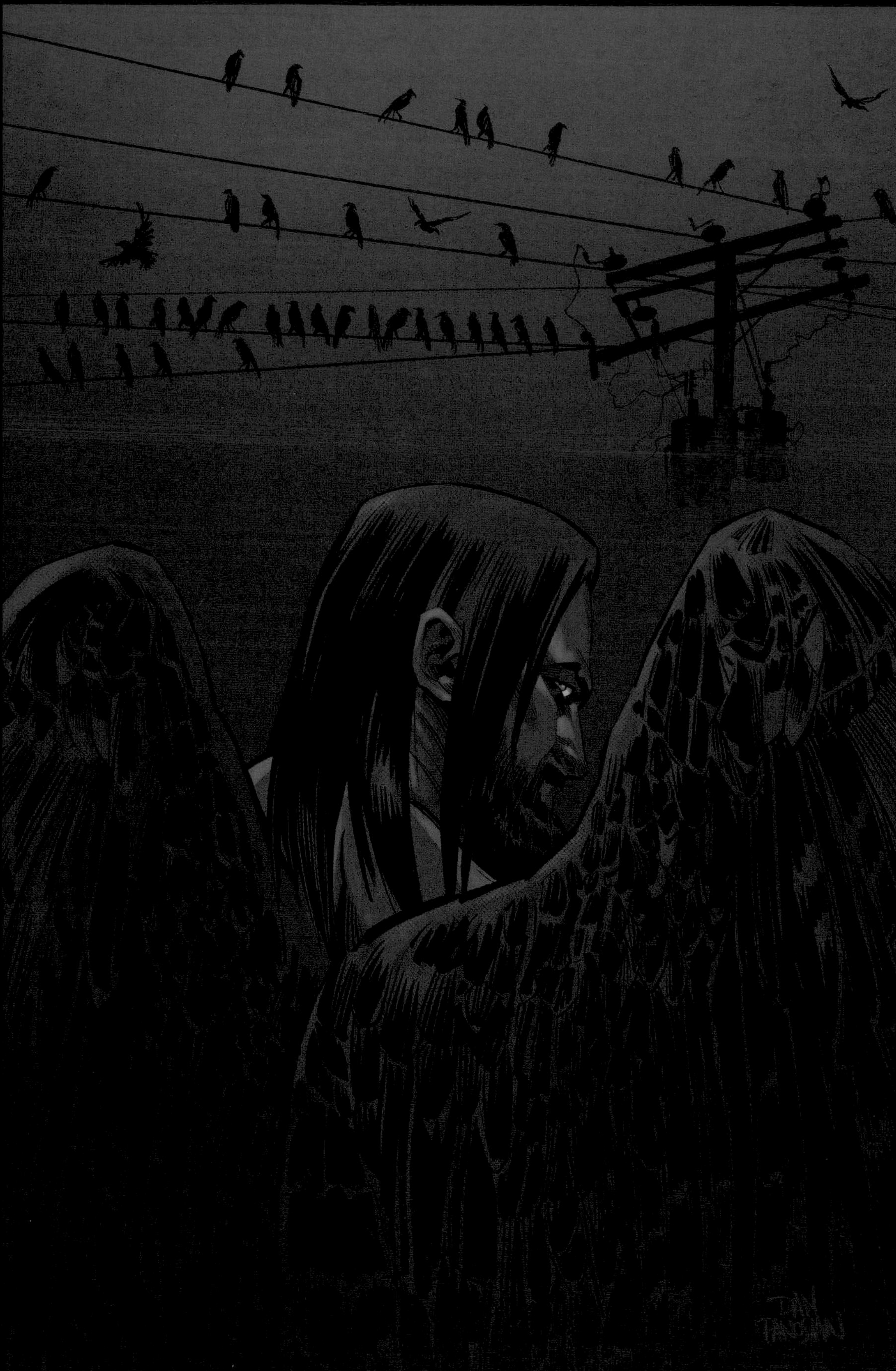

COVER 5C
DAN PANOSIAN

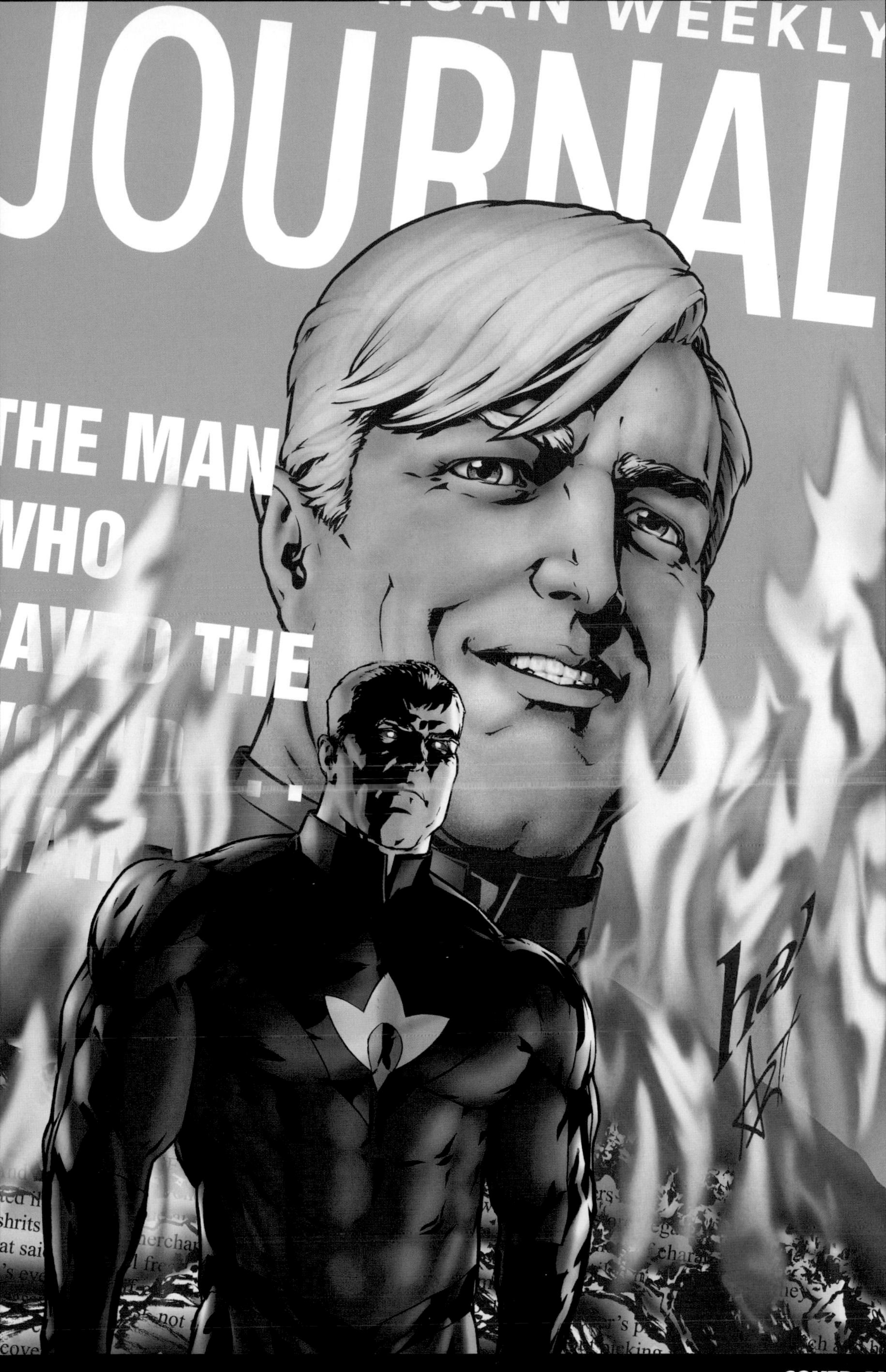

COVER 6A
GENE HA / COLORS BY ART LYON

BY JEFFREY SPOKES

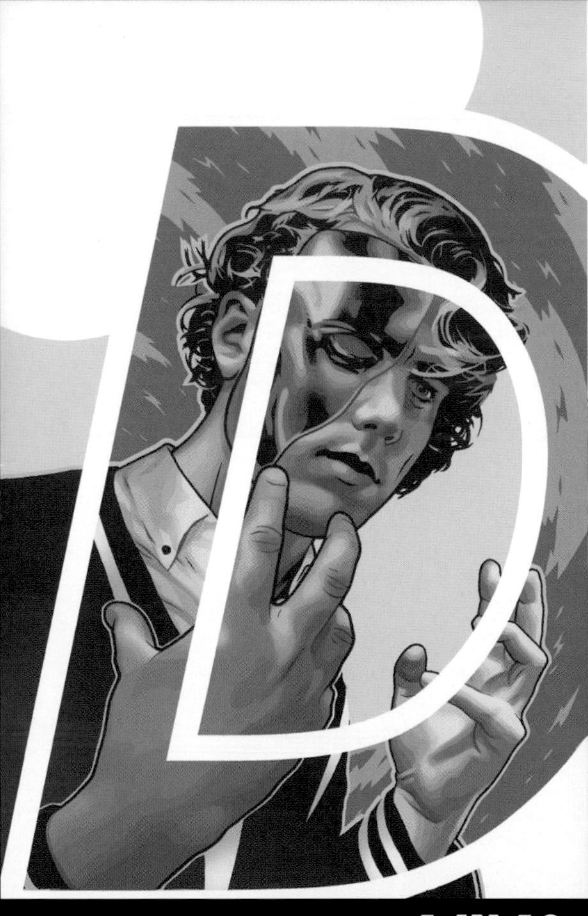

1 IN 10

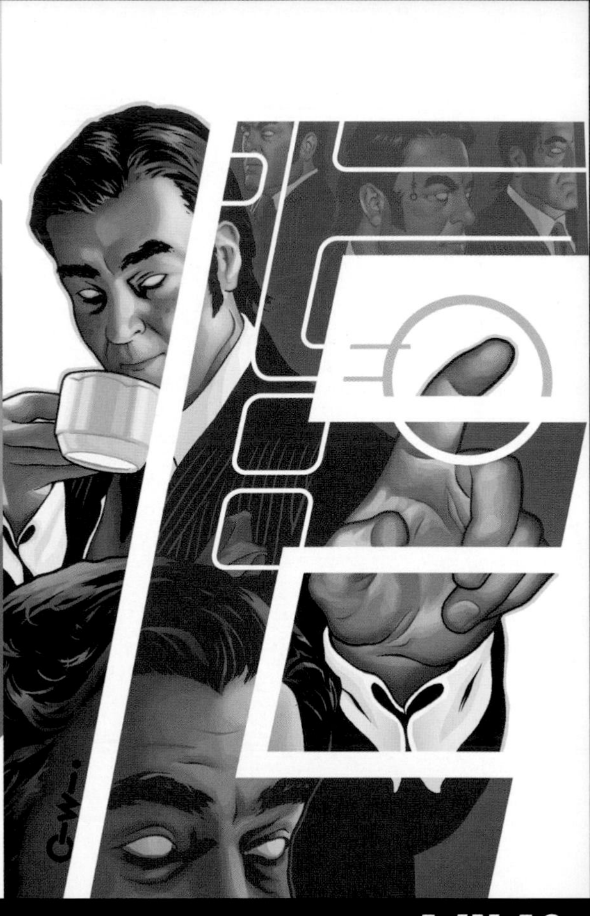

1 IN 10

COVERS 5-8

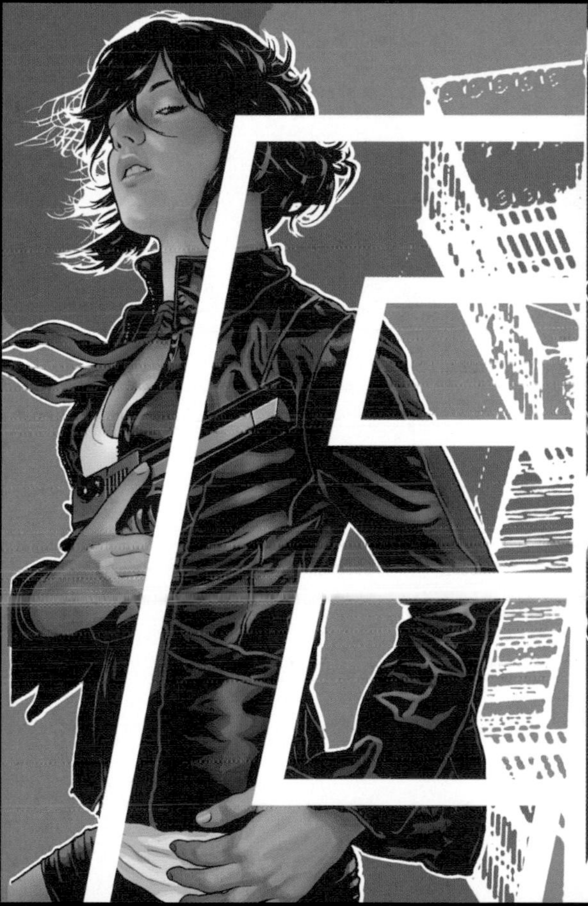

1 IN 10

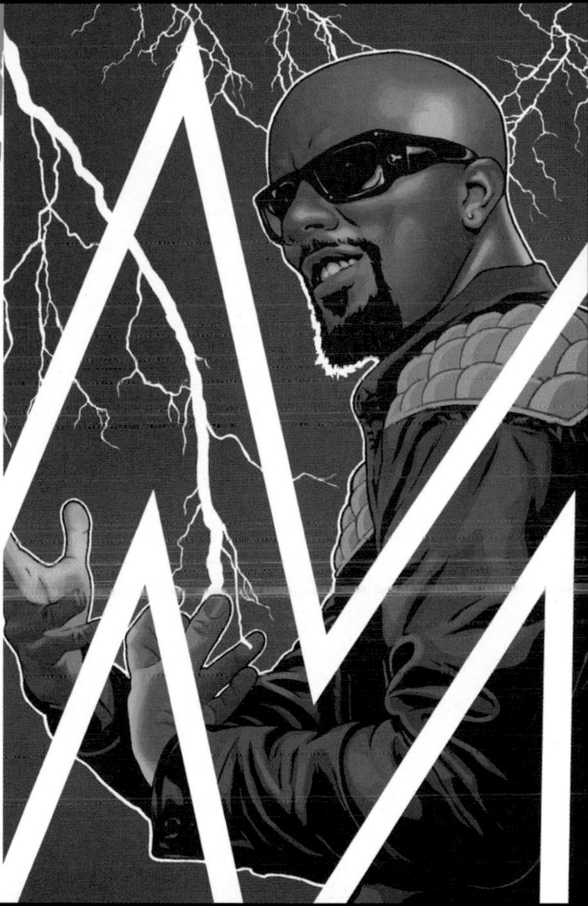

1 IN 10

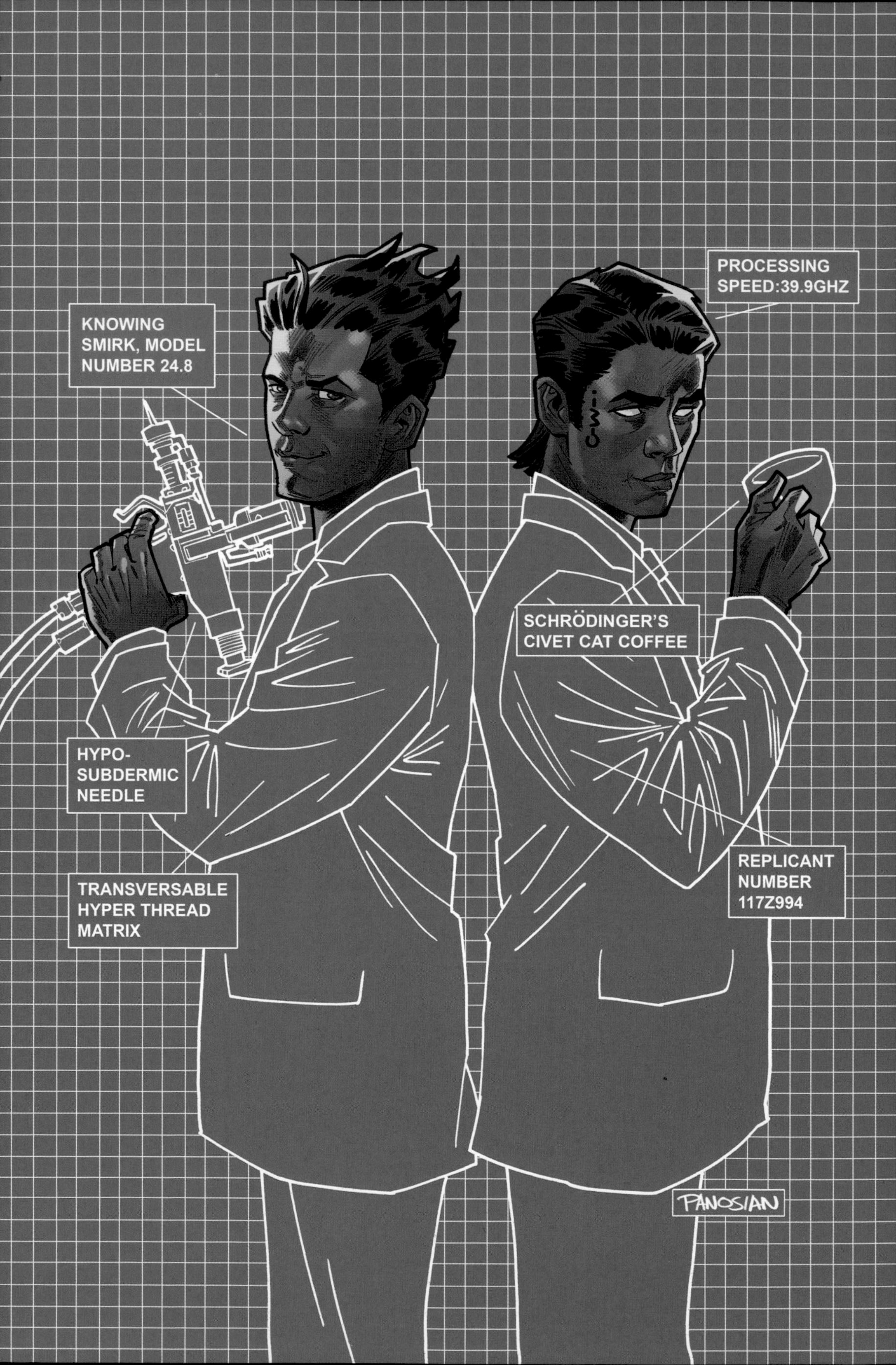
KNOWING SMIRK, MODEL NUMBER 24.8
PROCESSING SPEED:39.9GHZ
SCHRÖDINGER'S CIVET CAT COFFEE
HYPO-SUBDERMIC NEEDLE
REPLICANT NUMBER 117Z994
TRANSVERSABLE HYPER THREAD MATRIX
PANOSIAN

COVER 6B
DAN PANOSIAN

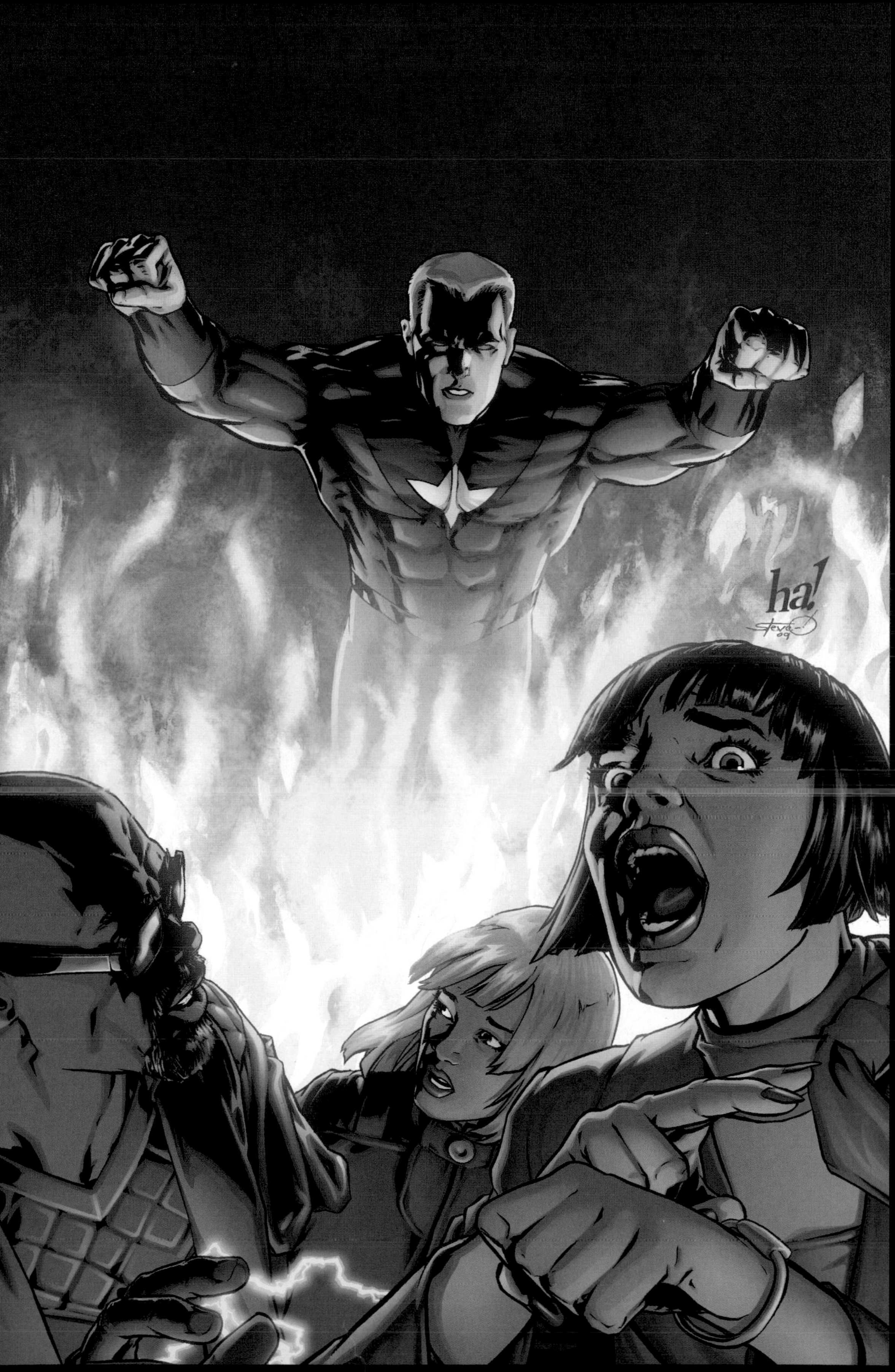
ha!

COVER 7A
GENE HA / COLORS BY STEPHEN DOWNER

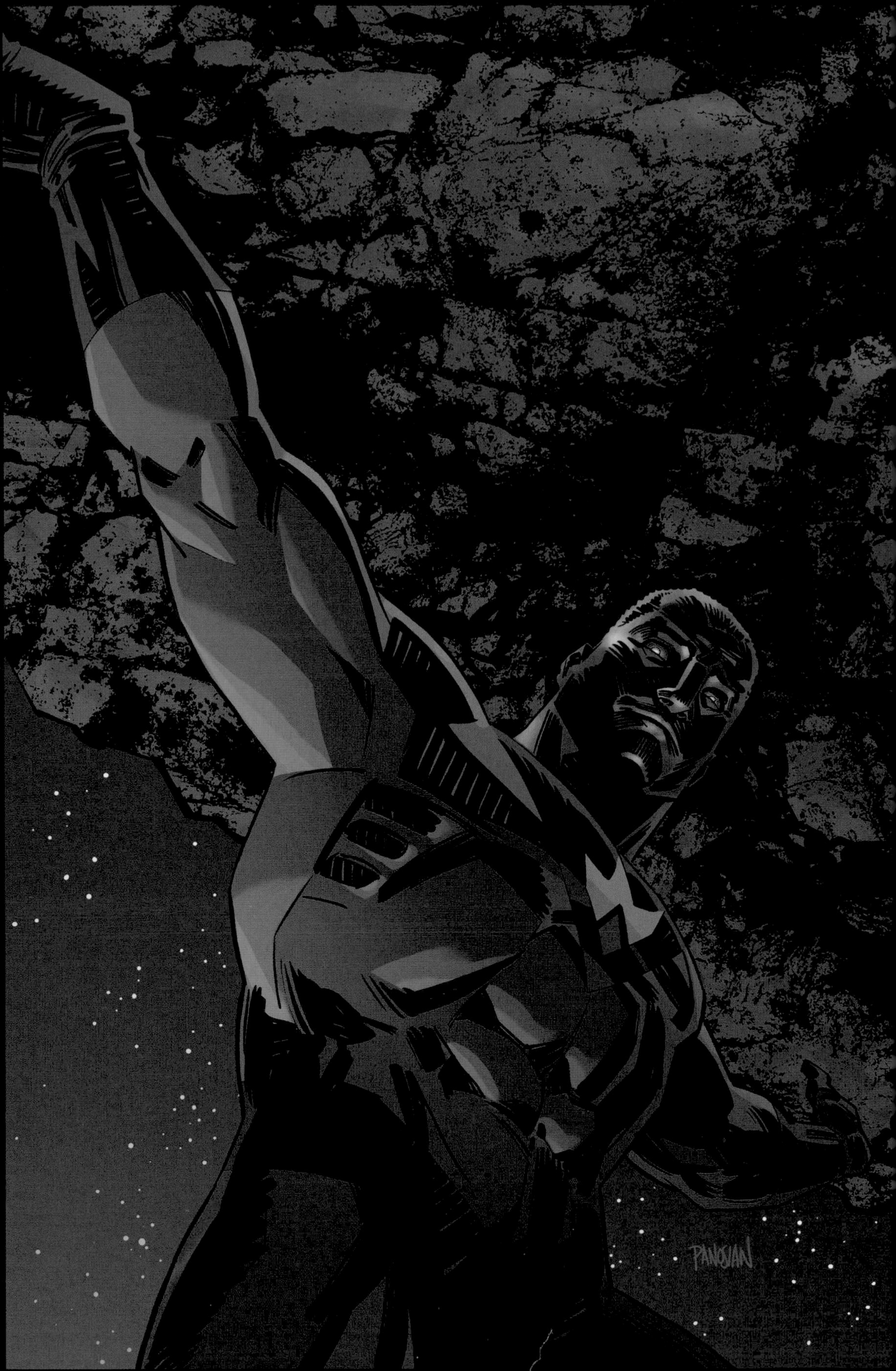
PANOSIAN

COVER 7B
DAN PANOSIAN

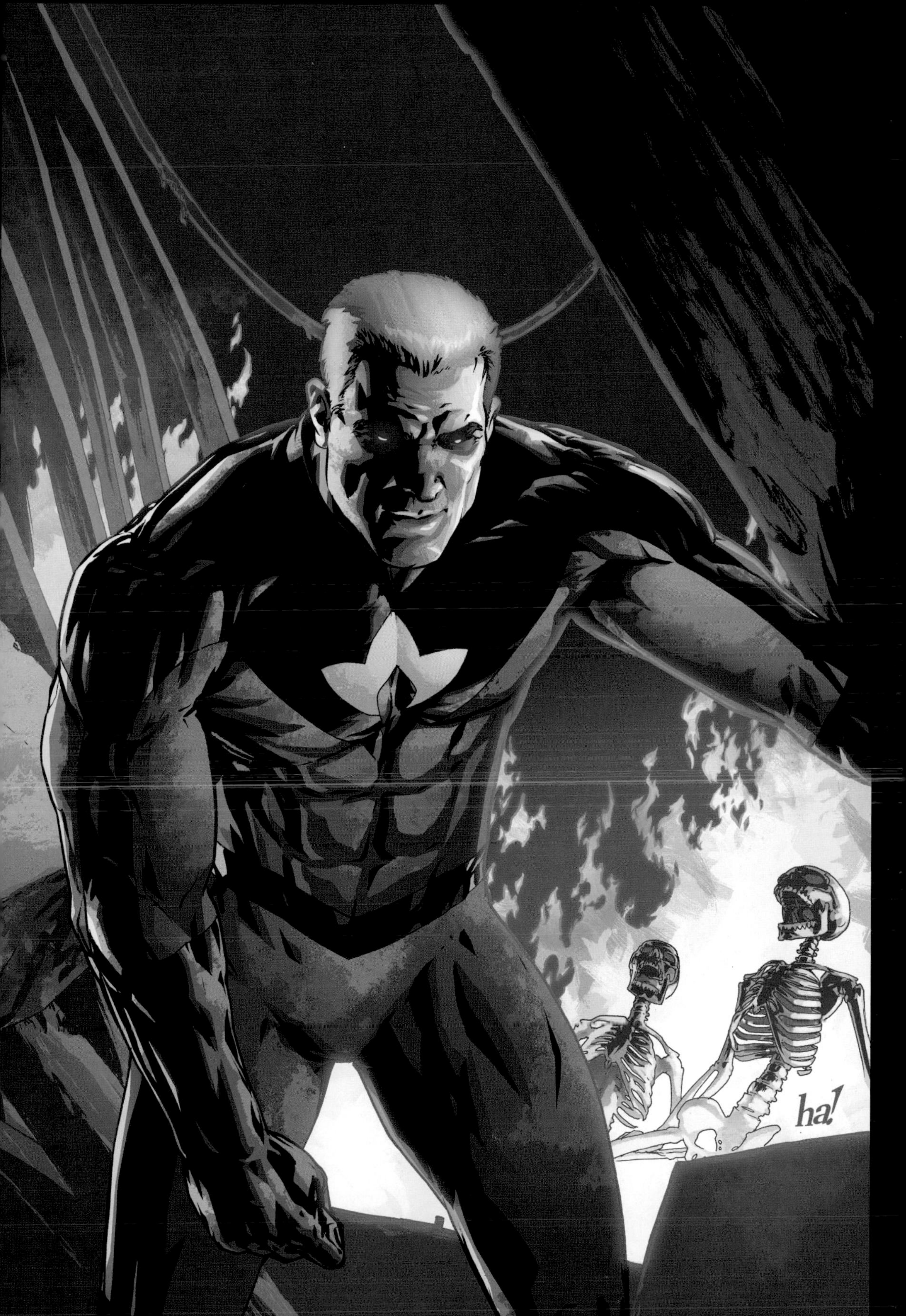
ha!

COVER 8A
GENE HA / COLORS BY MATTHEW WILSON

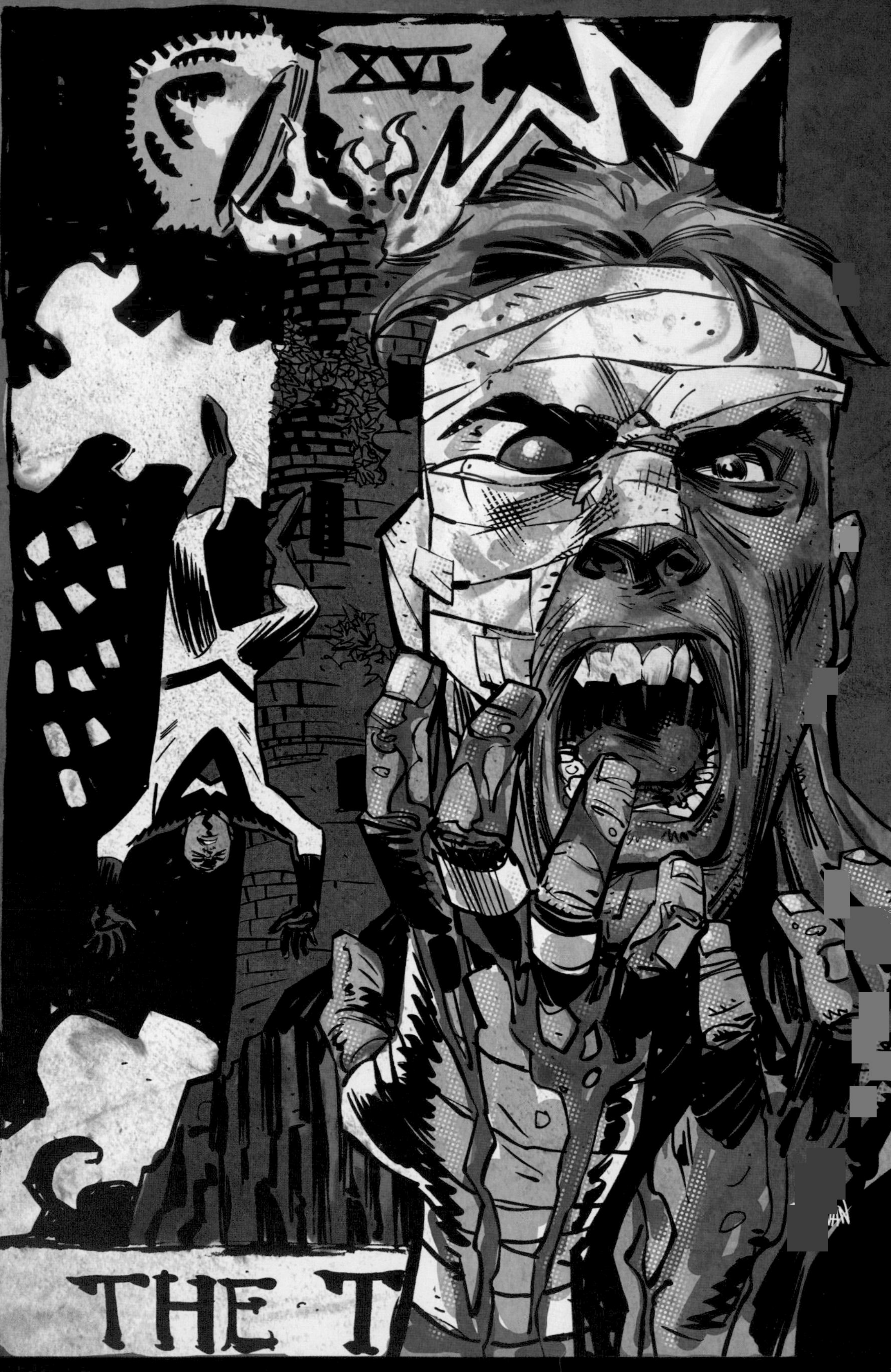
XVI
THE T

COVER 8B
DAN PANOSIAN

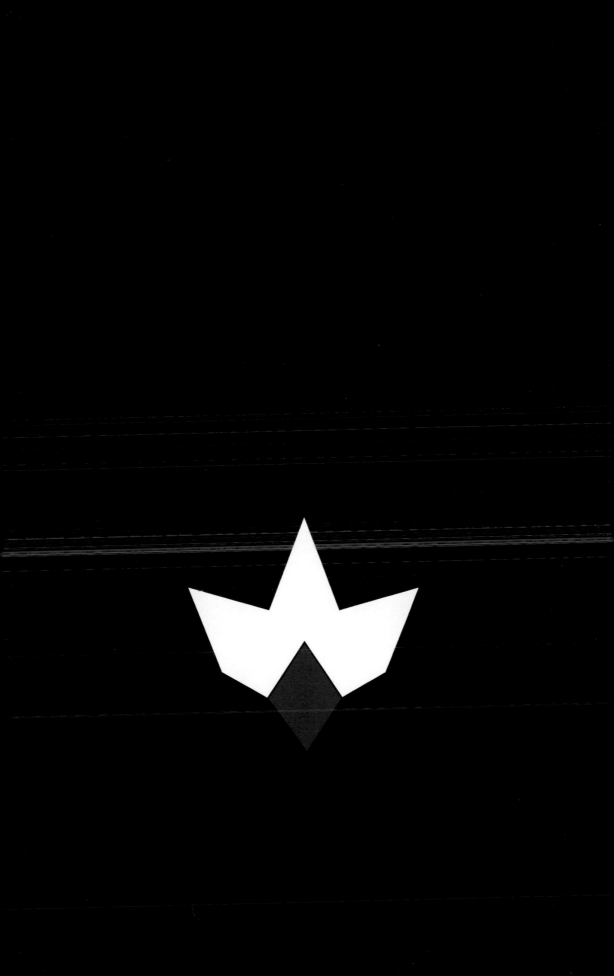

MARK WAID   PAUL AZACETA
POTTER'S FIELD

INTRODUCTION BY **GREG RUCKA**

FIRST TIME IN TRADE PAPERBACK!

A NEW VISION OF NOIR FROM LEGENDARY WRITER MARK WAID, AUTHOR OF THE MULTIPLE EISNER AWARD-WINNING KINGDOM COME, AND AMAZING SPIDER-MAN ARTIST PAUL AZACETA IN THEIR FIRST EVER COLLABORATION.

ISBN: 978-1-60886-052-4 / DIAMOND CODE: APR110885

14 PAGE POTTER'S FIELD PREVIEW!

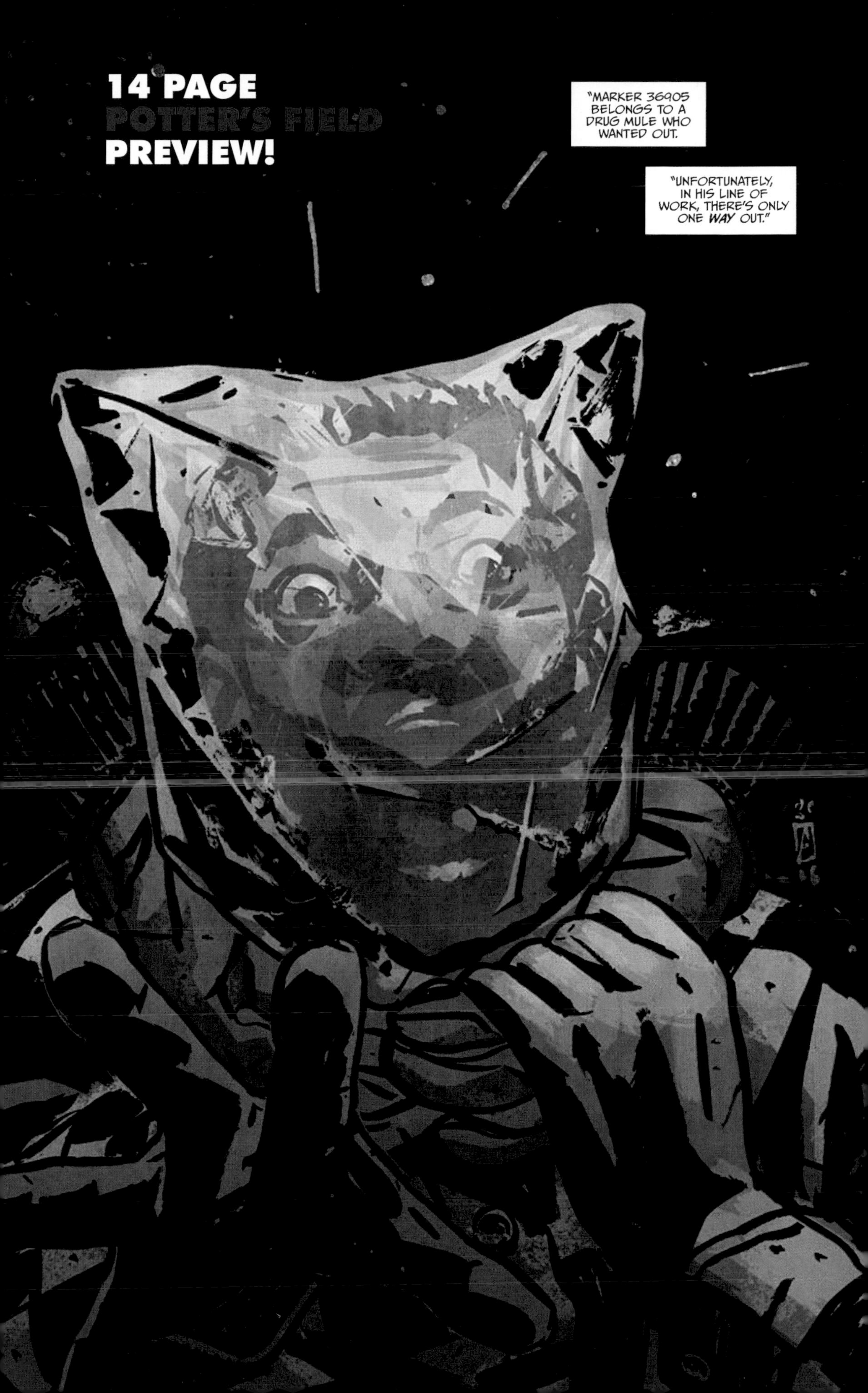
"MARKER 36905 BELONGS TO A DRUG MULE WHO WANTED OUT.
"UNFORTUNATELY, IN HIS LINE OF WORK, THERE'S ONLY ONE *WAY* OUT."

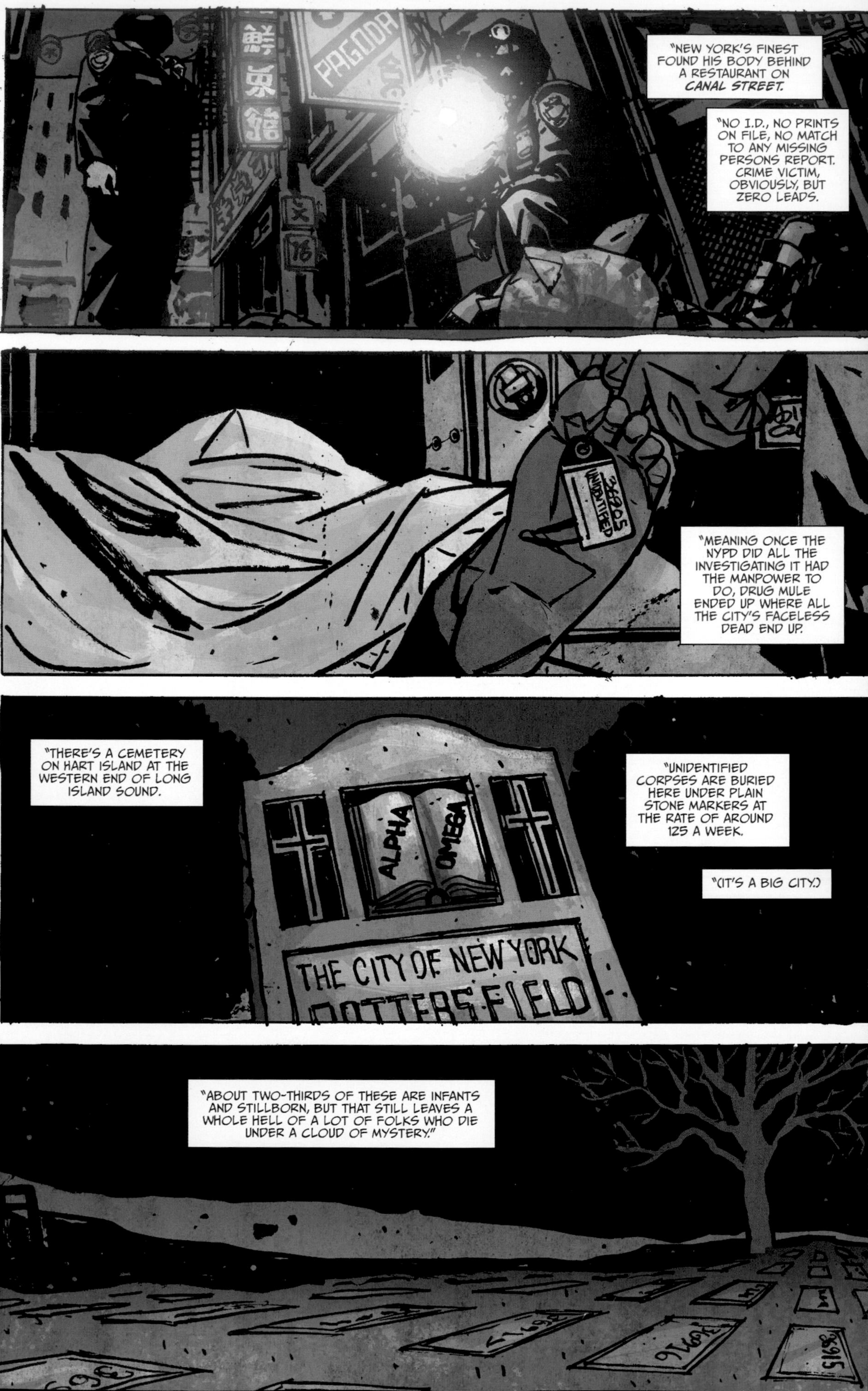
PAGODA
"NEW YORK'S FINEST FOUND HIS BODY BEHIND A RESTAURANT ON CANAL STREET.
"NO I.D., NO PRINTS ON FILE, NO MATCH TO ANY MISSING PERSONS REPORT. CRIME VICTIM, OBVIOUSLY, BUT ZERO LEADS.
36905 UNIDENTIFIED
"MEANING ONCE THE NYPD DID ALL THE INVESTIGATING IT HAD THE MANPOWER TO DO, DRUG MULE ENDED UP WHERE ALL THE CITY'S FACELESS DEAD END UP.
"THERE'S A CEMETERY ON HART ISLAND AT THE WESTERN END OF LONG ISLAND SOUND.
ALPHA OMEGA
THE CITY OF NEW YORK
POTTERS FIELD
"UNIDENTIFIED CORPSES ARE BURIED HERE UNDER PLAIN STONE MARKERS AT THE RATE OF AROUND 125 A WEEK.
"(IT'S A BIG CITY.)
"ABOUT TWO-THIRDS OF THESE ARE INFANTS AND STILLBORN, BUT THAT STILL LEAVES A WHOLE HELL OF A LOT OF FOLKS WHO DIE UNDER A CLOUD OF MYSTERY."

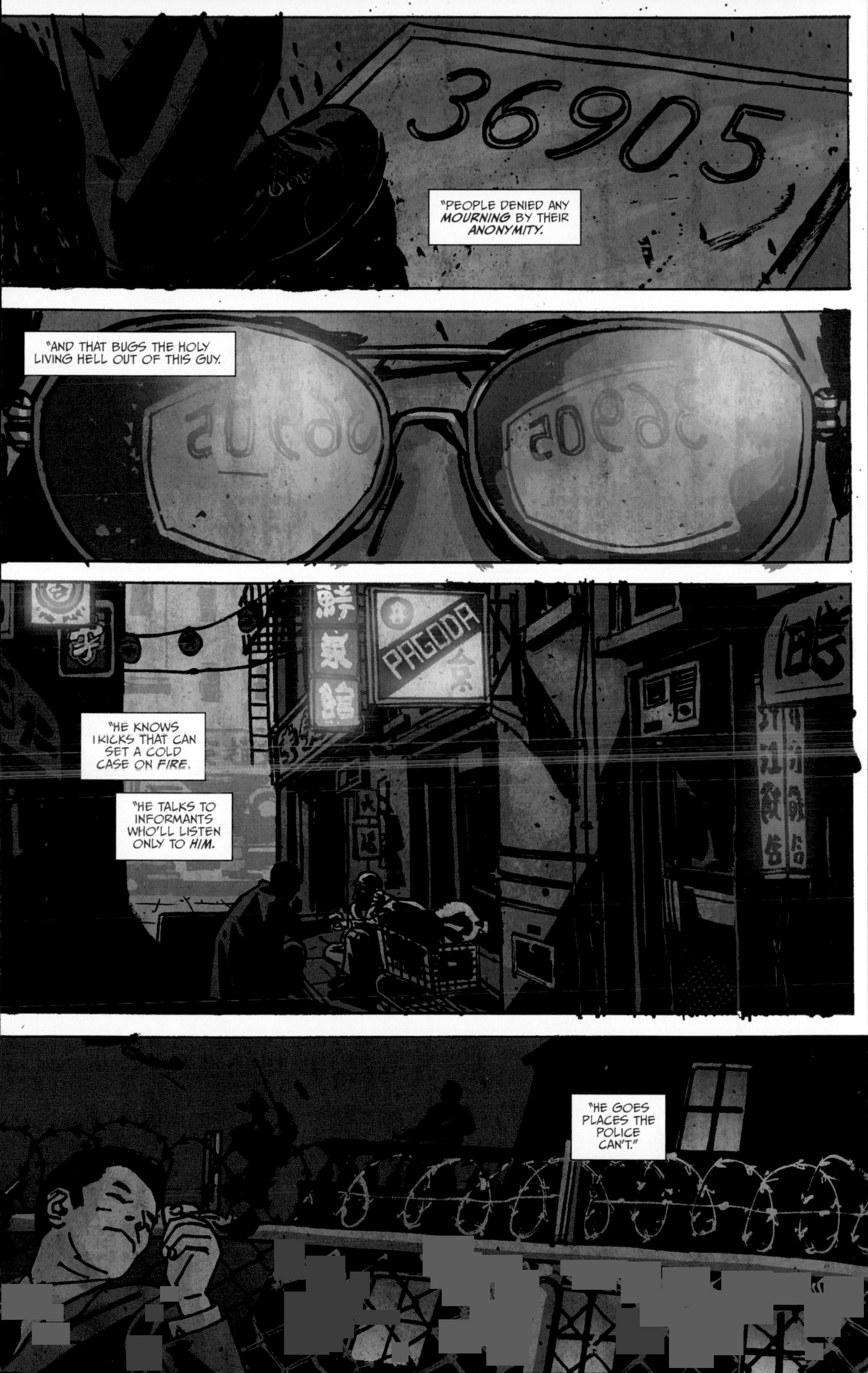

36905
"PEOPLE DENIED ANY MOURNING BY THEIR ANONYMITY.
"AND THAT BUGS THE HOLY LIVING HELL OUT OF THIS GUY.
PAGODA
"HE KNOWS KICKS THAT CAN SET A COLD CASE ON FIRE.
"HE TALKS TO INFORMANTS WHO'LL LISTEN ONLY TO HIM.
"HE GOES PLACES THE POLICE CAN'T."

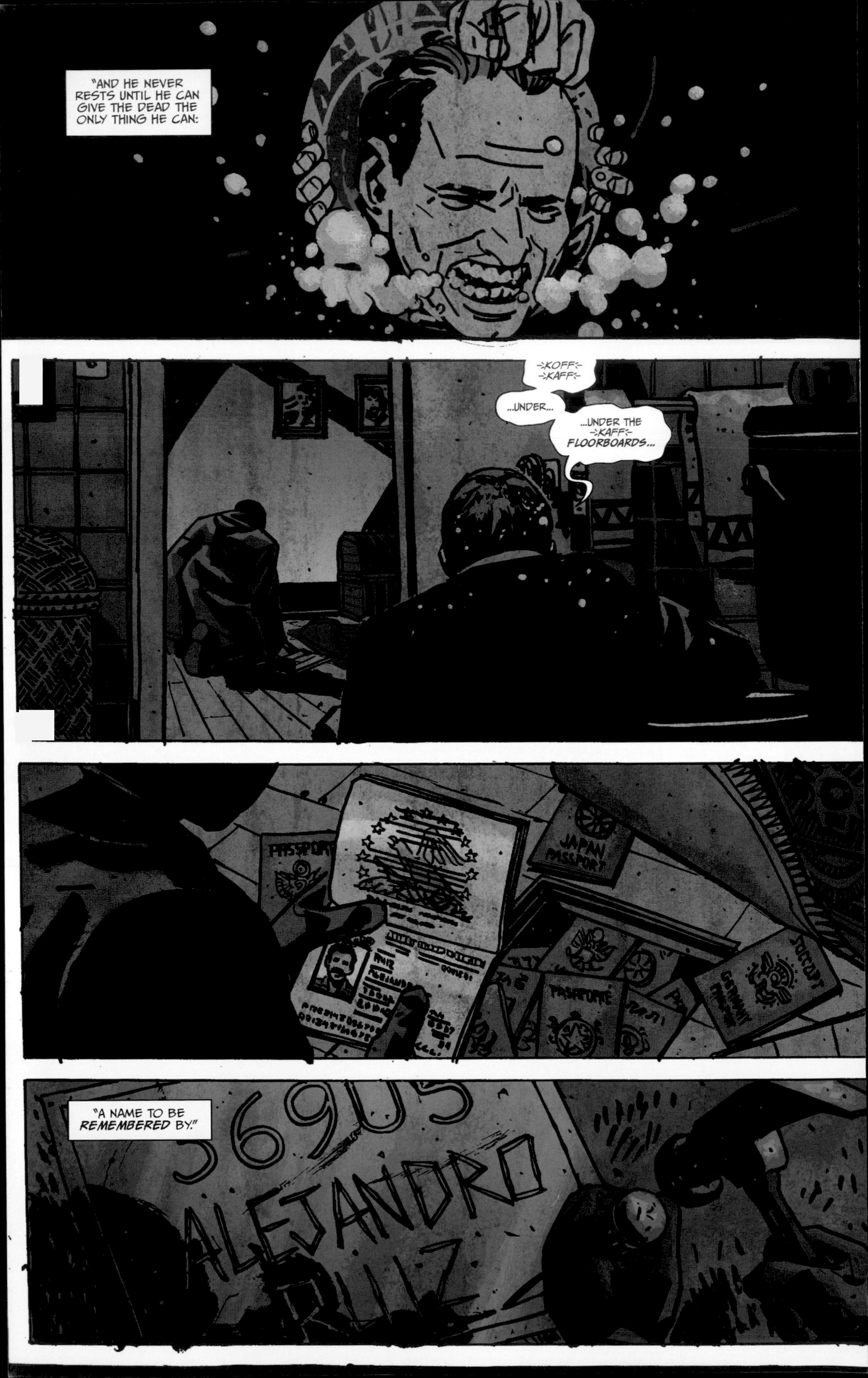

"AND HE NEVER RESTS UNTIL HE CAN GIVE THE DEAD THE ONLY THING HE CAN:
-KOFF- -KAFF-
...UNDER...
...UNDER THE -KAFF- FLOORBOARDS...
PASSPORT
JAPAN PASSPORT
PASAPORTE
"A NAME TO BE REMEMBERED BY."
56905
ALEJANDRO

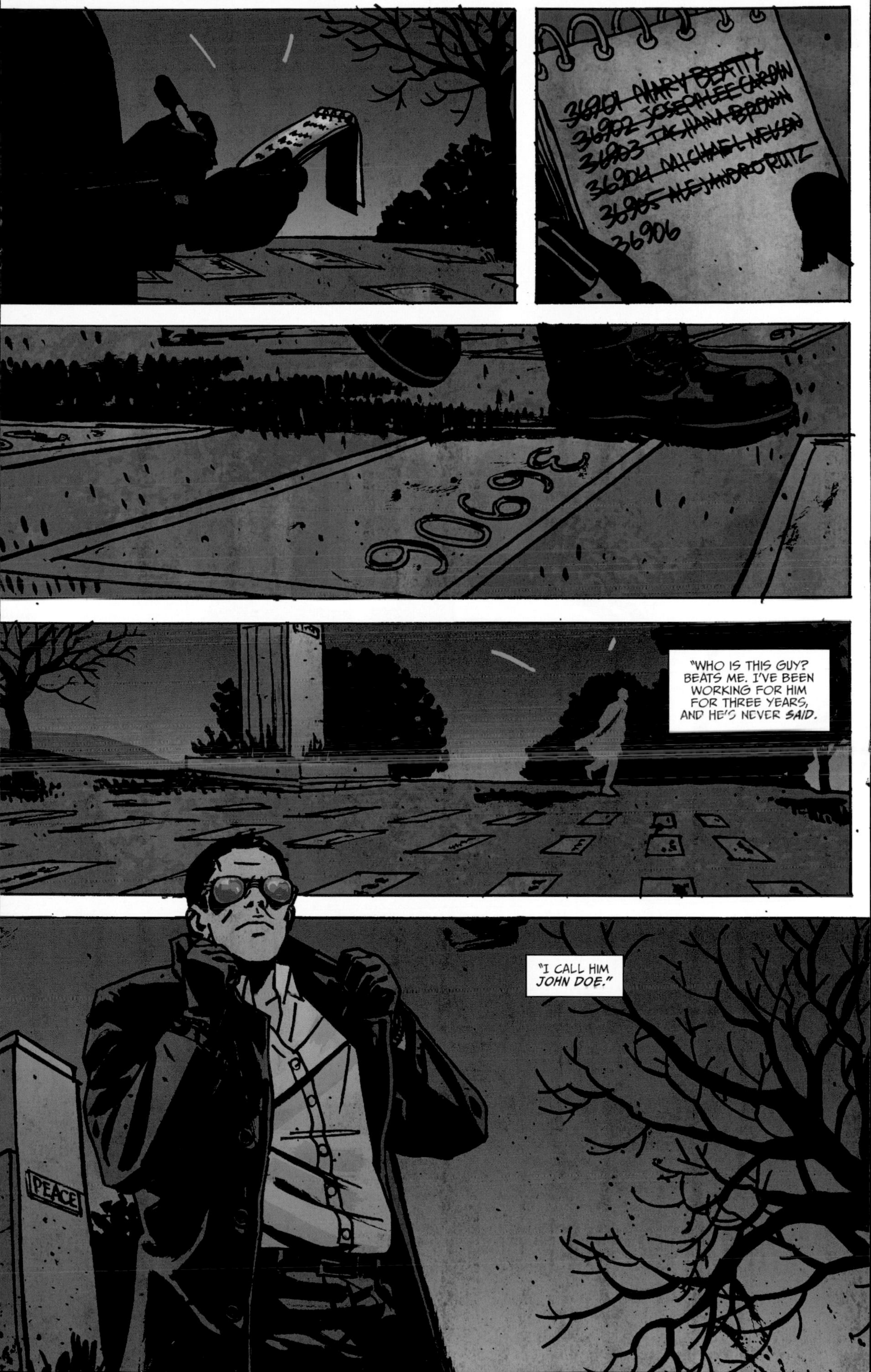
36901 MARY BEATTY
36902
36903
36904 MICHAEL NELSON
36905
36906
36906
"WHO IS THIS GUY? BEATS ME. I'VE BEEN WORKING FOR HIM FOR THREE YEARS, AND HE'S NEVER *SAID*.
"I CALL HIM *JOHN DOE*."
PEACE

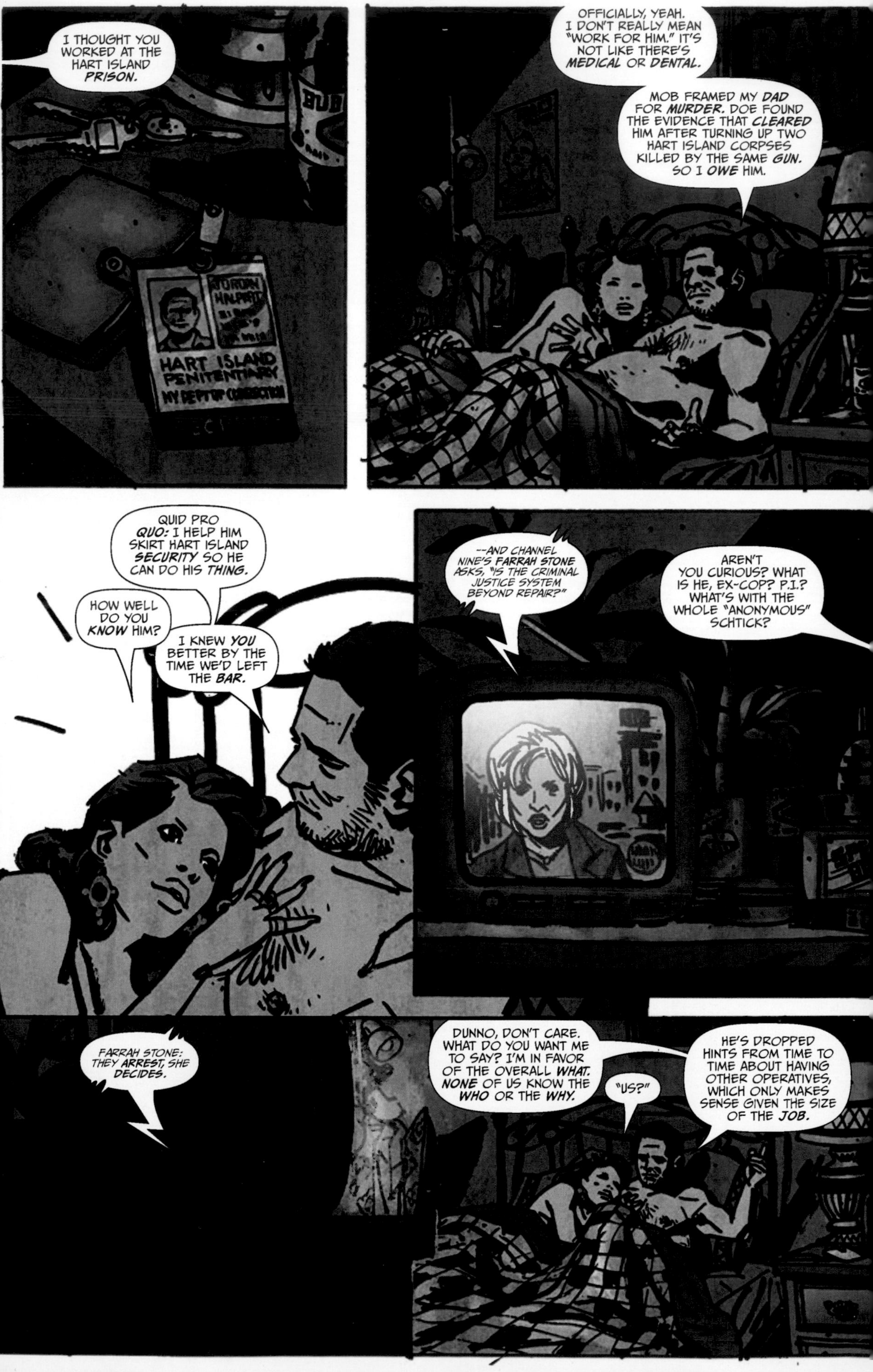
I THOUGHT YOU WORKED AT THE HART ISLAND PRISON.
HART ISLAND PENITENTIARY
OFFICIALLY, YEAH. I DON'T REALLY MEAN "WORK FOR HIM." IT'S NOT LIKE THERE'S MEDICAL OR DENTAL.
MOB FRAMED MY DAD FOR MURDER. DOE FOUND THE EVIDENCE THAT CLEARED HIM AFTER TURNING UP TWO HART ISLAND CORPSES KILLED BY THE SAME GUN. SO I OWE HIM.
QUID PRO QUO: I HELP HIM SKIRT HART ISLAND SECURITY SO HE CAN DO HIS THING.
HOW WELL DO YOU KNOW HIM?
I KNEW YOU BETTER BY THE TIME WE'D LEFT THE BAR.
--AND CHANNEL NINE'S FARRAH STONE ASKS, "IS THE CRIMINAL JUSTICE SYSTEM BEYOND REPAIR?"
AREN'T YOU CURIOUS? WHAT IS HE, EX-COP? P.I.? WHAT'S WITH THE WHOLE "ANONYMOUS" SCHTICK?
FARRAH STONE: THEY ARREST, SHE DECIDES.
DUNNO, DON'T CARE. WHAT DO YOU WANT ME TO SAY? I'M IN FAVOR OF THE OVERALL WHAT. NONE OF US KNOW THE WHO OR THE WHY.
"US?"
HE'S DROPPED HINTS FROM TIME TO TIME ABOUT HAVING OTHER OPERATIVES, WHICH ONLY MAKES SENSE GIVEN THE SIZE OF THE JOB.

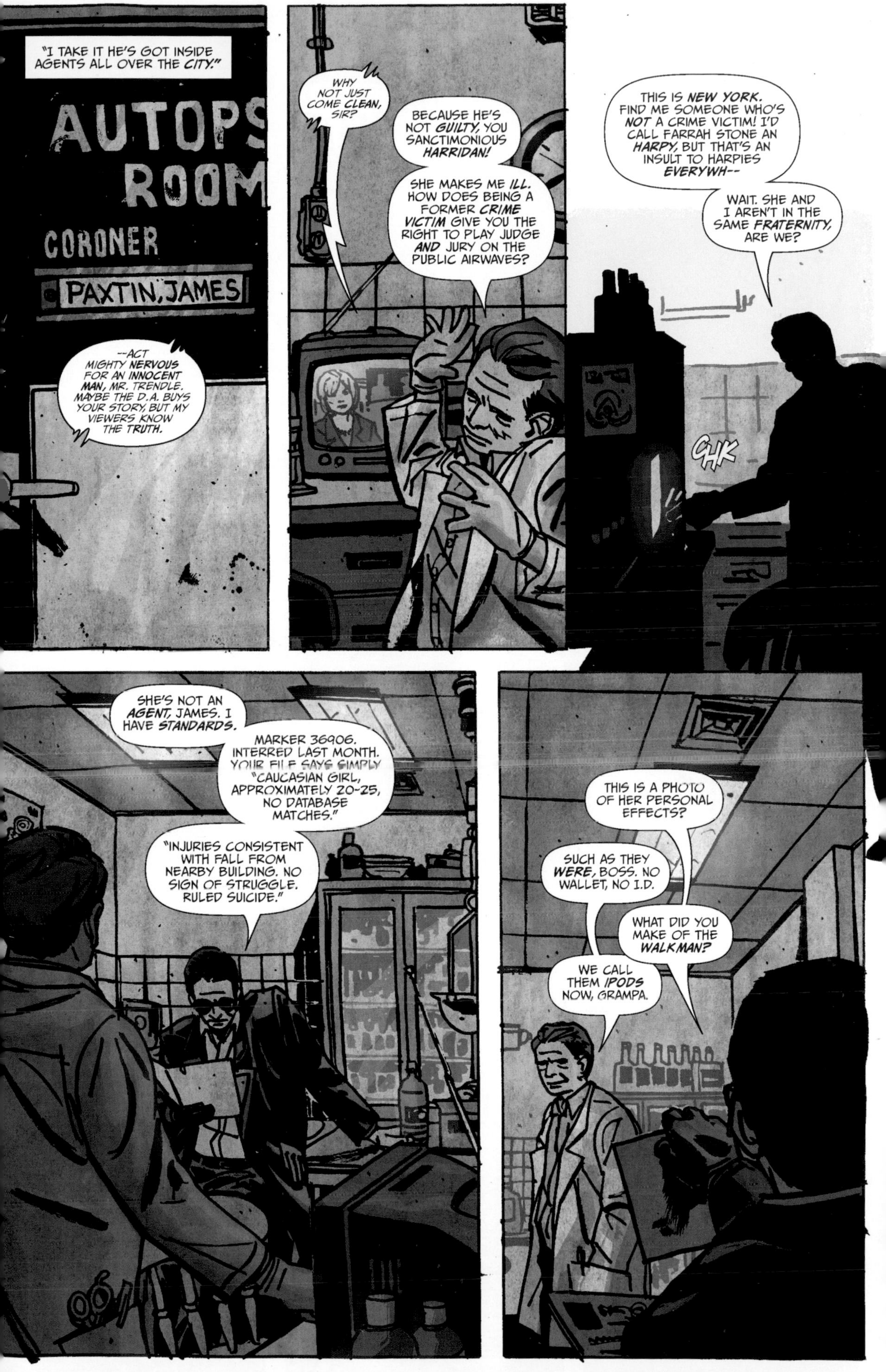
"I TAKE IT HE'S GOT INSIDE AGENTS ALL OVER THE CITY."
AUTOPSY ROOM
CORONER
PAXTIN, JAMES
--ACT MIGHTY NERVOUS FOR AN INNOCENT MAN, MR. TRENDLE. MAYBE THE D.A. BUYS YOUR STORY, BUT MY VIEWERS KNOW THE TRUTH.
WHY NOT JUST COME CLEAN, SIR?
BECAUSE HE'S NOT GUILTY, YOU SANCTIMONIOUS HARRIDAN!
SHE MAKES ME ILL. HOW DOES BEING A FORMER CRIME VICTIM GIVE YOU THE RIGHT TO PLAY JUDGE AND JURY ON THE PUBLIC AIRWAVES?
THIS IS NEW YORK. FIND ME SOMEONE WHO'S NOT A CRIME VICTIM! I'D CALL FARRAH STONE AN HARPY, BUT THAT'S AN INSULT TO HARPIES EVERYWH--
WAIT. SHE AND I AREN'T IN THE SAME FRATERNITY, ARE WE?
CHK
SHE'S NOT AN AGENT, JAMES. I HAVE STANDARDS.
MARKER 36906. INTERRED LAST MONTH. YOUR FILE SAYS SIMPLY "CAUCASIAN GIRL, APPROXIMATELY 20-25, NO DATABASE MATCHES."
"INJURIES CONSISTENT WITH FALL FROM NEARBY BUILDING. NO SIGN OF STRUGGLE. RULED SUICIDE."
THIS IS A PHOTO OF HER PERSONAL EFFECTS?
SUCH AS THEY WERE, BOSS. NO WALLET, NO I.D.
WHAT DID YOU MAKE OF THE WALKMAN?
WE CALL THEM IPODS NOW, GRAMPA.

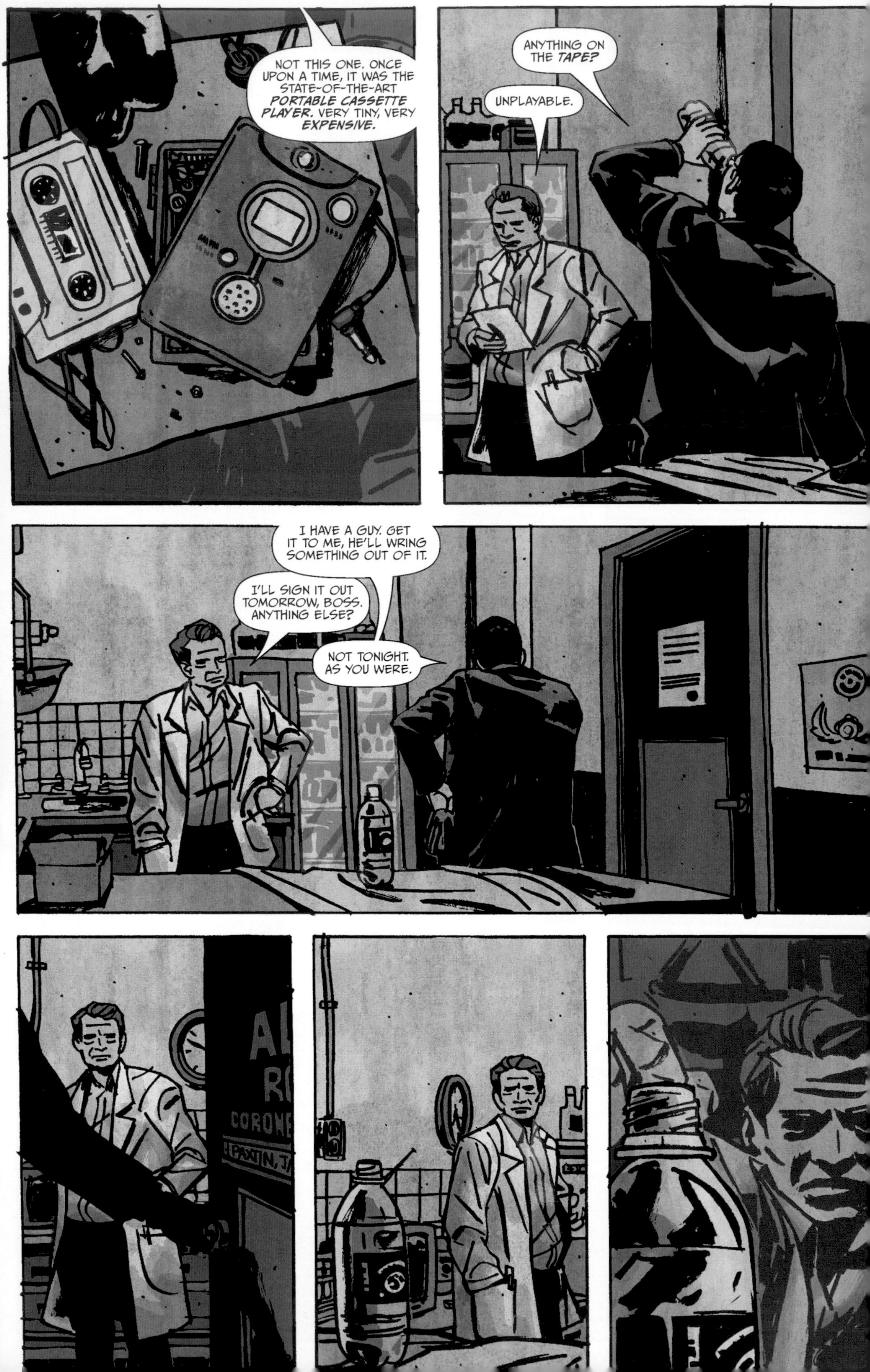
NOT THIS ONE. ONCE UPON A TIME, IT WAS THE STATE-OF-THE-ART *PORTABLE CASSETTE PLAYER.* VERY TINY, VERY *EXPENSIVE.*
ANYTHING ON THE *TAPE?*
UNPLAYABLE.
I HAVE A GUY. GET IT TO ME, HE'LL WRING SOMETHING OUT OF IT.
I'LL SIGN IT OUT TOMORROW, BOSS. ANYTHING ELSE?
NOT TONIGHT. AS YOU WERE.

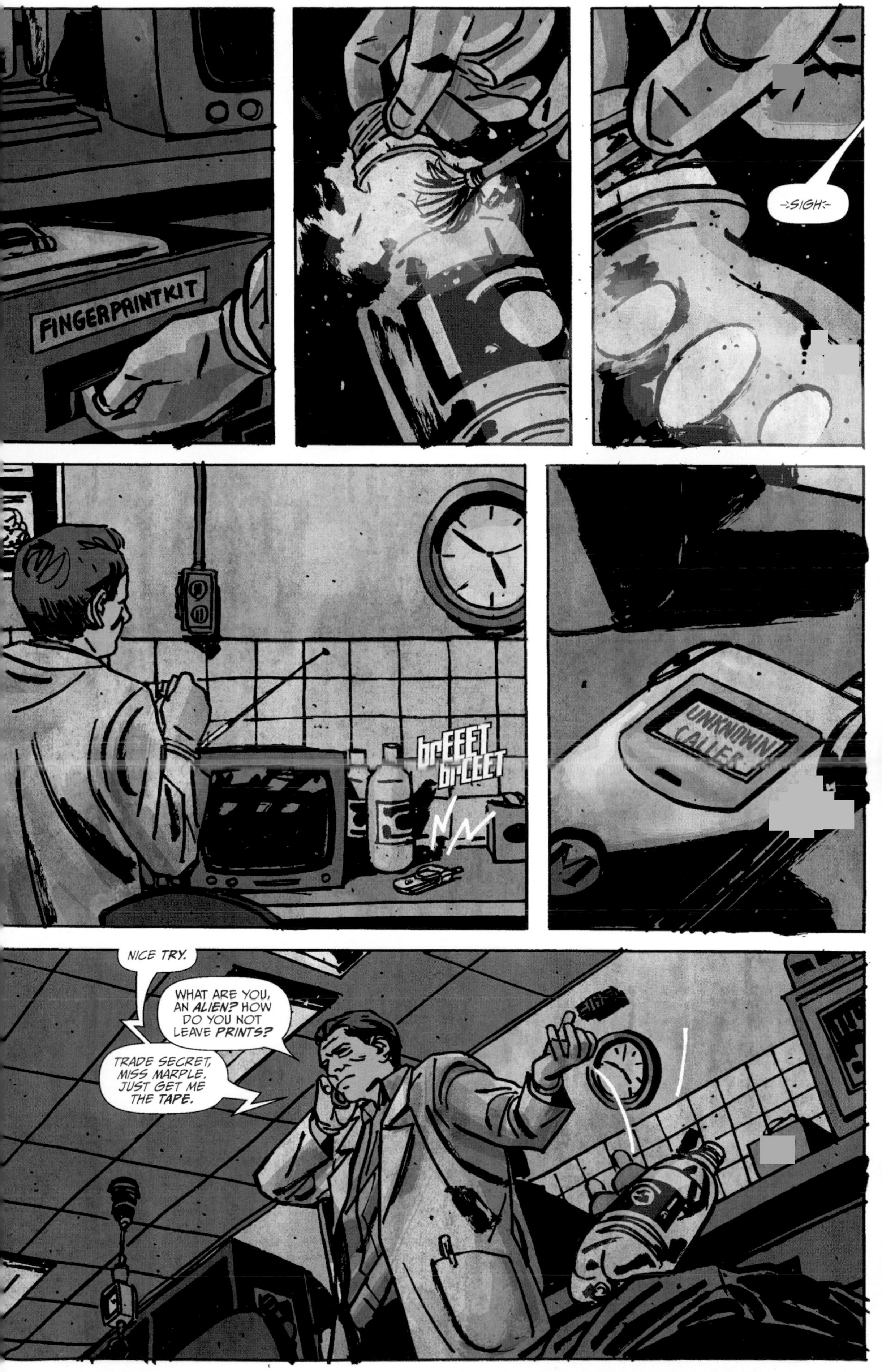
FINGERPRINT KIT
-SIGH-
brEEET
brEEET
UNKNOWN CALLER
NICE TRY.
WHAT ARE YOU, AN ALIEN? HOW DO YOU NOT LEAVE PRINTS?
TRADE SECRET, MISS MARPLE. JUST GET ME THE TAPE.

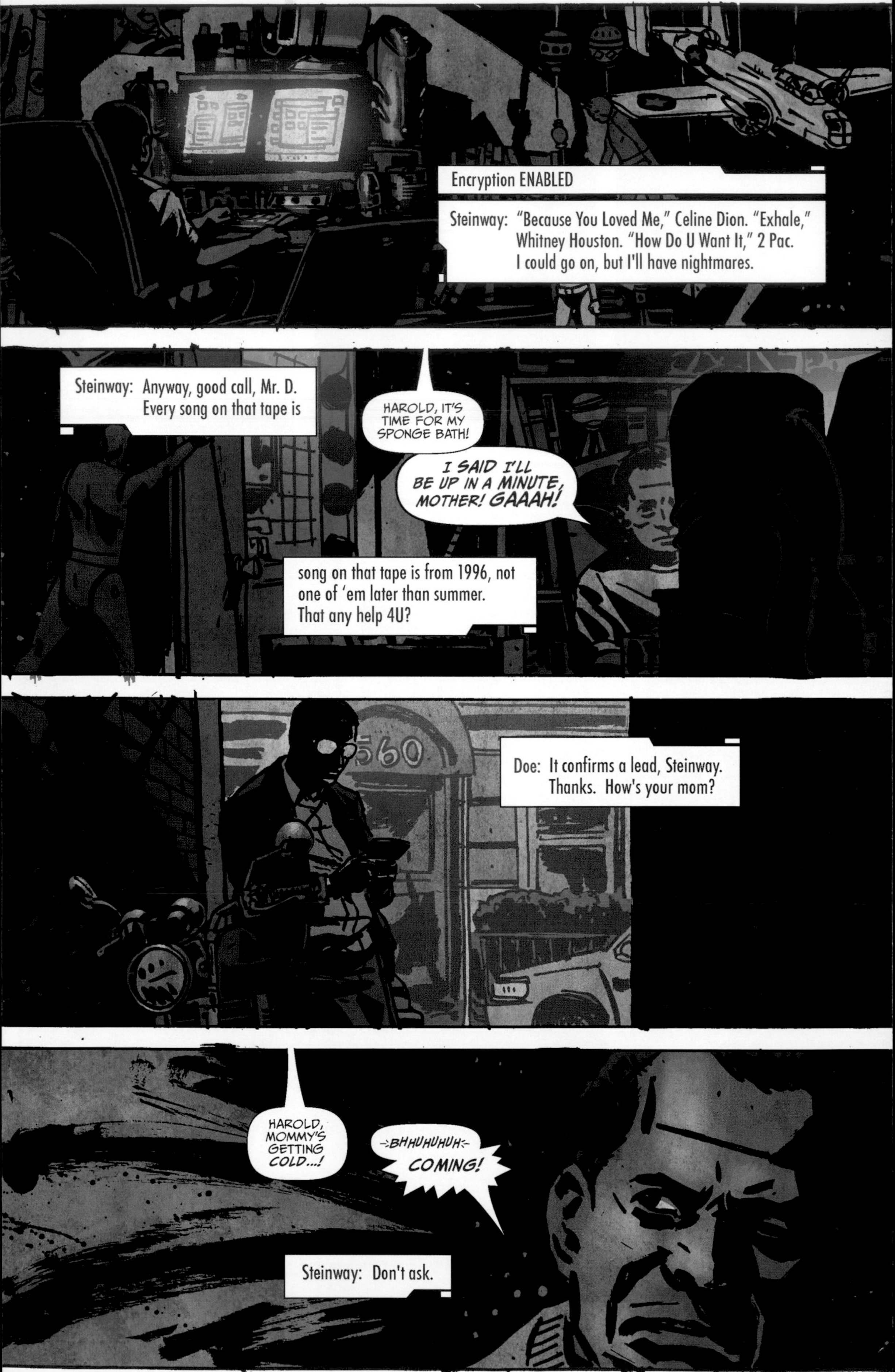
Encryption ENABLED
Steinway: "Because You Loved Me," Celine Dion. "Exhale," Whitney Houston. "How Do U Want It," 2 Pac. I could go on, but I'll have nightmares.
Steinway: Anyway, good call, Mr. D. Every song on that tape is
HAROLD, IT'S TIME FOR MY SPONGE BATH!
I SAID I'LL BE UP IN A MINUTE, MOTHER! GAAAH!
song on that tape is from 1996, not one of 'em later than summer. That any help 4U?
560
Doe: It confirms a lead, Steinway. Thanks. How's your mom?
HAROLD, MOMMY'S GETTING COLD...!
BHHUHUHUH
COMING!
Steinway: Don't ask.

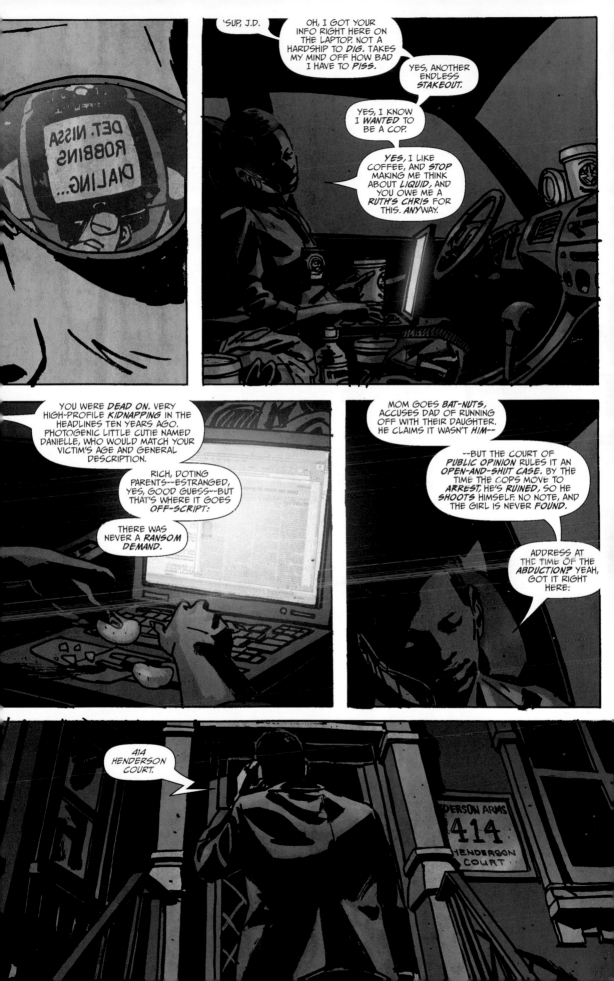

'SUP, J.D.

OH, I GOT YOUR INFO RIGHT HERE ON THE LAPTOP. NOT A HARDSHIP TO *DIG*. TAKES MY MIND OFF HOW BAD I HAVE TO *PISS*.

YES, ANOTHER ENDLESS *STAKEOUT*.

YES, I KNOW I *WANTED* TO BE A COP.

YES, I LIKE COFFEE, AND *STOP* MAKING ME THINK ABOUT *LIQUID*, AND YOU OWE ME A *RUTH'S CHRIS* FOR THIS. *ANYWAY*.

DET. NISSA ROBBINS DIALING...

YOU WERE *DEAD ON*. VERY HIGH-PROFILE *KIDNAPPING* IN THE HEADLINES TEN YEARS AGO. PHOTOGENIC LITTLE CUTIE NAMED DANIELLE, WHO WOULD MATCH YOUR VICTIM'S AGE AND GENERAL DESCRIPTION.

RICH, DOTING PARENTS--ESTRANGED, YES, GOOD GUESS--BUT THAT'S WHERE IT GOES *OFF-SCRIPT*:

THERE WAS NEVER A *RANSOM DEMAND*.

MOM GOES *BAT-NUTS*, ACCUSES DAD OF RUNNING OFF WITH THEIR DAUGHTER. HE CLAIMS IT WASN'T *HIM*--

--BUT THE COURT OF *PUBLIC OPINION* RULES IT AN *OPEN-AND-SHUT CASE*. BY THE TIME THE COPS MOVE TO *ARREST*, HE'S *RUINED*, SO HE *SHOOTS* HIMSELF. NO NOTE, AND THE GIRL IS NEVER *FOUND*.

ADDRESS AT THE TIME OF THE *ABDUCTION?* YEAH, GOT IT RIGHT HERE:

414 HENDERSON COURT.

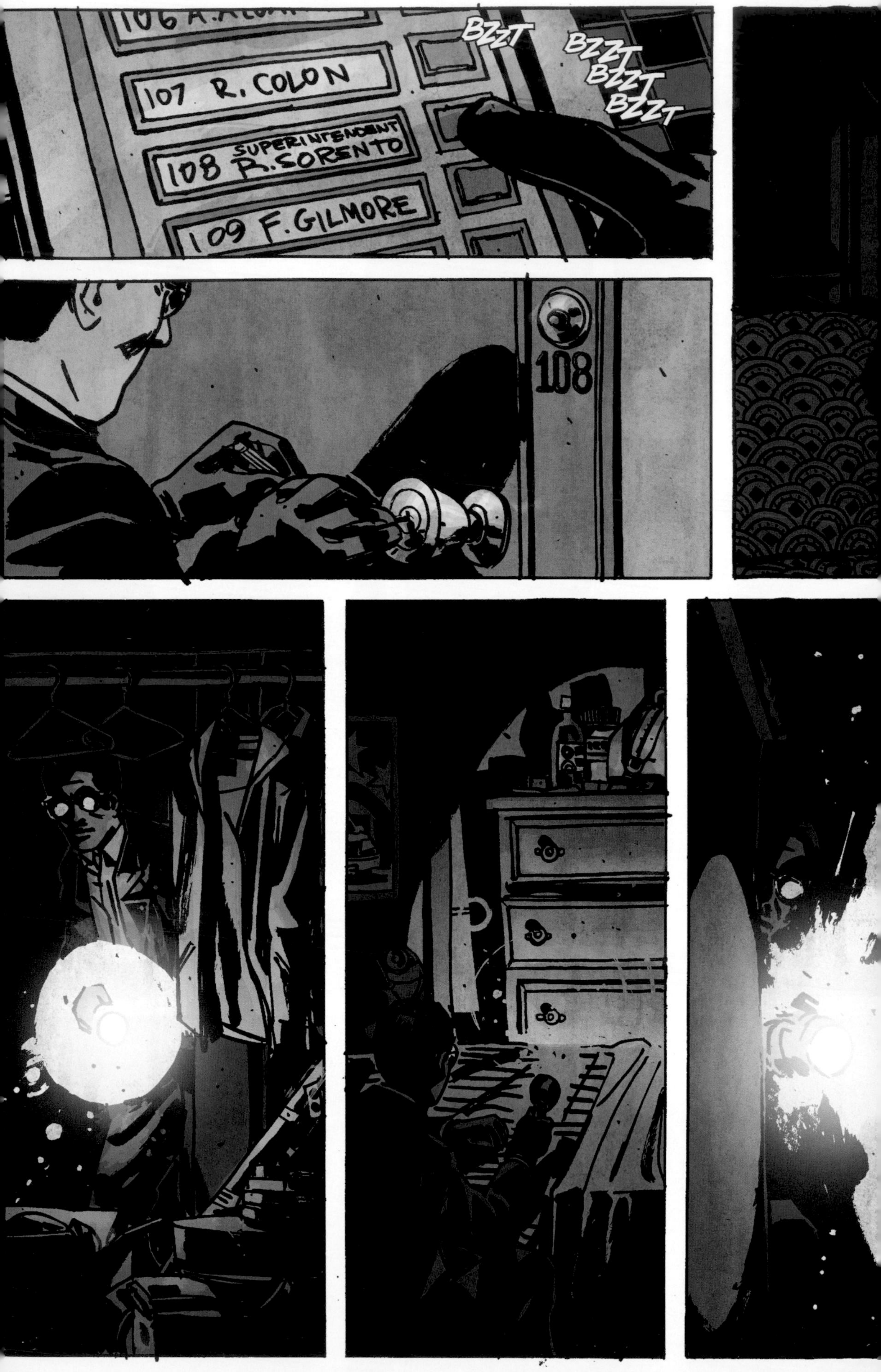
107 R. COLON
108 SUPERINTENDENT R. SORENTO
109 F. GILMORE
BZZT
BZZT
BZZT
BZZT
108

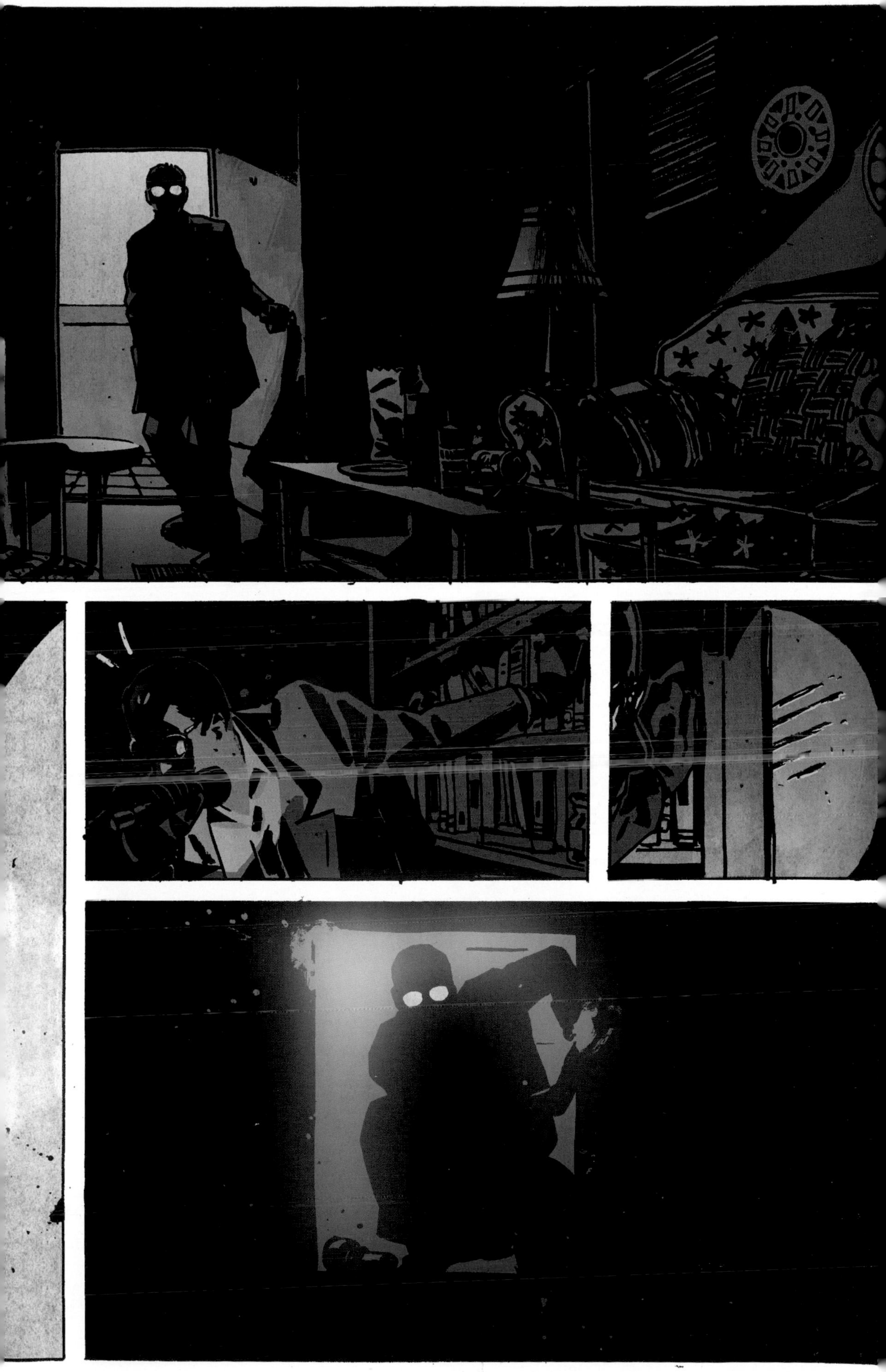

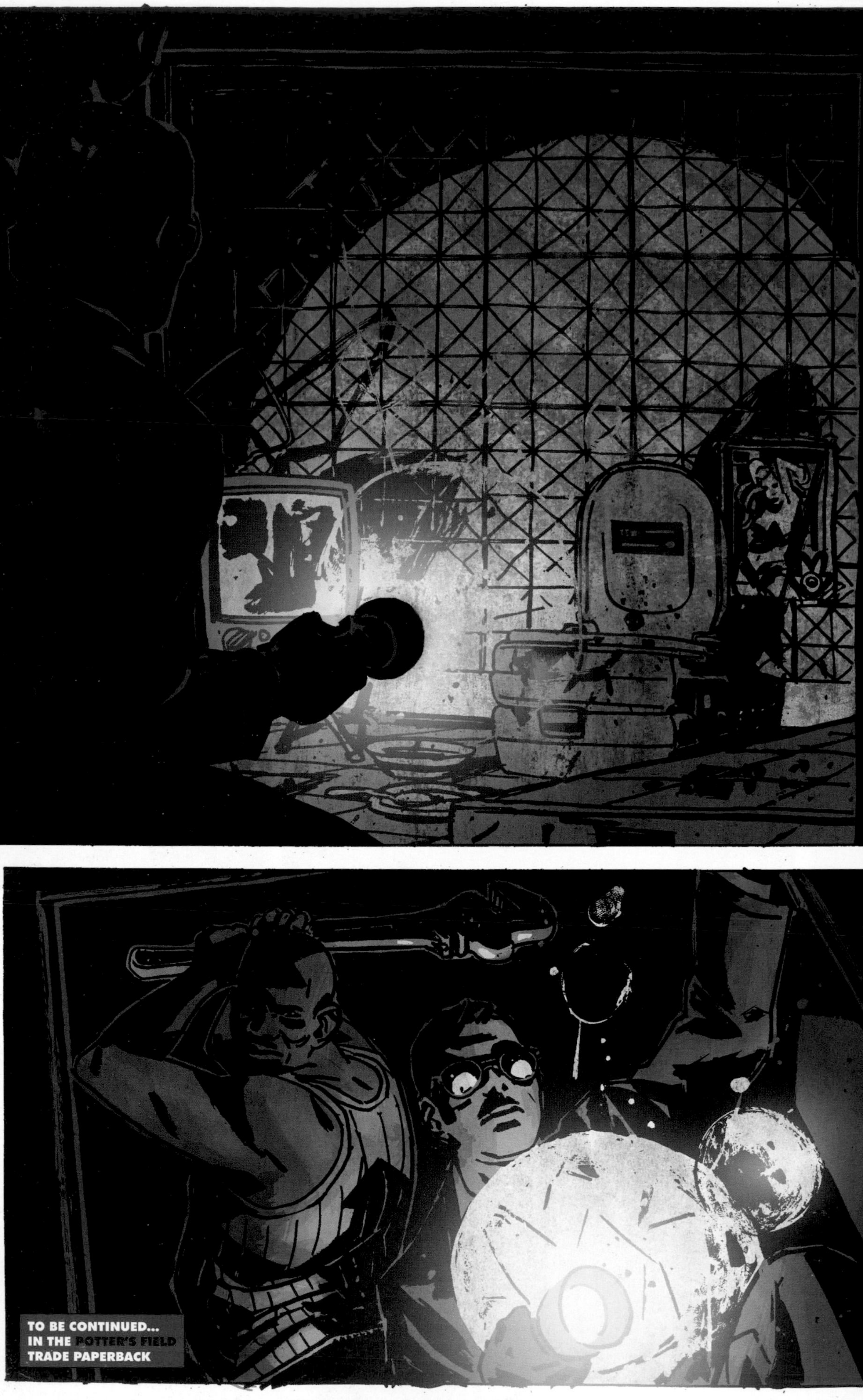
TO BE CONTINUED...
IN THE POTTER'S FIELD
TRADE PAPERBACK